THE WINE LIST 2004

THE TOP 250 WINES OF THE YEAR MATTHEW JUKES

headline

To Toby

Copyright © 2003 Matthew Jukes

www.thewinelist2004.com
www.expertwine.com

The right of Matthew Jukes to be identified as the Author of the Work has been asserted by him in accordance with the Copyright, Designs and Patents Act 1988.

First published in 2003 by
HEADLINE BOOK PUBLISHING

10 9 8 7 6 5 4 3 2 1

All information regarding recommended prices is correct to the best of the publisher's and author's knowledge at the time of going to press. No responsibility can be taken by the publisher or author if prices or availability change.

A CIP catalogue record for this title is available from the British Library

ISBN 0 7553 1249 X

Printed and bound in France by Pollina - n° L90330
Designed by Fiona Pike, Pike Design

Headline Book Publishing
A division of Hodder Headline
338 Euston Road
London NW1 3BH

www.headline.co.uk
www.hodderheadline.com

At last, a wine guide that lists only outstanding and affordable wines – all tasted by the 'palate of the people'

- The top 250 wines of the year – how much they cost, where to buy them and what they taste like

- An A-Z of invaluable advice on matching food and wine

- A global gazetteer of the best wine estates in the world

- A complete list of all the UK's best wine merchants

Whether you're a keen glugger or an experienced oenophile, THE WINE LIST is the only guide you'll ever need

'Buy this and you'll *never* drink another bad bottle'
Mirror magazine

'An **easy,** *quick* guide' **Guardian**

CONTENTS

THE WINE LIST has now been the number one wine guide in the UK for two years in a row. Thank you all so much. I am absolutely delighted with your support and obvious thirst for great wine. This year's book is totally updated and I hope it serves you well.

I have kept the exact same recipe this year – apart from a few refinements, a new vintage table and funky tricolour cover design. **THE WINE LIST 2004** is still the only book you'll ever need to track down the best wines in the world. There are so many ordinary bottles out there (and sadly hundreds of stinkers), but if you follow my suggestions, you'll never drink anything other than superb wine. Grab a corkscrew and some nice wine glasses, sit back and enjoy!

The **A-Z of food and wine** covers all of the ingredients and dishes you'll come across in the course of eating out and entertaining in. Flick through and find your dish, then read on to discover what style of wine is best suited to it. If I have left out any major food groups or dishes, do let me know and I will include them next year!

The **Top 250** is a distillation of over 25,000 of my tasting notes into a shorter list of around 500. Once completed, I ruthlessly cull this collection of wines into the final hard core 250. Fifty and a half weeks of non-stop tasting ends and ten days frantic writing begins. But what criteria do I use to decide if a wine is worth listing? Apart from awesome flavour, pinpoint-accurate winemaking and great value for money, I have made sure that each of the wines is ready to drink now. This means you can uncork or unscrew any of the bottles the second you get home. One thing to watch out for is that there is only a finite amount of each of the wines on the shelves. Each year, a few sell out extremely quickly so, if you want to grab some of the rarer bottles, you'll have to move fast. However, six months or so into the life of TWL03, two hundred and twenty wines were still available.

The Gazetteer is *the* comprehensive list of the finest wineries in the world. It can be used when you are on holiday, shopping for fine wine, or when you are in a restaurant with an unfamiliar wine list.

And, finally, the Directory is an essential list of the top independent wine merchants in the UK, plus their home town or post code, telephone number and, if they have one, e-mail address or website. I have also included the HQ hot lines for each of the major supermarket and specialist wine retail chains. Make use of this crucial list – it is the best way to track down and order any wine you are after.

As I write every word of this book myself and don't use other people's tasting notes or industry databases, all the research is mine. Of course, this means that any errors are mine, too. I have checked and rechecked every phone number, price and stockist, but things do change. Some shops may sell a little over my RRP, while others may sell under – I have noted the 'official' list price. Some of the wines are stocked in supermarkets, others in small independent merchants, but just because a shop is not on your doorstep, don't let it stop you buying their wines. Club together with some winey friends and order a case over the phone. Every merchant in this book delivers nationwide. This year I have issued a few of them with **THE WINE LIST** stickers to let you know which wines on their shelves have made my Top 250.

So, what happened in the Top 250 this year? Well, Australia and New Zealand combined have an excellent 65 entries, and South Africa consolidated its position with 17. South America dropped the ball a bit with only 9 (down 9 on last year). And, despite receiving a fair amount of bad press over the last year because of its perceived lack of good value wines, California has gone up 3 to 9. But, it's been the year the Old World fought back. Europe has had a blinder – France has 73 wines (up 11 on last year) and Italy, Spain and Portugal now represent a mighty 66 between them! Hungary, England, Austria, Greece and Germany all make it in single figures, and it all adds to the Old World team total – 150 wines to the New World's 100. What a result!

The gossip in the wine trade this year has centred around the relative pricing policies of the supermarkets and wine shops. Supermarkets have been accused of reducing margins with BOGOF (buy one get one free) and constant promotions, while chain stores have been hit by accusations of upping their margins to ridiculous levels. While it is good for the consumer to be able to take advantage of deals, it is important that they don't get into the habit of shopping by price rather than taste. I always welcome companies making a profit by increasing margins, so long as the wines they are selling are well chosen and represent good value. The mark of a talented wine buyer is someone who can find great-tasting wines that make a decent profit for their company and still represent great value to the consumer. We are lucky in the UK to have a number of very skilled buyers working in the wine trade, and we must support them and their companies by buying their wines.

I would like to thank everyone I have met over the last year, both in the UK wine trade and abroad, for their time, energy, enthusiasm and, crucially, bottles of wine. There are far too many of you to name individually, but you have all helped enormously and without you I would never be able to put this book together. This is an immensely enjoyable guide to work on and I look forward to doing it all again next year. Special thanks must go to Nathalie for her unstinting support, Isadora and Elspeth for keeping me sane, Ma and Pa for their encouragement, Robert Kirby for keeping me going, and the team at Headline, especially Jo Roberts-Miller for her amazing eye for detail and James Horobin for helping to keep me firmly in the No. 1 spot.

A-Z OF FOOD
AND WINE
COMBINATIONS

INTRODUCTION

This A–Z of dishes and ingredients is designed to point you in the
direction of some fantastic food and wine matches. One of my
jobs over the last fifteen years has been consulting to restaurants
around the world, writing wine lists and training wine waiters.
During this time I have tasted a huge range of food and wine
combinations – some of these were totally amazing, others an
awful clash of aromas and flavours. Now I know that wine and,
for that matter, food appreciation is a matter of personal taste –
clearly not everyone loves everything, as tastes differ. This is, of
course, good news, because if we were all alike there would be
no point in making oceans of different wines, or cooking the
innumerable dishes the world has to offer. And while I recognise
and celebrate this diversity, for each of the following listings,
I have endeavoured to guide you to a group of wines, styles or
grape varieties that should suit the food in question well. Your
task is to make the final selection of which bottle you are going
to uncork, bearing in mind your own personal palate. You could
do this by using any one of the wines in my Top 250, by scouring
the Gazetteer section for the world's best winemakers, or just by
going 'off piste' and searching for good matches yourself. You will
see some wine styles popping up more often than others. These
are multipurpose, multitalented styles like the refreshing, dry,
white grape Sauvignon Blanc or juicy, black fruit-driven New
World Cabernet/Merlot blends – try to keep a few bottles of
these styles of wine at home, in readiness for unexpected guests
or impromptu enthusiastic cooking. Perhaps surprisingly, Beaujolais,

food and wine

one of the most ridiculed styles of wine, is incredibly versatile in the kitchen – it pops up over twenty-five times in this section! One thing is certain, if there is a wicked food and wine combo in the world, you'll find it here.

And just to prove it works – I recently hosted a dinner for eight people in a smart restaurant. My challenge was to match a bottle of white wine to our starters. The problem was that between us we had chosen six very disparate dishes indeed. I grabbed the wine list and started to mentally break down the vast array of flavours we would be dealing with. Eventually I came up with what I hoped was a complementary wine. But the acid test was whether my guests thought the match worked. The dishes were *Crab, mussel and artichoke salad with saffron*; *Warm salad of smoked eel and bacon with Jersey royals*; *Grilled focaccia with creamed tomatoes, mint and parmesan*; *Pimentos with tuna and Niçoise relish*; *Brown shrimp and pea risotto*; and *Baltic herrings à la crème*. The wine I chose was 2002 Chapel Hill Verdelho, McLaren Vale, South Australia (interestingly this was in the Top 250 last year, with a retail price of £7.99!). It was a triumph. The ripe, tropical nose perked up the senses. The fine texture on the palate and zesty acidity cut through some of the more difficult ingredients like saffron, Niçoise dressing and eel. The lack of oaky nuances added to the persistent palate and extraordinary length made this wine the consummate all-rounder. As the wine mellowed, it unravelled, relaxed and its full array of aromas came out. Everyone was amazed, particularly when I made them guess the price of the wine. Who'd have thought that the weird but great value white grape Verdelho could have such a broad repertoire of food, wine and crowd-pleasing skills?

APÉRITIF WINE STYLES

Pre-dinner nibbles like *dry roasted almonds*, *bruschetta*, *cashews*, *canapés*, *crostini*, *crudités*, *olives* and *gougères* (devilish cheese puffs, served with alacrity in Burgundy and Chablis) are designed to give your palate a kick-start and get your juices flowing before a meal. It is crucial at this stage of the proceedings not to swamp your taste buds with big, juicy, powerful wines. Save these for later (you'll want them with the main course) and aim for refreshing, palate-tweaking styles that set the scene, rather than hog the stage: Champagne is the hands down winner if you're feeling flush but, if not, then sparkling wines from the Loire (Saumur), the south of France (Limoux) or Crémant de Bourgogne (Burgundy) would do the job. Italy offers up superb, dry, palate-cleansing fizz in the form of Prosecco, from Veneto, or some more serious sparklers from Trentino or Alto Adige. I am not usually a Cava fan (unless I'm in Barcelona), but Spain has a few worthy versions to sample. The real Champagne-taste-alikes come from the New World, with the added bonus that they are very good value – New Zealand, Australia (particularly Tasmania) and California are the places to go to find awesome quality. Fino or manzanilla sherries are wonderful palate cleansers, ever so foody, and, although seemingly perpetually 'out of fashion', will ensure you are regarded as a purveyor of fine taste – whether it be refreshingly retro or light years ahead of your time. The least expensive option (and often safest, particularly if you are eating out) is a zesty, uplifting, zingy dry white wine. There are thousands of these around and loads of first-class examples in this book. Stick with unoaked styles and keep the price down so that you can step up a level or two with the next bottle when the food hits the table. A neutral, dry white can always be pepped up with a dash of Crème de Cassis to make a Kir or use the same liqueur to turn a dry, sparkling wine or inexpensive Champagne into a glitzy Kir Royale.

STARTERS AND MAIN COURSES

Anchovies Strongly flavoured whether they are fresh or cured, anchovies need dry, unoaked, tangy, acidic whites or juicy, bone-dry rosés. Try Italy, Spain or France and keep to a low budget – a fiver should do it. There are a few worthy rosés from the New World, but tread carefully as they can be a little high in alcohol. Dry sherry is also a safe haven.

Antipasti The classic Italian mixed platter of *artichokes*, *prosciutto*, *bruschetta*, *olives*, *marinated peppers* and *aubergines* enjoys being serenaded with chilled, light Italian reds like Valpolicella and Bardolino, or clean, vibrant, refreshing whites like Pinot Grigio, Pinot Bianco, Frascati, Greco, Est! Est!! Est!!!, Orvieto, Verdicchio or Fiano.

Artichokes Dry, unoaked, fresh whites are best here, especially if you are dipping the artichokes in *vinaigrette* (see 'Vinaigrette'). Alsatian Sylvaner or Pinot Blanc, any Loire Sauvignon Blanc or Aligoté from Burgundy are perfect partners, as are the same Italian whites listed above for 'Antipasti'.

Asparagus Because of its inbuilt asparagusy characteristics (sniff a glass of Sancerre!), Sauvignon Blanc is the perfect match here. New World styles like Chilean, Australian or New Zealand Sauv have tons of flavour and would be better suited to asparagus dishes that have *hollandaise*, *balsamic vinegar* or *olive oil* and *Parmesan*. Old World styles, like those from France's Loire Valley are great if the dish is plainer. Northern Italian whites like Pinot Bianco or Pinot Grigio, as well as South African Sauvignon Blanc (somewhere between New Zealand and Loire in style) would all do the job well.

Aubergines If served grilled, with *pesto* or with *olive oil*, *garlic* and *basil*, you must identify the most dominant flavours in the dish. In both of these cases they are the same – garlic and basil – so tackle them with dry Sauvignon Blanc. Plain aubergine dishes are fairly thin on the ground as these glossy, sleek, black beauties are often used within veggie recipes (for example, *ratatouille* or *caponata*). If cheese or meat (*moussaka*) is involved those flavours take over from the aubergines, so light, youthful reds are required. Southern Italian or Sicilian Primitivo, Nero d'Avola or Aglianico, southern French Grenache-based blends, Chilean Carmenère or Argentinean Sangiovese or Tempranillo are all good matches. Just make sure they are not too oaky or heavy. If the dish is hotter or spicier, or the aubergines are *stuffed*, you will need a more feisty red, but don't be tempted by anything too weighty (avoid brawny red grapes like Cabernet, Zinfandel and Shiraz). *Imam bayildi*, the classic aubergine, onion, olive oil and tomato dish is a winner with juicy, slightly chilled Chilean Merlot, youthful, bright purple Valpolicella, spicy Sardinian Cannonau or black-fruit-imbued Montepulciano d'Abruzzo.

Australian The masters of fusion Down Under manage to juggle the freshest of land and sea ingredients and weave into the mix the best of Asia's spices and presentation. This beguiling and thoroughly delicious style of cuisine is a real hit worldwide, as the cooking is virtually fat free and packed with zesty, palate-tweaking flavours. It is no surprise that in trendy Sydney and Melbourne eateries they bathe their palates in Clare and Eden Valley Rieslings, fresh Verdelhos, zippy Adelaide Hills and Tassie Sauvignon Blancs and assorted Pinot Gris, Sémillon/Sauvignon blends and keen, balanced Chardonnays. Aussie reds are not all huge and porty, with Canberra or Frankland Shiraz, Tassie or Yarra Pinot and cooler Margaret River Cabernets really leading the field. It is no wonder they are all so fit down there, with such glorious local produce!

Avocado If the avocado is *undressed*, you need light, unoaked whites, in particular Loire Sauvignon Blanc, Muscadet or Bourgogne Aligoté. If *dressed* with *vinaigrette* or with *Marie Rose sauce* for a prawn cocktail, richer Sauvignon Blanc, Pinot Gris or Australian Verdelho are spot on, as are young, white Rhônes and Alsatian Pinot Blanc. *Guacamole*, depending on its chilli content, needs cool, citrusy, dry whites to quench the thirst.

Bacon This usually pops up as an ingredient in a dish and not often as the main theme, unless you've got a hangover and need a miracle cure – *bacon sandwich*! So, if you feel like a glass of wine to accompany this classic sarnie or your *full English breakfast* (I know I do) then chilled red Côtes-du-Rhône or Beaujolais would be superb, as would sparkling Shiraz from Down Under. If, however, you are using grilled *pancetta* or *lardons* in a salad, remember that the salty flavour and/or the smoked taste could suggest a move away from a salady white wine to a juicy, fresh red. Red Burgundy is heavenly with *bacon and eggs*, if a little decadent.

Barbecues The unplanned, spur of the moment, ever-so-slightly dangerous nature of the English barbecue, combined with monster mountains of meat, spicy marinades and intense, smoky sauces, ensures an informal (often hysterical) and flavour-packed occasion. Aim for inexpensive New World gluggers (white or red), so long as they are assertive, juicy and fruit-driven. Lightly oaked Chardonnay or Sémillon for whites, or inexpensive Zinfandel, Merlot, Carmenère, Cabernet Sauvignon or Shiraz for reds. Try Chile, Argentina, Australia, South Africa or New Zealand for likely candidates.

Beans With *baked beans* you simply need fruit-driven reds, as the tomato sauce flavour tends to take over. Any youthful reds with refreshing acidity, such as those from the Loire, Spain or Italy, should work well. Remember to keep the price down – it is not worth spending over a fiver for a *beans-on-toast* wine! Not surprisingly, anything goes with *green beans*, as they are hardly flavour-stuffed vegetables. You'd have to tiptoe with a fairy light, dry white to let a green bean truly express itself. *Tuscan bean salad* demands a chilled, light red or a tart, zingy white to cut through the earthy flavours in the dish. If you throw some beans into a stew, such as *cassoulet* or a wide variety of Spanish dishes, then Grenache-dominant wines from the south of France (Fitou, Corbières, Faugères or Minervois), or Garnacha-based wines from Spain (Navarra, Terra Alta, Priorato or Tarragona) will deal easily with the beanie ballast. *Black bean sauce* requires a few moments contemplation. The gloopy texture and intensity of sweetness must be countered by huge, juicy, mouth-filling, velvety smooth reds – Zinfandel is the only red grape with its hand up! *Refried beans*, either in *tacos* or other *Mexican* dishes, have a fair degree of sludginess and an earthy character that needs either rich whites like New World Chardonnay (Chile, South Africa and Australia make the best value) or fresh, fruity reds. I would try Bonarda, Sangiovese or Tempranillo from Argentina as a starting point, then head over to Chile for some Carmenère if you have no joy. My favourite bean is the noble cannellini, the base of all great beany soups. But you'll have to wait with spoon, glass and corkscrew at the ready until the 'Soup' entry to see what to uncork.

Beef There are so many different beef dishes, so it is lucky that the rules are not too demanding. Reds are the order of the day, but it is the size and shape of them that determines just how good the match will be. *Roast Beef* (or *en croûte/Beef Wellington*) served up for Sunday lunch demands a degree of formality. When you gather around the table do, by all means, push the boat out. It is at times like these when old-fashioned gentleman's claret (red Bordeaux) really performs well. Don't ask me why, but fine wines such as claret, Bandol, erudite northern Rhônes – Hermitage, Crozes-Hermitage, Cornas, St-Joseph or Côte-Rôtie – or even Italy's answer to an Aston Martin Vantage, the Super-Tuscans, are simply magnificent with this king of the beef dishes. As you'd expect, not one of these wines is remotely affordable. They are all special occasion wines, so if you are looking to shave a few pounds off the budget, I would recommend heading towards the top Cabernets from Australia's Margaret River (Western Australia) or Coonawarra (South Australia), or the Napa Valley in California. You've guessed it, again fairly dear, but these reds will give you the richness and complexity that you are craving. If you are on a strict budget, then replicate the flavours of the aforementioned great reds by choosing carefully – not all wines from Bordeaux are exorbitantly priced.

Try the less famous sub-regions like Côtes de Castillon, Bourg, Blaye and Francs, and choose a good vintage (see my Vintage Table page 235). These wines can really hit the spot, while Bergerac, Bordeaux's neighbour, or hearty Southern Rhône or Languedoc reds would also do very well. Most Aussie (try McLaren Vale in particular), South African, Chilean and Argentinean Cabernets or Cab/Shiraz blends around the tenner mark, offer charm, complexity and competence. It is at this price point that the New World leads the pack. But even if you drop down to a fiver you'll still have fun, just remember to stick to hotter climate wines, as claret at this price is pretty dire.

But how do you like your beef cooked? If you are a fan of *rare* beef, you can safely drink a younger, more tannic red wine, as harder tannins balance perfectly with juicy, rare meat. If you like your beef *well done*, then go for an older wine with smoother, more harmonious tannins. *Stews, casseroles* and *pies* need heavy, structured reds, particularly if meaty, stock-rich gravy is involved. Cabernet Sauvignon, Syrah (Shiraz), Pinotage, Piemontese (northern Italian) reds, Zinfandel and Malbec are but a few of the superb, hunky, chunky grapes to go for. Track down wines from South Africa, Australia, California and Argentina. Southern Rhônes like Gigondas, Lirac, Cairanne, Rasteau or Vacqueyras will be superb, as will Provençal or Languedoc reds made from a similar blend of swarthy red grapes. Portuguese wines are worth considering with rich beef dishes, as the red wines from Dão and the Douro Valley are woefully under-priced and mightily impressive. The great black wine from Cahors in southwest France also deserves a mention, as it is a gifted beef partner. *Bollito misto*, the Italian stew made from beef and just about everything else you could possibly think of, demands indigenous wines – Teroldego and Marzemino, from

Trentino in northern Italy, would be a good place to kick off, as would smart Valpolicella, Barbera and Dolcetto. *Boeuf bourguignon*, as the name suggests, usually pressgangs the help of red Burgundy. But please don't cook with anything expensive. Save your money for the 'drinking' wine and choose a more upmarket version of the wine you have used in your dish. *Steak and kidney pie* loves earthy, rustic reds with fresh acidity and pokey tannins. These slice through the gravy and sturdy kidneys – Madiran and Cahors from France, Malbec from Argentina and New World war-horses, like South African Pinotage and Syrah, also enjoy this challenge. *Cottage pie*, with carrot, celery, onions and minced beef rarely requires anything more talented than an inexpensive, fun lovin' red. You could even chance your luck with Bulgaria or Hungary (although I haven't road-tested this suggestion), or southern Italy or Sicily (much safer bets) and then go crazy and buy two bottles. A chunky *Beef stroganoff* also demands rusticity in its vinous partner, so search for southern Rhônes (Sablet, Cairanne or Vacqueyras); even Côtes-du-Rhône from the right Domaines can be a joy (see the Gazetteer page 187). *Hungarian goulash* would be all the more authentic if a Hungarian red wine joined it. Good luck, as I have yet to find the dream date, so if you want to be in more familiar territory, head straight for Rioja or Toro (Spain) or Chilean Cabernet Sauvignon. Straight *steak* has a more direct meaty flavour than a stew, so finer wines can be dragged out of the cellar (or offie). Try Chianti, Brunello di Montalcino, Ribera del Duero, Californian Merlot, Cab or Syrah, top-end Cru Beaujolais, Crozes-Hermitage, St-Joseph, and South African, Argentinean and New Zealand Cabernet Sauvignon. Watch out for *Béarnaise sauce*, which, though great with steak, can clog up the taste buds a little. With *steak au poivre*, the pungent, pulverised peppercorns make themselves known in each and every mouthful, so look for meaty (peppery) wines like northern Rhône reds (Syrahs) or their cousins from further afield – Shiraz from Australia or South Africa. *Burgers*, one of my all-time favourite dishes (homemade, not mechanically reclaimed!), often served with ketchup, bacon, cheese or relish (or all of the above), need fruit-driven reds like Italian Dolcetto, Spanish Garnacha, young Rioja Crianza, Californian Zinfandel, Chilean or South African Merlot, Australian Petit Verdot or Shiraz blends, or South African Pinotage. *Chilli con carne* is a difficult dish to match with wine but, as with burgers, it is necessary to search for fruitier styles like Aussie Merlot, or Negroamaro or Nero d'Avola from southern Italy and Sicily. *Steak tartare* is a stranger one, and I'm still not sure whether I actually really like it, but it works terrifically well with very light reds and rosés – Tavel (southern Rhône) and other Grenache-based rosés (try Spain or Australia) are perfect, as are nobby Pinot Noirs like Sancerre red or rosé. If you fancy splashing out, then rosé Champagne is the ultimate combo, if a little frivolous, but go easy on the capers, if they are served alongside. *Cold, rare roast beef salad*, and other cold beef dishes, need fresh, light reds with low tannins – Beaujolais, Valpolicella, red Loires (either Cabernet Franc or Gamay) or Argentinean Tempranillo or Bonarda would all work. The only occasion when you can break the red-wine-with-beef rule (there has to be one) is with *carpaccio* (raw/rare) or *bresaola* (air-dried). These wafer-thin sliced beef dishes can handle whites. Any dry, apéritif-style Italian white or light Montepulciano-style red would be perfect.

Cajun – see 'Mexican'.

Capers Sauvignon Blanc, from almost anywhere, or very dry Italian whites like Soave or Greco from Campania are good matches, as they can cut through the peculiar green, vinegary tanginess experienced when you munch on a caper. (For more suggestions see 'Apéritif'.)

Caviar Ridiculously decadent but if you can afford caviar you will no doubt be able to splash out on Champagne as well. Avoid rosé styles, though, and there is no need for prestige cuvées unless you're desperately trying to impress (or are a tasteless lottery winner). If the caviar is in a sauce, then consider the main ingredients of the dish. Smart Sauvignon Blanc (Sancerre, Pouilly-Fumé or Marlborough, New Zealand) is always a safe bet, but poached sea bass (for example) with a Champagne and caviar sauce would bankrupt you for a start and demand you follow the sea bass rather than the caviar in the wine-matching process, so read on for the 'Fish' section.

Charcuterie A selection of charcuterie (or *assiette de charcuterie* including *saucisson, salami, ham* etc.) contains diverse flavours along a similar textural theme. Characterful rosés, top quality, slightly chilled Beaujolais or Loire Gamay would be my first choices. Light to medium Italian reds, like Valpolicella, Morellino di Scansano, Montepulciano d'Abruzzo or Aglianico from the south would also be good matches. If you favour whites, then stick to firm, rich white grape varieties like Riesling, which usually manage to harness at least as much flavour intensity as the reds anyway. Do watch out for pickles, gherkins/cornichons or caperberries served with the charcuterie, as vinegar is going to go head-to-head with any glass of wine. Beware, a mouthful of gherkin will guarantee you'll not be able to taste the next mouthful of wine! My advice is to tap the pickles first, endeavouring to knock off as much vinegar as possible before eating. (For *chorizo* and *spicy salami*, see 'Pork'.)

Cheese (cooked) There is an entire cheese-board section at the end of this chapter, so flick on for after dinner nibbling. *Cauliflower cheese* (*Leek Mornays* etc.) and *cheese sauces*, depending on the strength of cheese used, need medium- to full-bodied whites such as New World Chardonnays or Sémillons. For reds, the quest for fresh acidity and pure berry fruit leads me to wines from the Loire (Saumur, Chinon or Bourgueil) or Chilean, Australian or South African Merlot, Italian Dolcetto or Freisa, or youthful Rioja, Navarra, Toro or Campo de Borja reds from Spain. *Fondue* needs bone-dry whites to cut through the waxy, stringy, molten cheese. If you are a perfectionist then you'd be langlaufing off in search of the inoffensive but innocuous wines from Savoie – Chignin-Bergeron, Abymes, Crépy or Apremont. This degree of food and wine fetishism would undoubtedly reward you with a senior job in the Attention to Detail Department of the V&A. However, if you are simply after pleasant-tasting, accurate-but-not-insanely-so wines, then well-balanced, fully ripe (as opposed to exasperatingly lean and teeth-strippingly acidic) styles like junior Alsatian Pinot Blanc, Riesling and Sylvaner, and Loire Sauvignon Blanc and Chenin Blanc would be ideal. You could even try dry Portuguese whites and various northeastern Italian single varietals like PG or PB. *Raclette* (urgh) fancies (but doesn't really deserve) light red Burgundies or Cru Beaujolais. With *cheese soufflé*, one of the masterpieces of the cooked cheese repertoire, you can really go out on a limb. Argentinean Torrontés, or any aromatic dry whites

food and wine

like dry Muscat (Alsace), Riesling (from Alsace or Clare Valley/ Adelaide Hills/Eden Valley/Frankland in Australia) or even lighter Gewürztraminer (from anywhere decent, but try Alto Adige in Italy or even Chile) would be delicious. If the soufflé has any other hidden ingredients remember to consider them before plumping for a bottle – with *smoked haddock soufflé* you'd have to follow the fish. *Mozzarella*, with its unusual milky flavour and spongy texture, is well suited to Italian Pinot Bianco, Pinot Grigio, good Vernaccia, Arneis, Gavi and Verdicchio. OK, they are all Italians, but what do you expect? *Grilled goats' cheese* is equally at home with Sancerre (after all the best goats' cheese hails from Chavignol, Sancerre's finest village) and all other Sauvignon Blancs from around the world. Lighter reds also work, particularly if you are tucking into a salad with some good ham hitching a ride as well. Goats' cheese is, all in all, pretty forgiving, but try to avoid oaked whites and heavy reds.

Chicken Chicken loves whites and reds alike, but be careful, as it is a touch fussy when it comes to precise grape varieties. Chardonnay is its favourite white, with Riesling coming in a close second. Pinot Noir is the bird's favourite red, with Gamay claiming the silver medal. This means that a well-educated chicken loves every bit of my beloved Burgundy region, and who can blame it? Lighter dishes like *cold chicken* or *turkey* are fairly versatile, so try picnic-style wines (see 'Picnics'). *Cold chicken and ham pie* goes well with lighter reds and macho rosés from the southern Rhône, Beaujolais and the Loire Valley. If you are feeling adventurous then try chilled Beaujolais-Villages – it's a super match. *Poached chicken* can handle the same sort of wines but perhaps with a little more weight – Old and, for a change, New World Pinot Noirs, for example. White wine companions could include lighter New World Chardonnays or French Country Viogniers. Possibly my favourite dish of all time, *roast chicken* once again follows this theme but takes it a stage further. Finer (by that I mean more expensive) red and white Burgundy, elegant, cooler climate Australian or Californian Chardonnay and Pinot Noir, and top flight Beaujolais are all wonderful matches. *Coq au vin* also works well with red Burgundy, but you can scale the wine down to a Chalonnais, Bourgogne rouge (from one of my reputable producers, of course) or Hautes-Côtes level (ditto) – none of these should cost more than a tenner. *Chicken casserole/pot pie* ups the ante further and it enjoys a broader wine brief. Medium-weight Rhône reds and New World Grenache-based reds, as well as mildly oaky Chardonnays, are all in with a shout. *Chicken and mushroom pie*, *fricassee* and c*reamy sauces* call out beyond Chardonnay to other varieties such as dry Riesling from Germany, Alsace (France), or Clare Valley, Frankland or Tasmania (Australia), Alsatian Tokay-Pinot Gris and funky Rhône whites. New World Pinot Noir (from California, New Zealand and Tassie and Victoria in Oz) is the only token red variety to feel truly at home here. OK, so far it has been fairly straightforward, but we are now going to throw a few obstacles in front of the poor bird, as *chicken Kiev* changes the rules completely. Full, rich and even part-oak-aged Sauvignon Blanc is needed to take on the buttery/garlic onslaught – white Graves (Bordeaux) and California does this well with their Fumé Blancs, but this style is starting to be made all over the world. Not content with this hurdle, *coronation chicken*, depending on who is making it, can also have a bit of a kick, so dry Riesling from New Zealand or Clare Valley/Eden Valley in Australia would be worth unscrewing. Lastly, *barbecued chicken wings* can be

food and wine

nuclear-hot and, in my experience, beer is usually the only saviour. If, for some reason, you're a mild-mannered person who would like to spare the palates of your guests, then a clean, inexpensive New World Chardonnay with a touch of oak would be agreeable.

Chilli *Enchiladas, chimichangas, fajitas, chilli con carne, diablo-style/dragon's breath pizzas* and any other fiery Mexican dishes all groan under the weight of a liberal dose of chillies. So thirst-quenching, chillable Italian red grape varieties like Primitivo, Nero d'Avola, Frappato or Negroamaro, or juicy New World Merlot are needed to cool you down and rebuild your taste buds. If you favour whites, then New World Chardonnay or Sémillon, thoroughly chilled, will have enough texture and body to handle the heat.

Chinese The perennial problem when matching wine to Chinese food is that one invariably feels drawn to sample a spoonful of every dish on the table (well I do anyway), thus mixing competing flavours wildly. Sweet-and-sour dishes ram-raid spicy ones, with poor old plain, stir-fried food struggling for a break in the non-stop palate action. This means Chinese-friendly wines must be multi-skilled, pure, fruit-driven offerings with all-important, firm acidity; tannic, youthful reds and oaky, full-bodied whites are completely out of bounds. White grape varieties to consider (in unoaked form) are Sauvignon Blanc, Riesling, Sémillon, Pinot Gris, Greco (southern Italy), Verdelho (Australia) and Gewürztraminer. Reds are a little more difficult, as there are only a few truly juicy varieties, but New World Merlot, Argentinean Bonarda and cheaper Californian Zinfandels are all good bets. It is no surprise that Antipodean wines work well with this style of cooking as Asia is on their doorstep.

Chutney see 'Pâté' and 'Pork'.

Duck *Roast* or *pan-fried* duck is often served with fruit or fruity sauces, so you need to counter this with fruity wine. Reds are essential here, with New World Pinot Noir, good Beaujolais, youngish Rioja, Italian Barbera or Negroamaro, Australian Chambourcin and any other super-juicy, berry-drenched wines doing the job. *À l'orange* changes the colour of wine to white, but full-flavoured, juicy wines are still the vogue. Alsace or top Aussie Riesling, Alsatian Tokay-Pinot Gris, or Southern French and Rhône Viognier all have enough richness and oiliness to crack this dish, as do top-end northern Italian white blends – but these can get expensive. With *cherries*, 'village-level' red Burgundy (utilising the cherry-scented grape Pinot Noir), top notch Barbera from Piedmont, smart Reserva Rioja and medium-weight Zins from California are excellent. The more robust dish of *confit de canard* demands meatier reds with backbone and grippy acidity and tannin to cut through the sauce and fat, like those from Bandol in Provence, from Languedoc, Roussillon or from the southwest of France, for example Madiran or Cahors. For an unlikely first-class combo, try *crispy aromatic duck* with chilled Chambourcin from Australia, or juicy, fruit-driven Californian Zinfandel – it is a dead-cert.

Eggs For *quiches, soufflés* or *light savoury tarts* think of the main flavours (ham, cheese, etc.) and consider its impact on the dish. Also, think about what you are eating with it. Once you have narrowed these flavours down, unoaked or lightly oaked Chardonnay would probably be a fair starting point – Chablis is the classic, but northeastern Italian Chardonnays would also be spot on.

Omelettes, frittata and *savoury pancakes* follow the same rules. However, for *oeufs en meurette* (the great Burgundian dish of poached eggs in red wine with lardons) a red wine is definitely called for – mid-priced Beaujolais or red Burgundy would be accurate. For *fried* and *poached* eggs, look at the other ingredients involved. If on a salad with stronger-flavoured elements, try Beaujolais, but if you'd rather not, then Alsatian Riesling or rich Pinot Blanc. For *quails' eggs*, see 'Apéritif Wine Styles'. Finally, *eggs Benedict* has an awful lot going on, from the muffin base, via the bacon or ham and ending with the gloopy, wicked hollandaise. Youthful Côtes-du-Rhône is a classic combination and is so delicious your guests will definitely want more.

Fish The flavour of fish depends not only on the sort of fish you are cooking, but also, crucially, on how it is cooked. The general rule is the milder the flavour, the lighter the white wine, and the richer the flavour, the heavier the white wine. Fish cooked in red wine is one of the few exceptions to this white-dominated section, as here a light red would simply meld better with the sauce. From Bianco de Custoza and Soave (Italy), Austrian Grüner Veltliner, Menetou-Salon and Sauvignon de Touraine (Loire), white Burgundy (Mâcon, Rully, Pouilly-Fuissé, Meursault and so on), fine Californian Chardonnay, zesty Jurançon Sec, heady Australian Pinot Gris, plump Marsanne or Sémillon, to any aromatic Riesling or Viognier – the opportunities are endless. Just remember that poaching and steaming are gentler, non-taste-altering ways of cooking, while grilling, searing, frying and roasting all impart distinctive charred or caramelised nuances to the fish. Also consider what you are cooking the fish with; check through the recipe for strongly flavoured ingredients, such as lemon, capers, balsamic vinegar, flavoured olive oil and pungent herbs. Often, the finer the piece of fish, the more money you can chuck at the wine. *Dover sole*, *lemon sole*, *turbot* and *sea bass*, at the top of my fish-league, are all pretty pricey, but if you've gone that far, you should complete the picture by splashing out on a serious bottle of white Burgundy. Failing that, for a tenner you could pick up a top South African Chardonnay, Australian Sémillon, Adelaide Hills/Eden Valley/Clare Valley/ Frankland Riesling or Chardonnay, Riesling from Alsace, posh Lugana or Gavi from Italy, dry white Graves (Bordeaux), white Rhône wines or trendy Spanish Albariño or Godello to go with these fish. *Halibut*, *John Dory*, *sea bream*, *skate* and *brill* all enjoy these styles of wine, too, while *swordfish*, *monkfish* and *hake* can take slightly weightier whites (or even a fresh light red, such as Beaujolais). *Salmon* (poached or grilled) also likes Chardonnay, whether it is from the Old or New World, but steer clear of oaky styles. *Trout* likes Riesling and add the all-time classic, Chablis, to this list as well. But, for an especially wicked combo, try to track down the unusually scented French Country wine, Jurançon Sec. *Fish cakes*, especially real ones with a high salmon content, go wonderfully with dry Riesling, richer Sauvignon Blancs or fresh Sémillons, particularly if you are partial to a generous spoonful of tartare sauce. *Red mullet* has enough character to handle rosé wines, making a pretty-in-pink partnership between plate and glass. *Kedgeree* is trickier, as the combo of smoked haddock, cayenne, parsley and egg may make you lean towards red. But don't, as rapier-like acidity is needed to slice through this dish and I'm sure you know which white grape does this best – Sauvignon Blanc. While we are on the subject, Sauvignon is the grape to enjoy with fish 'n' chips (*cod*, *haddock* or *plaice*) because it can handle the batter and, to a certain degree, the vinegar (but go easy). Sauvignon also shines with *fish pie*, with the poshest partnership being Loire all-stars Pouilly-Fumé or Sancerre. If you fancy a trip to the New World, then Marlborough in New Zealand has to be the starting point for fans of this zesty grape, with Australia's Margaret River giving the best Sem/Sauv blends. *Fish soups* and *stews* need more weight and one of the most accurate matches would be white Rhône made from Marsanne and Roussanne, or Viognier. Aussie Marsanne or Pinot Gris would also be a great option. *Sardines* require perky acidity to cut through their oily flesh; once again Sauvignon Blanc is the winner, but Italian Pinot Grigio, Arneis, Verdicchio or Gavi, Spanish Albariño, French Aligoté and even light reds, like Gamay, would be smashing. *Canned tuna* just needs unoaked, dry white wine. However, *albacore*, the finer, paler version, is more delicately flavoured so take care not to swamp it. The Italian trio, Lugana, Bianco di Custoza or Soave, would do this job inexpensively and with style. For *salad Niçoise*, see 'Salads'. *Fresh tuna*, seared and served rare, secretly likes juicy, fresh, light reds and chilled rosés. *Brandade* (*salt cod*), with its garlic and oil components, can stand up to whites with a little more poke. Albariño, from Galicia in Spain, is a perfect choice. However, Penedès whites and even light rosés are all within its grasp. *Herrings*, *kippers* and *rollmops* all have a more robust texture and aroma thanks to the curing process. Once again, dry whites and rosés work well, but steer clear of oaked whites, as the power of the barrel will overshadow the subtleties of the dish. *Smoked eel* is often served with crème fraîche, and cream is always a little problematic for wine, but look to Austrian Riesling or Grüner

Veltliner, top end Italian Pinot Grigio or bone-dry Riesling, and almost any dry wine from Alsace. These will all relish the challenge. *Smoked salmon* is perfect with Gewürztraminer, whether it is from Alsace or Chile – or anywhere else come to think of it. Just make sure you buy a bone-dry, not off-dry version. The scent and tropical nature of Gewürz works amazingly well, but so does Viognier and even Canadian Pinot Blanc. Don't forget Champagne or top-end Tasmanian or Californian sparkling wine, particularly if serving blinis topped with smoked salmon and caviar. *Smoked trout* or *smoked mackerel pâté* is a challenge – fishy, smoky and creamy flavours all in one dish. McLaren Vale Sémillon, Adelaide Hills Sauvignon Blanc and Pinot Gris (all Aussies), southern French Viognier, lighter Alsatian Riesling and Pinot Blanc are all perfect matches. Lastly, *curries* or *Asian* fish dishes often sport spices, such as turmeric, ginger and chilli, so turn back to our favourite saviour white grapes for a solution – New World Sauvignon Blanc's supreme confidence and Australia's mind-blowing array of Rieslings.

Frogs' legs Tasting more like chicken than any other creature I can think of, aim for smooth, mildly oaked Chardonnay from Burgundy, Australia, South Africa or New Zealand. Consider what you've cooked these cheeky blighters in and tweak your wine choice accordingly – if *garlic butter* is involved, stick to Sauvignon Blanc. Good Luck and keep the lid tight on the pan.

Game All flighted game, including *pheasant, quail, guinea fowl, woodcock, teal, grouse, snipe, wild duck* and *partridge* adore the magisterial red grape Pinot Noir. So red Burgundy would always be my first choice, with California, New Zealand, Tasmania and Oregon somewhere in the pack behind the leader. The longer the bird is hung, the more mature the wine required. I have enjoyed mature red Bordeaux, Super-Tuscan, northern Rhône, Spanish wines from Ribera del Duero or Tarragona and many other top reds with this heady style of cuisine. But it is important to aim for complex reds with layers of fruit and a bit of age, and this inevitably means spending up. *Hare* in *jugged* form often uses port and/or redcurrant jelly in the recipe, so a red wine is needed – and a big one at that. New-style Piemontese reds made from Nebbiolo or Nebbiolo/ Barbera blends would have the brawn, as would bigger Australian Shiraz (McLaren Vale, Frankland or Barossa Valley), Zinfandel from California or South African Pinotage. One cheaper and worthy source of full-bodied red is the Douro Valley in Portugal, which makes wine alongside port. Not only would you have a beefy wine, but it would also be in perfect synergy if you've used port in the recipe. *Rabbit,* as well as being a less athletic version of a hare, is also less pungent and has lighter-coloured flesh so, although big reds are essential, they don't need to be quite as insanely powerful as those suggested for hare. The classic combo of *rabbit with mustard and bacon* has some mighty flavours on board, so aim for fairly swarthy bottles with feisty tannins and a youthful, purple hue. Chianti, Carmignano, Vino Nobile di Montepulciano (all from Tuscany), Bandol (from Provence), Lirac, Rasteau, Vacqueyras, Cairanne and Gigondas (from the southern Rhône), Argentinean Malbec, South African Cabernet and Shiraz, and smarter Chilean Cabernet blends would be spot on. *Wild boar* again favours rich, brooding red wines. Depending on the dish, you could choose any of the aforementioned reds but, this time, add the two noblest of Italian wines, Brunello di Montalcino and Barolo, to the list –

although you might need to take out a bank loan to buy a bottle. *Venison* again loves reds and any wine in this section would do, including top Australian Cabernet Sauvignon and some of the better New Zealand Hawke's Bay Cabernets and Syrahs. Finally *game pie*, served cold, behaves like cold chicken and ham pie (see 'Chicken'), loving the company of lighter reds and richer whites. If served hot, open any wine suggested for steak and kidney pie (see 'Beef').

Garlic *Roast* garlic tends to pulverise fine wines so, if you are partial to shoving a few bulbs in the oven, keep the wine spend down and follow the main dish's lead. *Garlic prawns*, *mushrooms* and *snails* all need aromatic, bone-dry Sauvignon Blanc to save the day. If you fancy going out on a limb, then dry English white wines are also an excellent fit. *Aïoli* (*garlic mayonnaise*) can add excitement to chicken, potatoes, fish, soups and so on, but just watch out for it because you'll get a shock if your wine is not up to it. Once again Sauvignon can provide solace, but you will have to find one with a lot of character and punch. (For *chicken Kiev* see 'Chicken'.)

Goose The best wines for roast goose lie somewhere between those suited to game and those for chicken. In short, this means lighter red Burgundy and Pinot Noir are the reds to choose, while big, rich Chardonnays and Rieslings make up the white team.

Greek see 'Mezze'.

Haggis Traditionally Haggis is accompanied by a wee dram of whisky but, in truth, if it could speak for itself (a scary thought) it would plump for a rich, textural white wine. Depending on your palate, you could choose a broad, luscious New World Chardonnay at the rich end, or a scented, white Côtes-du-Rhône at the lighter end. If you really want to go over the top, try a Grand Cru Alsace Riesling or Tokay-Pinot Gris.

Ham Cru Beaujolais, Chilean Merlot or Carmenère, youthful Navarra or Rioja, Italian Nero d'Avola, Montepulciano or Negroamaro and youthful, inexpensive South African Merlot or Pinotage all have the essential juiciness to complement a glorious ham. The golden rule is to avoid any tannic or heavily acidic reds – stick to more mellow styles. *Parma ham and melon, prosciutto, jamón serrano* and *pata negra* all like dry German Riesling, many of the aromatic whites from Trentino, Alto Adige and Friuli (northern Italy), and Verdejo or lightly oaked Viura from Rueda (Spain). *Honey-roast ham* needs mouth-filling, textural, bone-dry whites like 'dry' Muscat, Viognier, Verdelho and Riesling. Search for these in Alsace, Australia, the Rhône Valley and from the vast array of terrific French Country wines (and grab some ripe figs to eat alongside while you're at it). *Ham hock* with lentils or boiled Jersey potatoes or beetroot or peas (I am so hungry writing this!) is a treat with posh, dry rosé, and there are a fair few out there, so head to Tavel in the southern Rhône or to richer examples of Sancerre rosé. *Smoked ham* has a fairly strong aroma and lingering flavour, so Tokay-Pinot Gris from Alsace would be exact, as would older Aussie Rieslings. If you favour red wine then choose a Merlot, a Cabernet Franc (from Australia or the Loire) or a Beaujolais, and chill it a degree or so to retain the freshness. *Gammon steak* (avoiding the time-honoured but grim addition of pineapple or peaches) makes a neat partnership with oily, unoaked whites. All Alsatian wines and most dry German

Rieslings would be delicious, as would the world-class Rieslings from Australia's Clare Valley, Eden Valley, Tasmania and Frankland. Sémillon rarely gets the call up for a specific dish, but Aussie versions and dry white Bordeaux (both with a smattering of oak) are simply stunning with it, too.

Indian Last year I had a full induction into matching Indian food with wine when I designed and wrote the wine list for the re-launch of top London Indian restaurant, Chutney Mary. After tasting all of the dishes, it was clear to me that unoaked or mildly oaked whites were to be the driving force in my selection. Smooth, juicy rosés were also essential, as were fruit-driven reds, avoiding any that were noticeably tannic. The surprise came when I made the final selection and found that Italy, Australia and New Zealand had claimed the lion's share of the list. There were a few wines from other countries but virtually no classics like claret, Burgundy or Rhône wines. Shock horror! This just proves that, depending on the style of cuisine, a wine list can be balanced, eclectic and hopefully thoroughly exciting, without relying on France. This year I can report that Chutney Mary won the Carlton Food Awards 'Best Indian Restaurant' accolade – yippee! The grape varieties or styles of wine that go particularly well with Indian food are: whites – Pinot Grigio, Verdicchio, Sauvignon Blanc, Pinot Bianco, Fiano, Torrontés, Riesling, Viognier, Verdelho, light Gewürztraminers and Albariño; reds – Valpolicella, Beaujolais (Gamay), Grenache (and Spanish Garnacha), Negroamaro, Pinot Noir, Nero d'Avola, Zinfandel, Barbera, Lagrein and Merlot. Other styles that work well include rich rosé, Prosecco (Italian sparkling wine), Asti (with puddings), rosé Champagne, Aussie sparklers and good quality ruby port.

Japanese *Sushi* is a strange one to drink wine with, as surely tea or saké would be more appropriate? However, sparkling wines and Champagne are a treat with the best sushi, and the ever-ready Sauvignon Blanc is there as a fully qualified stand-by. You could always look to zesty unoaked Italian whites for more joy – Vernaccia, Arneis and Gavi are all ideal. *Teriyaki* dishes are a nightmare to match wine to, as the sweetness and fruitiness in the glossy soy and saké glaze is particularly dominant on the palate. Zinfandel or rich Pinot Noir from California, super-ripe Chambourcin, lighter Shiraz or Merlot from South Australia, and Nero d'Avola or Negroamaro from Sicily would just about manage this huge challenge. You will always be offered a blob of nuclear green goo with your sushi, called wasabi. I'm afraid wasabi is a stealthy, committed and silent wine assassin – Wasabi 1, Wine 0.

Junk food What should you drink with a hamburger, cheeseburger, chicken nuggets, bargain bucket or any of the other palate-numbing, industrial, fast-food offerings? A fizzy soft drink, of course, for that all-enveloping burpy, bilious feeling that you are looking forward to enjoying, ten minutes after racing this glorious cuisine down your trap. If you are seriously considering opening a bottle of wine, though, you'll no doubt return to an even-colder-than-normal burger in its neon poly-box by the time you've found a bottle and glasses. You should, of course, eat outside your front door (to avoid any unwanted aromas inside) and then hose your palate down with a simple Chilean Carmenère, Aussie Shiraz, Kiwi Sauvignon Blanc or South African Chardonnay. After that, log on to the 'Slow Food' website, sign up for a lifetime membership and vow not to enter another fast-food joint… until next time.

Kidneys Lambs' kidneys generally absorb a fair amount of the flavour from the ingredients in which they are cooked and, as mustard is often used, keep the reds firm, chunky and with a lick of keen acidity – Chianti, Morellino, Barbera (all Italian), Rioja, Toro, Navarra (all Spanish), Languedoc and the Rhône Valley (both French) would all be worthy of consideration. (For *steak and kidney pie* see 'Beef'.)

Lamb Red Bordeaux is, strictly speaking, the classic combination with *roast lamb* or *lamb chops*. However, reds from nearby Bergerac and further afield Burgundy, South Africa's Pinotage and Shiraz, California's Merlot, Australia's Shiraz and Cabernet blends, Spain's Rioja, and Argentina and Chile's Cabernets and Merlots are all in with a shout. In fact, if you keep the wine firmly in the middleweight division, you will do well. You can, of course, go bonkers on the price of the wine or stick within a tighter budget; lamb is less critical than, say, beef or game. The way it is cooked, though, should influence your final choice. If cooked *pink*, the range of suitable wines is enormous (any of the above). If *well done*, then a fruitier style of red should be served, so head to the New World countries listed above. Watch out for gravy and mint sauce, as an abundance of either could trip the wine up. *Shepherd's pie* is incredibly easy to match to red wine. In fact, just open whatever you feel like – if it's red and wet, it will probably be spot on. *Lamb pot roast* and *casserole* tend to be a little richer than a chop or roast lamb because of the tasty gravy. Again, don't spend too much on the wine, as authentic Languedoc or southern Rhône reds should be perfect. Plain *lamb shank* is another relatively easy dish to match to red wine, with inexpensive European examples from Portugal,

Spain, Italy and France all offering enough acidity and structure to cut through the juicy meat. *Moussaka,* with cheese, onion, oregano and aubergines, is altogether different. Lighter, fruit-driven reds such as New World Pinot Noir, Primitivo or any other southern Italian red and inexpensive workhorses from Toro, Alto Duero or Campo de Borja in Spain will work well. *Stews* like *navarin* (with vegetables), *Irish stew, cassoulet* or *hot pot* all have broader shoulders when it comes to reds. Beefier southern French examples from Fitou, Corbières, St Chinian, Madiran, Faugères, Minervois or Collioure would be spot on. From further afield, Malbec from Argentina or Carmenère from Chile, as well as medium-weight, fragrant Aussie Shiraz (McLaren Vale, Pemberton or Yarra Valley), would suit these dishes. *Cold roast lamb* follows the same rules as beef and, to a certain extent, ham in that fruity, light reds and juicy medium- to full-bodied whites can work well. Beaujolais, served cool, not cold, is, again (surprise!), a great partner here, while Chardonnay in any of its following guises would enliven the dish – medium-priced white Burgundy, Chardonnay from Margaret River, Adelaide Hills or Yarra Valley (Australia) or Nelson or Marlborough (New Zealand), or lighter South African and Chilean styles. Lastly, we come to *kebabs*, one of lamb's noblest incarnations whether you've lovingly marinated and skewered the meat yourself or not. You would struggle to wrestle with a kebab and a glass of wine while staggering down the street after a late night out dancing. But on the off-chance that you make it home before tucking in, then a glass of sub-fiver Aussie Chardonnay or a Sémillon/Chardonnay blend from one of the reliable brands would be a useful thirst-quencher, and not something you'd regret having opened the next morning.

Liver *Calves' liver with sage* (yum) needs medium-weight reds with firm acidity. The texture of medium rare liver is relatively delicate, but the flavour is persistent and the acidity cuts through this with style. Loire reds made from Cabernet Franc are the pick of the bunch; Saumur-Champigny, Chinon, St Nic de Bourgueil or Bourgueil are all relatively inexpensive and a perfect match. I would stop there as the red Loires are such an underrated lot but, if you feel a little more racy, look to Northern Italy. Valpolicella, Trentino Teroldego, Lagrein, Marzemino and Cabernet (Franc or Sauvignon) all have the required fruit richness with balancing acidity, freshness and grip needed for this task. *Liver and bacon* needs a touch more spice, but not much more weight, in a red wine, so move to a warmer part of France or Italy (i.e. head further south). Red Bordeaux or Chianti would do, but this may push the budget up a tad.

Meat As in *balls* (see 'Pasta'), *pies* (see 'Beef') and *loaf* (see 'Terrines').

Mexican Mexican food – *fajitas, enchiladas, tortillas, quesadillas, tacos, burritos* and the like – loaded with chilli and *salsa*, leads to the consumption of copious quantities of lime-stuffed beer, which has undeniable thirst-quenching properties but precious little flavour. But, if you fancy a glass of wine, you must go in search of juicy, fruity, chillable red grapes like Nero d'Avola, Negroamaro and Primitivo (from southern Italy), Carmenère and Merlot from Chile, budget Zinfandel from California and Cabernet or Merlot cheapies from Oz to cool you down and smooth out your battle-worn palate. As for whites, inexpensive New World mildly oaked Chardonnay or Sémillon (or a blend of the two), chilled down ice-cold, will allow you to taste the food and the wine in turn, without suffering from chilli or refried bean reflux. Interestingly, Cajun cookery follows a similar pattern to Mexican food when it comes to wine styles, as cayenne, paprika, oregano, garlic and thyme all cook up a storm and need to be tempered with juicy whites and reds.

Mezze (or *Meze*) This is the chance for dry Greek whites to shine. And there are enough out there of sufficiently high quality really to hit the mark (check out the Top 250). If you are unable to track them down, then try Muscat, Pinot Blanc or Sylvaner from Alsace, New Zealand Sauvignon Blanc or Argentinean Torrontés. Also try to find dry Muscat from Australia, Spain or Portugal, another rarity but stunning with mezze. Greek reds, I believe, are still lagging behind the whites in terms of quality. The cheapies are fine, if a little coarse, but I would avoid spending more than a tenner, as you will be hard-pushed to justify it with so much global competition out there. I would probably head to Italy or Spain for refuge.

Mixed grill A very important inclusion in my A–Z, mixed grill is the dish of choice on Mount Olympus – I'm told Hercules is a particularly avid fan. You need a rich, manly red with this hearty fare and there is nothing more macho than a feisty southern Rhône red (see the Gazetteer for a list of top performers) or its New World counterpart, a 'GSM' blend (utilising Grenache, Shiraz and Mourvèdre) from Australia. Hoohah!

Moroccan/North African The most important thing to consider when matching this intriguing style of food with wine, are the spices. Counter the sensory bombardment with either aromatic wines, or go the other way and choose closed, neutral ones to act as a backdrop to the food – these let the dish capture your senses uninterrupted. Spain, Italy and France are the most obvious ports of call and, within these three great wine nations, my favourite aromatic white styles would be Albariño (from Galicia in western Spain), Viognier (south of France) and Ribolla Gialla, Traminer, Erbaluce, Tocai, Lugana and richer Pinot Grigios (northeast and northwest Italy). Reds that work well are Rioja or similar-style Tempranillo/Garnacha blends (Spain), chilled and ripe Côtes-du-Rhône (France), and Nero d'Avola, Aglianico, Frappato or Primitivo (southern Italy and Sicily). If you want to go the neutral route, choose Beaujolais as a red, or Alsace Pinot Blanc or Loire Sauvignon Blanc as a white. If you feel the need to stray further from the Med, aim for more Sauvignon Blanc, this time from Chile or South Africa, for its herbal, lime-juice characters, and Barossa Valley Bush Vine Grenache (South Australia) for its pure red-berry fruit and herbal, smoky nose.

Mushrooms It is fair to say I am an unapologetic and often voracious carnivore, but I can happily sit down to a slap-up dinner, oblivious of the fact that I have forgotten to include meat, if mushrooms play a central role in my cooking. It is strange, and I try to feel cheated while doing the washing up, but I am replete, so, what's the problem? Clearly, veggies live a life of abstinence from many of the headings in this chapter, but can still experience 'meaty' food, in terms of intensity, flavour and texture, when mushrooms (and other ingredients) are wielded correctly. So, when matching wine to mushrooms, ignore the fact that they are fungi and look at the task they are employed to do in the dish. *Baked* or *grilled* mushrooms usually retain their essence and flavour, and cellar temperature reds (i.e. chilled a touch) should allow them to express themselves. Make sure that you choose loose, open reds with less dominant flavours that are ready to drink – simple Grenache blends, Gamay or Pinot Noir, for example. *Creamy sauces* are always tricky; if you overdo the cream, a robust, oaked Chardonnay or Sémillon is needed, but if the cream features only in a supporting, swirly role, then refreshing red grapes such as Merlot and Barbera would be superb. *Mushroom omelettes* and *mushroom tarts* are both classic examples of how a mushroom can hold its own in an eggy arena – here, again, light, fruit-driven reds enter the fray. *Wild mushrooms* can be intensely gamey and foresty, so turn to the 'Game' section and trade down a little in terms of weight (and price). *Mushrooms on toast* are thankfully back in vogue as a top-quality restaurant starter – good news, as there is nothing better for setting the palate up for a main (wintry/meaty) course. This is one of the easiest dishes to make at home and, even if you splash out on fancy bread and top shrooms, it is still a dead cheap dish. Wine-wise, look to whatever main course you are preparing and downsize the style a touch for the starter, leaving a bigger, better wine in reserve for the main course. If you are having a double serving as a stand-alone, make it in ten mins, in-front-of-the-telly dinner, then try Barbera or Dolcetto from northern Italy, for their truffley, black cherry aromas and flavours. These two varieties are becoming more widely available and won't half whiz this dish up to the top of the charts. *Stuffed mushrooms* depend on what they are stuffed with. I know it is obvious, but cheesy, veggie ones work well with light reds. Lose the cheese, though, and rich whites are in with a shout; medium-sized Chardonnays and Rieslings are ideal. For *mushroom risotto* see 'Risotto'.

Mustard Turn up the volume on any red or white wine if you are making a mustard sauce, dressing or an accompanying dish with a mustard theme. You do not need to go too far, but a notch up in quality and flavour is needed to counter the intensity of flavour – this will translate to a pound or two more spent on your bottle.

Olives See 'Apéritif Wine Styles' if you are nibbling them. But, if you're cooking with olives, say in a lamb recipe, take care not to introduce too much (if any) of the liquor (water, brine or oil), as it is very pungent (and often not of the highest quality) and can cast too strong an influence over the final taste of the dish. This will, in turn, affect your wine's chances of survival. As usual, the rule is to look to the main ingredient in the recipe and make sure that your chosen wine can be enjoyed alongside an olive, prior to its involvement in the dish. *Tapenade* is a funny old thing – vehemently unfriendly when it comes to wine (unless you love dry sherry), it is best to go for very dry whites from cooler-climate regions, for example Frascati, Soave, Lugana Greco, Falanghina, and Vernaccia (all Italian), or Sauvignon de Touraine, Cheverny, Muscadet, Bergerac Sec, Jurançon Sec or Pacherenc de Vic Bihl from France.

Onion As a stand-alone dish, onion must be at its best in a classic *onion tart* and Alsatian Riesling is the only wine to drink alongside this noble offering. If you stray from this advice, you'll receive a knock at the door from the long arm of the wine police. If you conform, you will be in no doubt about the virtues of food and wine matching. You may also see *caramelised* onions offered as a side dish; if so, tread carefully. The intense sweetness, albeit tempered by the rest of your food, can put a wine off. So eat and sip cautiously – I chickened out of this one! For *French onion soup* see 'Soup'.

Oysters see 'Seafood'.

Paella Not worthy of a listing really, except that it is such a cacophonic mix of ingredients and it often crops up in 'what do I drink with…' questions. The answer is chilled, ripe Cabernet Franc (red Loire), Albariño or Godello (Spanish white grapes) or French Grenache-/Spanish Garnacha-based light reds and rosés. Mmm!

Pasta Naked pasta tastes pretty neutral, which is why it is never served stranded on its own! So, the trick is to consider what you are serving over, under, around or in it. Stuffed styles like *cannelloni*, *agnolotti*, *cappelletti*, *tortellini* or *ravioli* can contain veg, cheese, meat and all sorts, so bear these ingredients in mind. *Spinach and ricotta tortellini* soaks up juicy Italian reds like Freisa, Dolcetto and Barbera from Piedmont, and young, simple Chianti, Franciacorta, Bardolino and Valpolicella. *Seafood* pasta dishes, including the all-time favourite *vongole* (*clams*), love serious Sauvignon Blanc (from anywhere), decent Frascati (over £5 if you can find it!), Soave (again, break over the fiver barrier), Lugana, Fiano di Avellino, Greco di Tufo and Vernaccia di San Gimignano. *Meatballs, spaghetti Bolognese, lasagne* and *meaty sauces* all respond to juicy reds. Keep the budget down and head for expressive, fruit-driven examples that work in tandem with the dish, as opposed to trying to score points. Any heavy reds would ruin the dish so try to be careful. Consider all of Italy, many New World regions, but steer clear of hugely alcoholic wines (read the label and stay under 13.5%) and, although heretical, anything bright and juicy made from Tempranillo or Garnacha from Spain. *Roasted vegetables* often pop up in pasta dishes allowing you to choose between richer whites and lighter reds. Not only is this an attractive veg-friendly dish, it also suits all wine palates (this makes it a safe dinner party dish for first-time guests). *Pesto* may be a classic pasta combo but it is remarkably hostile on the wine front. Oil, pine nuts, Parmesan and basil seem innocent enough, but combine them and you are forced into lean, dry whites for safety. Go to Italian regions Friuli, Alto Adige or Veneto as your guide. They grow Sauvignon Blanc up there, so at least you can rely on that stalwart grape but, otherwise, Pinot Grigio, Tocai Friulano and Pinot Bianco are all good bets. *Red pesto* is a different call altogether. This time go for light red wines and keep their temperature down to focus the fruity flavours. *Cheesy* and *creamy sauces* tend to be more dominant than the ingredients bound therein, so once again Bardolino, Valpol, Dolcetto, Freisa and Barbera (all from Piedmont), Montepulciano (from Marche) and medium-weight Chianti are all accurate. If, for some reason, you want to stray from the idyllic shores of Italy (I don't know why, as all of these wines are cheap and widely available) then there is plenty more choice; medium-weight reds and dry whites are everywhere. Just remember not to overshadow the dish, particularly with higher-alcohol wines. For *tomato sauce*, see 'Tomato'. For *mushroom sauce*, see 'Mushrooms'.

Pâté Regardless of its ingredients, pâté is very keen on white wines. The only reds that work are micro-featherweights such as Beaujolais and Bardolino. In the white world, you need to hunt down fruity, aromatic wines from any decent estate in my Gazetteer, but make sure they have a degree of sweetness. All styles from technically dry (but still ripe and fruity – Riesling, Gewürztraminer, Muscat, Chenin Blanc and so on) up to genuine sweet wines can be considered. Pâté is usually served as a starter, so pouring a sweet wine can seem a little about face. But if you are serving pudding or cheese later on in the proceedings, by selecting your menu carefully, you can happily open a bottle of sweet wine, serve a few small glasses for starters and finish it off during cheese or pud. Many sweet wines are sold in half or 50cl bottles, so if it's a small gathering, anything up to six, you'll not waste any. *Chicken liver pâté* favours dry to medium-dry German Riesling, Alsace Riesling, Pinot Blanc, or mildly sweet white Bordeaux styles (Loupiac or Saussignac) and older Aussie Rieslings. *Country pâté*, a clumsy catch-all term that often hints at a coarser texture of pâté of indeterminate origin, again likes light white wines with a degree of sweetness. If you are pushed into choosing from a short wine list or are confronted with a sparsely stocked off-licence, then play safe, buy a dry white and hope for the best. But if you have the luxury of choice, then Alsace is a great region to start with. Riesling and Tokay-Pinot Gris are the plum choices here. Head to the New World and you'll find Riesling in abundance in Australia, while Chilean Gewürztraminer is an unusual, but rewarding style. *Duck pâté* can be delicious but, if you want the real thing, plump for *foie gras (goose liver)*. We are now firmly in sweet wine territory. Sauternes, Loire and Alsace sweeties, Aussie botrytised Riesling and Sémillon, and with a tighter budget, Monbazillac, Ste-Croix du Mont, Loupiac, Cadillac and Saussignac, Sauternes' taste-alike neighbours. If you have never tasted this heady food and wine combo, you are in for a very pleasant surprise indeed. *Parfait*, the smoother, creamier, whipped-up version of pâté, tends to reveal its secret brandy ingredient more than a coarse pâté, so make sure your sweet wine is rich enough to cope with this. If you don't want to sip a sweet wine, then nearly-sweet or rich whites from Alsace also work. Vendange Tardive (late-picked) wines offer richness without cloying, sugary sweetness and will appease the non-sweet wine fans. Grapes to consider are Tokay-Pinot Gris, Gewürztraminer and Riesling. *Smoked salmon pâté* and other fish pâté incarnations are well served by aromatic whites (see 'Fish'). One thing to remember with pâté dishes is that occasionally *chutney* (or *onion confit/onion marmalade*) is served alongside, giving an intense fruit or veg explosion of flavour, which may confuse the wine. Not so Alsatian Vendange Tardive wines, mentioned above, whose spice and richness of fruit will welcome the added flavours – drier wines will suffer. I have already talked about gherkins and capers in the 'Charcuterie' section, so keep them well under control.

Peppers Fresh, crunchy, raw peppers crackle and pop with zingy, juicy, healthy flavours. It is no surprise that Sauvignon Blanc (from almost anywhere) is the best grape for salads and raw peppers, as 'capsicum' is a classic tasting note for this variety. It is a marriage made in heaven, but if you want to try something different, then dry Chenin Blanc from South Africa or Italian Pinot Grigio would also be splendid. *Piemontese peppers* are a favourite Saturday lunch dish of mine, and with the olive oil, garlic, black pepper and tomato ingredients, dry whites are required, especially if the traditional anchovy fillets are criss-crossed on top of the glistening tomato hemispheres. Assertive Sauvignon Blanc is the best option, although Verdicchio, Orvieto, Greco, Fiano and Gavi (or less expensive Cortese-based Piedmont white) would be appropriate. A *stuffed pepper* depends more on the stuffing than the pepper itself, so look to the filling for guidance. Generally speaking, meat or cheese stuffing goes well with light Italian reds. *Peppers marinated in olive oil* love any dry white wines; for consummate accuracy Italian is best, so find some Soave, Frascati or Friuli single varietals such as Pinot Grigio, Pinot Bianco, Traminer or Sauvignon Blanc. For *gazpacho* see 'Soup'.

Picnics You simply must buy screwcap-sealed bottles for picnics. There is no need for a corkscrew, you can reseal the bottle with ease and also not have to worry about anyone knocking it over. These days there is a massive choice of wines out there, but for all-round picnic-matching skills, rosé has to be the first port of call. It is multitalented when it comes to all manner of cold food dishes, and if you chill the bottles down ice cold for departure, it will drink like a white early on, and as the day hots up (if it does!), will behave more like a red. This should coincide with your move from crudités and dips, via smoked salmon, to rare roast beef and finally some good cheese (yes, I do make my own picnics and, no, I don't have an account at Fortnum's!). Other varieties that enjoy *al fresco* food are Sauvignon Blanc for whites and Beaujolais for reds. Once again, chill all your wines right down prior to departure and, to enjoy them all at their best, drink them in order from white, via rosé to red.

Pigeon see 'Game' but spend less!

Pizza I love pizza and, if prepared well, there is nothing to touch it. Incidentally, if you are a fan and fancy a cunning twist to the trad tomato sauce, then make too many Piemontese peppers for lunch and keep a few aside. Skin the peppers when they cool and then whiz them up with the garlic, oil and tomatoes. You'll be left with a reddy-orange sauce with one hell of a kick – perfect for painting liberally over your pizza bases. And you thought this was a wine book! Heroic pizzas, like these, rarely allow white wines enough space to be heard. However, I suppose a simple vegetable or seafood pizza might need a feeble, dry white wine. Assuming you have a tomato (or red pepper!) base and some mozzarella cheese on top, the real point of a pizza is the unlimited number of palate-expanding toppings that you sling aloft – mushroom, onion, anchovy, caper, olive, beef, ham, egg, pepperoni and, crucially, chillies. A real man's pizza has these and more, so you will have to find a feisty red and chill it down. My all-Italian pizza wine line-up includes: whites – Arneis, Soave, Bianco di Custoza, Verdicchio, Pinot Bianco, Pinot Grigio and Orvieto; chillable reds – Sardinian Cannonau, Freisa, Barbera and Dolcetto from Piedmont, Marzemino and Teroldego from Trentino, Bardolino and Valpolicella from Veneto and Montepulciano d'Abruzzo, Morellino di Scansano, Sangiovese di Romagna, Primitivo di Puglia, Nero d'Avola di Sicilia, Negroamaro and Aglianico from further south. If you insist on drinking non-Italian wines with pizza, then you're gonna get nicked by the wine police (again, because I bet you shirked with the onion tart, too).

Pork Porky pig has so many different gastronomic guises that I have given the gallant *sausage* its own section. And, no doubt, *pâté* and *terrine* lovers are delighted that these two dishes also won their own headings. I have also dealt with *charcuterie, cassoulet, bacon, full English breakfast* and *ham* in other sections. Here I endeavour to cover any other porcine dishes not otherwise mentioned. So, first in the queue is the princely *pork pie* and its less exciting, ever so slightly oddly coloured, asteroid cousin, the *Scotch egg*. A good pork pie is a real treat, and while I'm sure that a pint of real ale is more than likely the ideal partner, a glass of Cru Beaujolais is also a perfect fit. The Scotch egg somehow crops up in pubs and picnics more than at the dinner table (not really surprising, would you want one in your fridge?) and real ale is the only sensible choice. But you wouldn't be putting a foot wrong by ordering a juicy Merlot either. If you like a dollop of Branston or Piccalilli on the plate with your pie, then be ready for the wine to be sent into a tailspin. There is no way out, your palate will go down in flames. *Chorizo* and *salami* fall into the aforementioned 'Charcuterie' section, but do remember that the spicier the salami, the greater the need for cool red wine. A plate of chorizo is excellent with dry sherry – manzanilla and fino are the two best styles. Next on the agenda, *spare ribs* (my iron-stomached brother is a devotee, so I have taken advice on this one). Whether drenched in barbecue sauce or not, they are prehistoric fare, so cave-man reds are needed to slake your thirst. Juice and texture are the essential ingredients, so head to the New World in search of Argentinean Sangiovese, Bonarda or Tempranillo, Chilean Carmenère or Australian Cabernet/Shiraz blends. Californian Zinfandel would also work well, although it would be disproportionately expensive to the dish. *Rillettes*, which can also be made from duck or rabbit, is one of pork's lighter sides. This mild, oddly fondanty, savoury dish is often served as part of a plate of cold meats. White wine is called for,

food and wine

with Pinot Blanc, Sylvaner and Riesling from Alsace all working well. As usual Aussie Riesling will find this a doddle, too. I have left the big daddy to last – *roast pork*. There are a number of ways to serve roast pork, so when it comes to matching this dish to wine, the brief is fairly open. One thing is certain – if you are going to serve a red, make it light (Pinot Noir is best). Pork is far more excited to be associated with white wine, particularly if there is apple sauce moored alongside. Classy, unoaked Chardonnay from Chablis or Burgundy would be exact, although New World Chardonnays can hack it as long as they are not too overtly oaky. Riesling (dry and luxurious), Condrieu (the super-dear northern Rhône Viognier), Vouvray (make sure it says *sec* – dry – on the label) and southern Rhône whites (thin on the ground but a lot of bang for your buck) are all worth a substantial sniff.

Quiche (and posh tarts?) see 'Eggs'.

Rabbit Rabbit *rillettes* love a little more scent and exoticism in their wines than pork rillettes, so Marsanne, Roussanne and Viognier from anywhere in the world (Rhône is your starting point, maybe California or Australia next) or Pinot Blanc and Riesling (the richer styles from Alsace) would be mouth-wateringly spot on. All other bunnies, see 'Game'.

Risotto Generally, the richness and texture of a risotto needs to be 'cut' with the acidity of a clean, dry white wine, but what else have you folded into your risotto? It is these magic ingredients that matter when finding the perfect wine to counter the creamy, cheesy (if you've whacked in a spot of Parmesan and butter alongside the stock!) rice. Light reds can work with *wild mushroom* risotto but, even with this, I prefer scented, cool whites. *À la Milanese*, with saffron, can force a light, dry white into submission unless it has enough fruit and 'oomph'– Arneis or Gavi from Piedmont are worth a go, as is Riesling from a good Australian or Alsatian producer. *Chicken and mushroom* risotto likes Chardonnay and lighter Pinot Noirs, just as a non-risotto dish might. *Primavera* favours fresh, zingy, green whites – Sauvignon Blanc anyone? For *seafood* risotto see 'Seafood'.

Salads A huge subject that more often than not just needs a spot of common sense. Basic *green* or *mixed* salad without dressing is virtually tasteless, as far as wine is concerned, but be careful if it's dressed – particularly if vinegar is involved because this changes all the rules. People will tell you that light whites are always best with salad, but you are hardly going to order a glass of white to accompany your *pousse and shallot* salad after having downed a rare steak and chips. Just chomp through the salad, having a break in the red, and then bring it back into view when you've finished. Don't worry, the salad is a palate cleanser and knows that it is not the main show. *Seafood* salad enjoys the white wines that go well with seafood (obvious, I know, see 'Seafood'); *Niçoise* likes tangy Sauvignon Blanc, Sauv blends and neon green Margaret River Sémillons (Australia); *chicken* salad works well with Rhône whites and middle-weight Chardonnays; *feta* salad, not surprisingly, is perfect with dry Greek whites; *French bean and shallot* salad likes lighter, inexpensive Alsace Tokay-Pinot Gris and Pinot Blanc; *tomato and basil* salad is best matched with rosé or anything fresh, dry, keenly acidic, white and Italian; *Caesar* salad, if made properly, is great with Sauvignon Blanc or Gavi; *Waldorf* salad needs softer, calmer white grapes like Pinot Blanc and Sylvaner (Alsace), or South African Chenin Blanc; *pasta* salad can get a little stodgy, so uplifting, acidity-rich, dry whites are essential. Every country in the wine world makes salad-friendly wines, even the UK, where the better dry white grapes like Bacchus, Reichensteiner and Seyval Blanc, in the right hands, can be a joy (you know where to look!).

Sausages (meaty ones, please, as opposed to fish or veggie!) Any sausage dish, including *toad-in-the-hole* and *bangers and mash*, needs manly, robust, no messin' reds. Cahors, Garnacha blends from Tarragona, Shiraz or Cabernet from Western Australian or McLaren Vale, Malbec from Argentina, any Languedoc or southern Rhône reds, Barbera from northern Italy, Primitivo from southern Italy, and Chinon or other red Loires are all suitable. Zinfandel, Merlot and Cabernet from California would also be awesome, as would a bottle of plain old claret. Hurrah for sausages and their global compatibility with red wine! They're not fussy and nor should you be.

Seafood Muscadet, Cheverny, Menetou-Salon, Sauvignon de Touraine, Quincy, Pouilly-Fumé, Sancerre (all Loire – seafood specialist wines), Chenin Blanc (South Africa), Albariño (Spain), Lugana, Verdicchio, Soave and Pinot Grigio (Italy) and any bone-dry, unoaked New World whites are all perfect with seafood. *Squid* and *octopus* both need very dry whites with aromatic fruit like Sauvignon Blanc, northern Italian or Penedès (Spain) whites, and resinous Greek whites if the dish is served in its ink. The curious, bouncy texture of both squid and octopus does not embrace wine in the same way fish does, so concentrate on the method of cooking and the other ingredients to help you make your final choice. *Crevettes grises*, or the little grey/brown shrimps, eaten whole as a pre-dinner nibble, are stunning with Muscadet or Loire, Australian or Kiwi Sauvignon Blanc. *Crayfish* and *prawns* are a step up in terms of flavour and dry English whites, simple, dry Riesling, and Sauvignon or Sémillon/Sauvignon Blanc blends are all lovely. If you are a *prawn cocktail* fiend (I am), then smart Sauvignon Blanc (no need to spend over £8) is dry and aromatic enough to wade through the livid pink Marie Rose sauce. *Lobster*, the noblest of all crustaceans, served cold or in a salad, should tempt you to delve into the deepest, darkest corners of your cellar and uncork the finest whites. Burgundy (no upper limit), Australian and New Zealand Chardonnay (only the best – not too oaky), Californian Chardonnay (elegant as opposed to blockbuster) and Viognier, (from its spiritual birthplace in Condrieu, in the northern Rhône) will all set you back a fortune but, hey, you've bought lobster in the first place, so go the extra light year and finish the job properly. *Lobster thermidor* is not my favourite dish, as I feel that lobster loses its magical texture and elegant flavour when served hot, but you can easily uncork richer (but less expensive) whites like Aussie Sémillons or South American Chardonnays. If you feel like a slice of lobster class, but for a slightly reduced price, then *langoustines* (or *bugs/yabbies* if you're mad for crustacea and on hols in Australia) are the answer. Lobster-wines are perfect here, just adjust the price downwards by a few quid or more. *Dressed crab* is a fabulous dish and, once again, Loire whites, like Muscadet (only £4–£5 for a good bottle) are spot on. Dry whites such as Ugni Blanc from Gascony, Jurançon and simple Chablis are also good, but Sauvignon Blanc is again probably the pick of the grapes (it always is). Don't just look at the Loire, though, as the white wines from Bordeaux and Bergerac often have a fair slug of Sauvignon in them and, of course, Sauvignon is grown all over the world. *Mussels* probably do best in *gratin* or *marinière* form when dry Riesling, Barossa Valley Sémillon, New Zealand Pinot Gris and New World Sauvignon Blanc are all worthy contenders. *Scallops* can take a little more weight in a white wine (mildly oaked Sauvignon Blanc, for example). They can even handle a spot of light red. *Scallops sauté Provençal* (with tomatoes and garlic) and *scallops wrapped in bacon* are wicked with smart rosé. *Scallops Bercy* (with shallots, butter, thyme, white wine, parsley and lemon juice) are superb with top Sancerre or Pouilly-Fumé – spend up, it will be worth it. *Oysters* are traditionally matched with Champagne, but not by me – I prefer a simple dry white like Muscadet, with its salty tang, or a 'village' Chablis or Sauvignon de St-Bris. And lastly a *plateau de fruits de mer* – all of the above, plus whelks (yuk) and winkles (too fiddly, what's the point?) – really only needs a first class bottle of Sauvignon de Touraine or Muscadet. You'll thank me, because after you receive the bill for this heavenly platter of seafood you'll be delighted to spend a fraction of that on a bottle of slottable wine. Finally *seafood risotto* – here dry Italian wines including decent Frascati, Vernaccia di San Gimignano, Arneis, Verdicchio Classico, Greco and Fiano, along with South African Sauvignon Blanc and Chenin Blanc make a rather delicious combination. Remember that Chilean Sauvignon is often cheaper than both South African and New Zealand versions, so if you are having a big risotto party then look here for a volume purchase. For *clams*, see 'Pasta'.

Side dishes see 'Vegetables'.

Snails Oh yeah! See 'Garlic'.

Soups Dry sherry is often quoted as soup's knight in shining armour. But it seems a bit silly to crack open a fresh bottle of fino every time I fancy a bowl of soup. And, what's more, it isn't the best wine for the job, as the soup family is a diverse collection of individuals – no one wine can expect to cover all of the flavours. *Minestrone*, with its wonderful cannellini bean base, and *ribollita* (the stunning, next-day minestrone incarnation, re-boiled with cabbage and bread thrown in for extra body) like to keep things Italian, with Teroldego or Marzemino from Trentino and Valpolicella being superb candidates. If you want to hop over the mountains to France, then simpler southern Rhônes (a well made C-d-R would do) make a refreshing and accurate alternative. *Spinach and chickpea* soup goes well with bone-dry whites like those from Orvieto, Frascati, Greco, Verdicchio (Italy), Penedès or Rueda (Spain), or Sauvignon Blanc from New Zealand, South Africa or Chile. *Vichyssoise* (*chilled leek and potato* soup) needs creamy, floral whites, such as simple Alsatian Riesling, South American or French Viognier, or light, white Rhônes. *Lobster* or *crayfish bisque* also has a creamy texture coupled with a deceptive richness, so dry sherry could conceivably make an appearance here. If you don't fancy that, then white Burgundy is best. *Bouillabaisse with rouille*, the serious fish, garlic, tomatoes, onion and herb broth with floating toasty crostinis topped with garlic, chilli and mayo, is a mighty dish and yet only needs tiddly little whites like our old favourites Muscadet and Sauvignon de Touraine. *Consommé* is a definite dry sherry dish (at last). *Gazpacho* (*chilled tomato, cucumber, onion, pepper and garlic* soup) likes nothing more than Spanish new-wave (unoaked) Viura or cheeky Verdejo from Rueda. *Mushroom* soup is another dry sherry candidate (as presumably you've used some in the recipe), while *French onion* soup goes well with dry Riesling from Alsace or South Australia. *Oxtail* demands hearty reds – rustic, earthy inexpensive southern French bruisers are ideal. *Lentil and chestnut* and *lentil and bacon* soups both crave dry sherry (this time try an amontillado, for complexity), while *clam chowder* is basically a fishy soup with cream (and sometimes potato), so Sauvignon Blanc, Chenin Blanc and all seafood-friendly whites are perfect. *Vegetable* soup can be dull but it can also be excellent; either way, rustic reds at the bottom of the price ladder are sound. *Tomato* soup is a strange one. Always avoid oak. I favour light reds or dry whites – Gamay (Beaujolais or Loire) or Sauvignon Blanc (Pays d'Oc, Loire, South Africa or Chile) all do the job admirably.

Sweetbreads Classically cooked with *butter and sorrel, sauce ravigote* (mustard, red wine vinegar, capers and tarragon) or *sauce gribiche* (like ravigote but with chopped hard-boiled eggs and parsley as well), sweetbreads demand aromatic, decadently textured, self-confident white wines. Alsatian or South Australian Riesling, with a bit of age, would be my first choice. If you can't find any, then try creamy, oily, nutmeg- and peach-scented Rhône whites. All of these wines are dear, but there is no real way around this quandary. *Ris de veau aux morilles* (veal sweetbreads with a very rich, creamy wild mushroom sauce) needs the most intense Rhône whites or Alsatian Rieslings.

Tapas Sherry and dry white wines, preferably Spanish, avoiding oaky ones, are perfect partners for these addictive Spanish snacks.

Terrines A terrine is a more robust pâté, generally served in slices. So what's good enough for a pâté is often good enough for a terrine. One of the classics is *ham and chicken* which loves white Burgundy or elegant, non-French, mildly oaked Chardonnays. Another white Burgundy lover is *jambon persillé*, the sublime parsley, jelly and ham dish. This is not surprising as it is a Burgundian recipe in the first place. Beaujolais, Alsatian Gewürztraminer, Riesling and Tokay-Pinot Gris love *rabbit*, *hare* and *game* terrines, particularly if there are prunes lurking within. *Fish* terrines follow the lead of fish *pâtés* and *mousses* with Sauvignon Blanc, Riesling, clean, fresh Chardonnays, like Chablis, and finally the enigmatic Spanish stunner, Albariño.

Thai Along the same lines as Vietnamese and other 'Asian but not overly so' styles of cuisine, it is best to look to the main ingredient and then concentrate on appropriate southern hemisphere, fruit-driven wines. Likely candidates are: Australian or New Zealand Riesling, Viognier, Sémillon, Verdelho, Pinot Gris and Sauvignon Blanc. New World sparkling wines in general work well, as do dry Muscats from Portugal and Pinot Gris or Viognier from Argentina.

Tomato Strangely, tomatoes are pretty fussy when it comes to wine matching (see 'Soup'). Pinot Noir works but, generally, New World versions perform better than their Old World counterparts, as they often have more fruit and lower acidity. Other reds, like Sicilian Nero d'Avola, Aglianico, Primitivo (southern Italy) and any juicy, warm-climate Merlot or Zinfandel are accommodating. When raw, as in a salad, rosé is a good choice. A *tomato sauce* demands dry, light whites and Italy is the best place to look for these, as they are often ripe and cheap. Tomato *ketchup*, while delicious, is so sweet and vinegary that it gives wine a hard time, so use sparingly on your burger if you like drinking fine wine. Drench it if you're gunning down a cheap glugger.

Truffles Truffley, foresty, feral and musky – yum! You have a choice of similarly scented wines to match this unusual life form – Burgundian Pinot Noir, Piedmont's magnificent Nebbiolo and Barbera, and Syrah (French and serious, please). If you want to cook chicken or fish with truffles, then vintage Champagne (you could even go crazy and find some vintage rosé Champs) or top Alsatian Riesling would be nothing short of spectacular.

Turkey The thing to watch out for with *roast* turkey is the cranberry sauce factor. Often a fresh, young Crianza Rioja or juicy New World Pinot Noir complements this outlandish red-fruit flavour well. At Christmas, Rioja is again a winner as mountains of cocktail sausages, bacon, sprouts and the rest take the flavour spotlight away from the turkey. If you are very brave, totally ahead of your time, or just a little mad, then sparkling Shiraz from Australia would be fantastic, celebratory and original. Otherwise, see 'Chicken'.

Turkish I have already covered lamb kebabs (with lashings of chilli sauce) in the 'Lamb' section but, essentially, Turkish food is best with Greek wines (endeavouring to be non-political) as the cuisine styles are linked and the resinous, aromatic whites and purple, violet-scented reds are spot on.

Veal There are some mightily good dishes in this section, but sadly there is no hard and fast rule as to what to follow on the wine front, so read carefully. Veal does, however, prefer to keep the company of grown-up white wines and classy, lighter reds. *Saltimbocca*, the terrific veal, sage and prosciutto dish, needs a wine to 'jump in the mouth'. Pinot Nero (Italian Pinot Noir) would be fine, but is hard to find. If your search is unsuccessful, try another weirdo – Trincadeira from Portugal makes an inexpensive, inspirational substitute. *Vitello tonnato* (stunning), the thinly sliced, braised veal dish, served cold and drizzled in a sauce made from marinated tuna, lemon juice, olive oil and capers, is one of the world's most sumptuous starters. Take the tuna and anchovy (used in the braising stage) as your lead – fresh, sunny, seaside whites like Verdicchio, Greco and Vernaccia work especially well. *Wiener schnitzel*, fried veal in egg and breadcrumbs, can often taste a little on the dry side, so what else is on the plate? If there is nothing of enormous character to deflect your mission, give it the kiss of life with a juicy, mildly oaked Chardonnay. *Blanquette de veau*, the French classic with a cream sauce, is definitely a white wine dish. Again Chardonnay will do, but for perfection go for Viognier, Roussanne or Marsanne blends from the Rhône. *Osso bucco*, veal shin with wine, tomatoes, parsley, garlic and zesty gremolata, is a lighter, more heady stew than most, and Tasmanian, Yarra Valley, Adelaide Hills (Aussie), New Zealand or Oregon Pinot Noir would be great, as would huge, full-on Chardonnays from anywhere in my Gazetteer.

Vegetables Vegetables (served on their own or as an accompaniment) taste, on the whole, relatively neutral. But, depending on how they are cooked, they can require a moment or two's thought. Any *gratin* (*baked with cheese*) or *dauphinoise* (*thinly sliced potato baked with cream and garlic*) dish needs light reds or firm, self-confident whites. *Beetroot* is a tad tricky, but Alsatian whites generally have the texture and flavour to make it through. *Cabbage, leeks, spinach, parsnips, cauliflower, sprouts, courgettes, carrots, peas* and *potatoes* are usually innocent so don't worry about them, but *gnocchi* (plain or flavoured with spinach) needs juicy, fruit-driven wines with perky acidity to cut through their texture and lubricate the palate. *Marinated vegetables* and *polenta* love Italian whites – Pinot Grigio, Soave, Verdicchio etc. *Lentils* often dry the palate out and rustic, earthy reds are essential. Look to French Country wines or to Chile and Argentina. *Corn on the cob* is a dead ringer for New World Sauvignon Blanc. Open a bottle and, with some wines, you'll actually detect a canned sweetcorn aroma!

Vegetarian If you are a strict vegetarian or vegan, look at the label on the wine bottle – many now advertise their credentials. If you are still unsure, ask your wine merchant.

Vinaigrette A passion killer for wine, vinegar is strongly flavoured and makes any wine taste flat for a few seconds. Dressing made with lemon juice and oil is more wine-friendly and healthier.

Vinegar See above! Balsamic vinegar seems to be more accommodating than most.

Welsh rarebit Always finish on a good note, and cheese on toast is a must for survival. Whether you make these for late night nibbling or as a traditional savoury after pudding, you deserve a meaty little rustic red swimming alongside. Anything from the south of France, southern Italy or Spain would be a delicious match.

PUDDINGS

There is nothing better than finishing off dinner with a glass of sweet wine to accompany your pudding. Read on for a comprehensive list of my favourite puddings and their dream wines. There is only one rule to remember when matching wine to sweet dishes – you must make sure the wine is at least as sweet as the pudding, otherwise it will taste dry. Most wine shops have a few sweet wines lurking on the racks, but sadly not as many as one would like. You may have to find a decent independent merchant to get a good selection of sweeties so check out the 'Directory' on page 203 for a merchant near you. Also run through my Top 250 for a serious list of sweet wines that between them cover all the dishes in this section.

Almond tart Despite its heavenly flavour and decadent texture, this needs fairly careful handling on the wine front, as an overbearing sweet wine would crush the delicate almondy nuances. Lighter, youthful sweeties like Muscat de Beaumes-de-Venise, Muscat de Rivesaltes, Moelleux (sweet) Loire whites and Jurançons would all be spot on. Stick to these styles if your almond tart has fresh fruit on top. *Bakewell tart*, while perhaps not as elegant as a fresh fruit tart, likes these sweeties, too, but you could go for a little more age on a sweet Loire wine.

Apple *Strudels*, *pies*, *fritters* and *crumbles* all enjoy varying degrees of nutty, cinnamony, buttery pastry and brown-sugar-toffee flavours. These overlay the intrinsic fruitiness of the filling and demand a richer, heavier style of pudding wine. We are still, however, in the foothills of sweetness! German Riesling (of at least Auslese status), late-picked Muscat or Riesling from Australia, classic French Sauternes (don't spend too much) or New World botrytised Sémillon and lighter, youthful Hungarian Tokaji (lower number of Puttonyos!) are all runners. *Baked apples* (assuming they are served warm/hot) ought to have ice-cold, light, fresh German or Austrian Riesling (Spätlese or Auslese level) and clean, light Muscats. This will give your palate a marvellous and invigorating sauna then plunge pool sensation every time you take a sip. See below for *tarte tatin*.

Apricot A sensationally accurate apricot combo is Vendange Tardive (late-picked) Condrieu (from the northern Rhône) with *apricot crumble* (especially if Ma Jukesy makes it). Unfortunately this wine is extremely rare and exceedingly expensive (best to buy it on hols in the Rhône), so where else should you look? The answer is sweet Jurançon (Moelleux), bursting with tropical quince and peach flavours, or Monbazillac, a friendlier priced Sauternes-style offering from the southwest of France.

Bananas *Raw* – either it's breakfast, you're on some madcap diet or you are Tim Henman – all of you, put the corkscrew down! *Banoffee pie*, the hideous Fraken-pud of sticky toffee and rude bananas, can only be tamed by the most outrageous of sweet wines – Hungarian Tokaji (don't waste it!), Australian liqueur Muscat (much more accurate and affordable) and Malmsey Madeira (if you are sooo cool and don't care what your friends think). With comedy *banana splits*, the candied Willy Wonka toppings and ice cream flavours are more dominant than the neutered banana, so watch out on the wine front. I would serve mini-milkshakes, as surely you are hosting a kiddie's birthday bash. You could always tuck some amaretto into the adults' shakes! Hee hee.

Berries
Black, goose, blue, rasp, logan, huckle, straw, mul, cran, bil and his secret lover *damson* pop up in many different recipes. Whether they are served *au naturel*, in a juicy *compote*, or cooked in a *summer pudding*, they all love the talented sweet wine superhero Sémillon and his sidekick Muscat. Track down these grapes from France – Sauternes, Saussignac, Monbazillac, Loupiac and Cadillac all fall neatly into the Sémillon camp; while Muscat de Rivesaltes, de Beaumes-de-Venise, de Frontignan and de Lunel all advertise Muscat on the label, so are easier to spot. Aussie late-picked Muscats are all great and inexpensive, but watch out for liqueur Muscats, as they are wildly different and will stomp all over a *fruit purée*.

Biscuits/Biscotti (and proper shortbread)
Vin Santo is the top choice for the biscuit family. Sweeter Madeira styles and cream sherry also work well, counter-pointing the crumbly texture and buttery ingredients well. None of these wines need be served in large quantities, as they are all sipping styles. Sauternes (heady sweet white Bordeaux) or New World botrytised Sémillon (same style, much better value) come in a worthy second. Other, lighter biscuits enjoy the company of simpler sweet wines, but I would stick to Sémillon or Chenin Blanc-based French versions.

Brandy snaps
God, I love brandy snaps, but can I make 'em at home? No way! If I do try, I always have to make sure the local burns unit and wooden spoon manufacturers are on standby.

Once again, try Australian liqueur Muscat, you'll love it – just try to stop when you've got through the first batch and bottle.

Bread and butter pudding You need wines with a bit of power and acidity for a traditional B & B pudding. Weightier Muscat-based wines are my favourites for the job – Moscatel de Setúbal from Portugal and Moscato or Passito di Pantelleria from the volcanic island off the south of Sicily would be a delight. Take it steady, though, as these are addictive, gloriously moreish and hugely alcoholic. Buckle up for a late night.

Cakes What's wrong with a cup of tea? Well, quite a lot, actually, when you could be enjoying a teeny glass of cream sherry or a schooner of Aussie liqueur Muscat with *coffee* cake, Bual or Malmsey Madeira with *Dundee*, *Battenberg*, *brownies* or a traditional *fruitcake*, or demi-sec Champagne with *Victoria* or *lemon sponge*. The perfect match for *doughnuts*, by the way, is Homer Simpson.

Cheesecake Whether it is cherry (the only one I'll eat) or any other style, the 'cheesiness', not the fruit, controls the choice of wine. Botrytised Sémillon and Riesling from the New World, Coteaux du Layon and other sweet Loire wines, Austrian Beerenauslese, and Alsatian Vendange Tardive Riesling and Tokay-Pinot Gris all work. The trick is to keep the sweetness intense and fruit-driven, without resorting to heavyweight styles of high alcohol/fortified wines.

Cherries In *pie* form, cherries behave like berries and prefer the company of mid-weight sweet wines. Cherries served with *chocolate* in a *marquise* or *Black Forest gâteau* can handle a much richer wine. Try Amarone, the wickedly intense red wine from Veneto in Italy, Maury or Banyuls from Roussillon (France) or really juicy Californian Zinfandel for a bizarre match. It works, honest.

Chocolate A deluxe *choccy cake* can, if it is not too intense, retreat into lighter Muscats and botrytised Rieslings. Chocolate *mousse, petits pots au chocolat* and chocolate *soufflé* all head towards Orange Muscat, with its pervading aroma and flavour of orange blossom. This is one of the finest food and wine combinations of all, as orange and chocolate are natural partners (just ask Dawn French). Australia and California make two examples that I know of, so well done Brown Bros and Andrew Quady respectively, your culinary credentials in choccy heaven are guaranteed. Chocolate *pithiviers*, the single most decadent dish in the pudding repertoire, needs unctuous fortified wines with a touch of burnt nuttiness – Banyuls or Maury (Roussillon, France), liqueur Muscat and liqueur Tokay (Australia). And while we are on the subject of top choccy, *St-Emilion au Chocolat* is no slouch. Match any of these ridiculously insane dishes with the following list of galactically serious wines – Passito di Pantelleria (for its mind-boggling orange zest aroma), Tokaji, black Muscat (space-age, careful, get ready for re-entry), liqueur Muscat, PX (short for Pedro Ximénez, the boozy, black, teeth-rottingly sweet turbo-sherry), botrytised Sémillon from the New World, Maury and Banyuls (the mega, port-like sweet Grenache wines from the south of France) and, finally, young, punchy, underrated, tawny port.

Christmas pudding During the festive period, it is useful to have a wine that lasts well once opened – you've got to make it from Christmas Eve to New Year's Day, after all. Liqueur Muscat from Australia and tawny port, as well as Malmsey Madeira, all fit the bill. You'll find that you can squeeze twelve glasses out of a bottle without short-changing anyone. Not bad, hey?

Cinnamon rolls A heavenly creation – but ever so naughty! You need considerable levels of sweetness and toffeed aromas in the wine to cope with the intensity of sugar. Vin Santo, Hungarian Tokaji, liqueur Muscat and old oloroso sherry would be stunning. Old-fashioned *Lardy cakes* are, sadly, hard to find these days, but if you are keen to have a tipple, then stick to Malmsey Madeira.

Crème brûlée As I only like the top, crunchy, caramelised bit, as opposed to the silky creamy bit, I can only make a stab at the best match. I reckon the sweet-spot would be somewhere between my almond tart and my cheesecake wines. Loire sweeties, made from Chenin Blanc, appear in both sections, so they must be spot on; Coteaux du Layon, Moelleux Vouvrays, Bonnezeaux (pronounced 'Bonzo'!) and Quarts de Chaume are your choices. You could always look for some South African Chenin Blanc sweet wines, as the grape is widely planted down there.

Crème caramel Sadly another pud that you won't get me near (it's a texture thing – too slippery), but I have it on good authority that light, delicate sweeties are required. German Auslese Rieslings from the Mosel and youthful, fairy-light Muscats would be ideal.

Crêpes Suzette Clairette de Die, the little-known sparkling wine from the Rhône (see The Top 250, for a great one), or Asti (Italy's frothy Moscato) would be the cheaper but worthy options, with demi-sec Champagne being the grown-up but expensive choice.

Custard As soon as you start waving custard around, say, on a spotted dick, you are giving your palate and the wine much more to think about. Intense creaminess craves acidity in a wine. With custard being the ultimate in eggy creaminess, the big guns like Malmsey Madeira, liqueur Muscat and Tokaji must be let out of their cages.

Doughnuts see 'Cakes'.

Fruit *Raw* fruit of any kind has a much lighter flavour than you would expect when pitted against a sweet wine. So, stay with dainty Asti, German or Austrian Spätlese Rieslings, demi-sec Champagne, fresh, clean Muscats, Italy's Recioto di Soave, Spain's Moscatel de Valencia or very light, young Sauternes. Oh, if you fancy a lychee, then find a sweet Gewürztraminer, as it has remarkable lychee characteristics on the nose and palate. *Poached* fruit, like peaches or apricots, picks up sweetness from the added sugar and can be pretty intense, so tread carefully. You may need a rich Coteaux du Layon from the Loire to see you through. For *pies* see 'Berries'.

Fruitcake see 'Cakes'.

Gingerbread A wonderful creation that, along with *ginger cake* and *ginger biscuits*, is made even better when accompanied by a glass of cream sherry or Malmsey Madeira.

Gooseberry fool A heavy, oleaginous sweet wine would trample this refreshing, palate-cleansing pud. What you need is young, botrytised Sémillon, like Sauternes, Saussignac, Monbazillac or Loupiac, or Asti or demi-sec Champagne. Try to keep the price down, as more expensive wines will usually taste finer and often more intense. A good idea would be to grab a bottle of fresh, young, Riesling Auslese (Mosel, Germany) for a fruit-cocktail-style, grapey flavour – it will also be much cheaper.

Ice cream Years ago I did a tasting where a rosé Sancerre ended up being the perfect partner for Chunky Monkey (or was it Chubby Hubby). So, as you may be able to guess, matching wine with ice cream is not always straightforward. If you want to play safe then *vanilla*, *chocolate*, *rum and raisin*, *coffee*, *toffee* and *cookie-dough* ice creams all love Pedro Ximénez (PX), the intensely coffee-and-raisin-drenched sweet sherry. You could always try sweet liqueur Muscats from Australia as well. If you have a *fruity ice cream* or *sorbet*, just leave it alone – you need a few minutes without a flagon in your hand. If you want to go crazy and experiment, you're on your own, but do let me know any perfect combos – I'll put them in next year's A–Z.

Jam tart You have to find a very sweet wine. This is the only rule, as you can't get sweeter than jam. Icewine (made from pressing grapes that have frozen on the vine) from Canada might be a relatively inexpensive way of tackling this dish. Other than that, you are looking at a monstrous price tag (with Trockenbeerenauslese from Germany) and, you'd have to ask, is the tart worth it?

Jelly Light, sweet German Riesling should not interfere too much with the jelly. Sorry, I take that back. Are you seriously thinking about matching wine to jelly?

Lemon meringue pie German Riesling would work – make sure it's sweet, but not too sweet. Recioto di Soave (Italian) or Loire Chenin Blanc would also handle this citrus theme well. The good thing is that these styles of wine are relatively inexpensive and pretty easy to come by. *Tarte au citron*, my preferred choice in the lemon/pastry arena, is stunning with Coteaux du Layon (Loire).

Meringue On their own, meringues are virtually tasteless and often a bit dusty, so if served with fruit (*pavlova*), it is the fruit that concerns you – see 'Fruit'.

Mince pies I generally follow the Christmas cake/Christmas pud lead of rich, sweet Madeira, youthful tawny port and blindingly brilliant liqueur Muscats. It will save you another trip to the shops and all of these brews are big enough to wrestle with brandy butter.

Pastries These belong to the same school as tarts and cakes, in other words, you are not really expected to crack open a bottle of wine for one – *pain au chocolat* and liqueur Muscat anyone? However, if you are in the mood, then Coteaux du Layon, Muscat de Beaumes-de-Venise, Saussignac and Monbazillac are France's best efforts. Botrytised Riesling from Australia and New Zealand, or sweet Muscat from California might also work well. Otherwise, try a German Spätlese Riesling but remember to keep the price down.

Peach melba Botrytised Riesling does the peachy thing well, as you can detect peach notes in the wine – so head Down Under or to Germany. Alternatively a late-picked Viognier from the Rhône would be stunning, but they are hard to come by and mightily dear. For *poached peaches* see 'Fruit'.

Pecan pie A well-deserved entry for one of the all-time classic Yankee Doodle dishes, which strangely needs to be drunk exclusively with Australian wine. Magill Tawny, from super-winery Penfold's, is the benchmark wine with these naughty, addictive slabs of pudding. Otherwise, Aussie liqueur Muscats or Tokays or, if you fancy something a little posher, try Malmsey Madeira.

Pineapple upside-down pudding Got to get a mention as one of the most irresistible menu items of all time. The caramel and pineapple team up to form a supremely exotic partnership in this dish and smart Sauternes would give a real result here. If you are cutting back, then Australian botrytised Sémillon would also work wonders.

Plum crumble Of the crumble family, plum is up there with blackberry and apple (essential Jukesy fodder) as one of the mightiest. A degree of concentrated sweetness is needed here, so head off to Canada for decadent Riesling Icewines, Hungary for sexy Tokaji, or to Italy for heroic Vin Santo.

Rhubarb crumble A relative lightweight next to the plum crum, rhubarb crumble likes to take it easy on the wine front. Exotically sweet Riesling from just about anywhere has rhubarby notes on the nose and palate, so this is the one and only grape to follow with rhubarb based puddings (including *fool*, *compote* and *ice cream*).

Rice pudding No idea, sorry. I haven't eaten rice pudding since school days – it was enough to put me off forever.

Rum baba By the very nature of the beast, a rum baba has a bit of a kick to it. Underneath the mild, genial exterior, a sweet-wine-bashing freak is waiting to get out. Rum baba is the Dr Lecter of the pudding world and you have to go for a fortified wine to stand a chance of survival. Our A-Team are tawny port, Bual or Malmsey Madeira and liqueur Muscat – go get 'em boys.

Sorbet see 'Ice cream'.

Steamed puddings I am writing this entry on my knees, as I am a devout fan of steamed puddings. The greatest syrupy, toffeed, old-fashioned puddings (*spotted dick*, *treacle sponge* and *suet pudding* included) deserve the most regal sweet wines. I don't care that suet is a beastly ingredient and that these recipes don't involve any tricky cooking techniques, they are celestial. All of these wines have been mentioned before but, hey, all do the business – top-flight botrytised Sémillon (from anywhere), decadent Madeira, Tokaji (spend up), Vin Santo (see the Gazetteer) and liqueur Muscat (from any one of the top Victorian specialists in Australia).

Strawberries Top quality strawberries love Asti and Moscato d'Asti (Italy), demi-sec Champagne and Clairette de Die (Rhône, France). These are all fizzy or frothy, with a touch of grapey sweetness.

Tarte au citron see 'Lemon meringue pie'.

Tarte tatin This is one of the greatest dishes of all time, along with tarte au citron. I haven't put it into the apple section, not because these days tatin is made with pear and all manner of other fruit (and savoury ingredients), but because the tatin method of cooking is the crucial factor in this dish. The rich, toffee/caramel gooeyness is what preoccupies the palate and, for that reason, honeyed Loire sweeties like Coteaux du Layon are right on the button. New World botrytised Sémillons would do, as well, and Sauternes would be a real treat.

Tiramisù A strangely unappetising dish, in my opinion, as coffee, mascarpone, chocolate and brandy are odd bedfellows, and never seem to fit truly well together in the same bowl. If you must, stay accurate with Vin Santo (to blot out the flavour) or Marsala.

Toffee apple Follow the rules for 'Tarte tatin'.

Treacle sponge see 'Steamed puddings'.

Treacle tart Treacle tart, particularly if you have included lemon zest to lighten the mood, is not as stodgy as you might expect. You could try Sauternes but, if in any doubt, then Hungarian Tokaji or youthful liqueur Muscat would probably be safest.

Trifle The marvellous old English creation, adorning vicarage sideboards up and down the country, must be delighted to have so many options on the wine front. German Riesling Beerenauslese is my top choice but any sweet Riesling would be lovely. Likewise, Sauternes and the family of worldwide sweet Sémillons all love this dish. If you are going to tip in a bit of booze, sherry is traditionally used and good quality cream sherry is probably best. Whatever you choose, I'll have a glass of pud wine please and politely refuse the trifle – it's the whipped cream, yuk.

Zabaglione Passito di Pantelleria, from the tiny volcanic island off Sicily, is the only wine to accompany this creamy concoction, unless the Marsala you use in the recipe is of sufficient drinking quality. If so, then you can cover two bases with one wine – and that must be the epitome of food and wine matching.

CHEESE

The old adage 'red-wine-with-cheese' is downright wrong. When pondering which wine to drink with your cheese, keep an open mind as surprisingly almost anything goes – white, red, sweet, dry and fortified. Try to keep your cheese board simple to limit the number of flavours and, therefore, wines needed – and watch out for chutney as its pungent flavour tends to trip wines up. I have listed the main categories of cheese from lightest to most pungent and mentioned, within each, some of my favourite styles.

Fresh cheese (*Cream cheese, feta, ricotta* and *mozzarella*) These usually pop up in salads or simple cooking and their flavours are not dominant, so drink what you fancy. Whites would be best and make sure they have some cleansing acidity on board. See 'Cheese (cooked)'.

Natural rind cheese (*Goats' cheese – Crottin de Chavignol, Sainte-Maure de Touraine, Saint-Marcellin* and *Selles-sur-Cher*) Sauvignon Blanc from the Loire Valley in France is benchmark with goats' cheese, with the stunning wines from Sancerre being the pick of the crop (Chavignol is one of the finest wine villages in Sancerre and the producer of the famous Crottin). If you're caught short, though, any dry, fresh, unoaked white would be OK. If you feel like drinking red, then Loire Cabernet Franc or Gamay work perfectly well.

Soft white cheese (*Camembert, Brie de Meaux, Pavé d'Affinois, Chaource, Bonchester, Pencarreg, Explorateur, Boursault, Gratte-Paille* and *Brillat-Savarin*) Once again, Sauvignon Blanc works terrifically well here, although, if you want more palate 'oomph', head to Marlborough in New Zealand, Elim in South Africa or Adelaide Hills in Australia. Remember that the richer the cheese, the bigger the white, so Chardonnay can be considered, too. For reds try Pinot Noir (either red Sancerre or lighter red Burgundies), fresh young Syrah from the Rhône or McLaren Vale in Oz and rosé Champagne. Gratte-Paille and Brillat-Savarin traditionally go well with youthful, inexpensive claret – stick to my favoured châteaux in the Gazetteer section to avoid the stinkers.

Washed rind cheese Milder examples like *Chaumes, Port Salut* and *Milleens* need nothing more than dry, fruity reds – light Loire red, Bordeaux or New World Merlot, for example. Smellier cheeses, including *Epoisses, Chambertin* and *Langres*, really enjoy white Burgundy (from Chablis in the north all of the way down to Mâcon in the south), Alsace Riesling or Tokay-Pinot Gris, and other controlled (i.e. not too oaky) Chardonnays from further afield. *Munster* loves Alsatian Gewürztraminer and *Vacherin Mont d'Or* loves red Burgundy, Beaujolais and lighter red Rhônes.

Semi-soft cheese This covers a huge selection of cheese. Try the following combinations: *Livarot* – Alsatian Tokay Pinot-Gris; *Maroilles* – Roussanne or Marsanne from the Rhône; *Pont-l'Evêque* – Viognier, also from the Rhône; *Raclette* – (assuming you are reading this halfway up a mountain in the Alps, you lucky thing) likes anything from the Savoie region, red or white; *Gubbeen* – Pinot Blanc or Sylvaner from Alsace; *Edam* – whatever, it's not fussy (light whites and reds); *Morbier* – Rhône whites; *Fontina* – light, Alpine Gamay or Valpolicella; *Reblochon* – this outstanding cheese likes much richer Gamay (smart Cru Beaujolais) and also red Burgundy; *Saint-Nectaire* – another heroic cheese, particularly the wild, farmhouse version, likes the same again, plus meaty red Côtes-du-Rhônes; *Tomme de Savoie* (we are in the zone here) – likes either Rhône whites or lighter reds; *Bel Paese* and *Taleggio* – Lombardy whites such as Lugana and reds like Franciacorta.

Hard cheese The largest category of all, ranging from mild, via medium and strong to extra-strong cheeses. As a starting point, get an idea of the strength and age of your chosen cheese and this will help your wine selection. Cheeses in this group are, among others – *Cheddar*, *Gruyère*, *Cheshire*, *Parmigiano-Reggiano*, *Pecorino*, *Cornish Yarg*, *Double Gloucester*, *Lancashire*, *Caerphilly*, *Gouda*, *Beaufort*, *Manchego*, *Cantal*, *Etorki*, *Comté*, *Emmenthal*, *Jarlsberg* and *Mimolette*. Listed from wines for mild cheese all the way up to wines for the extra strong ones: whites – Alsace Pinot Blanc,

Chablis, Jurançon Sec, white Burgundy, white Rhônes, New World Sémillons and, lastly, New World Chardonnays; reds – Loire reds, Chilean Merlot, Côtes-du-Rhône, spicy Italian reds like Primitivo, Old World Cabernet from Bordeaux or Margaret River (Australia), Shiraz from Frankland, Barossa Valley, McLaren Vale and Clare Valley (Australia), Vino Nobile di Montepulciano and Chianti (Italy), and Zinfandel (California); fortified – port (tawny, LBV and vintage), Madeira, Banyuls and Maury (both from France), and old oloroso sherries.

Blue cheese For *Stilton* look no further than rich, nutty Madeira, tawny port, LBV or vintage port; *Roquefort* and *Fourme d'Ambert*, in contrast, prefer sweet Sauternes, Monbazillac or Saussignac; *Dolcelatte* is a bit of a lightweight and, because of its unusual sweet flavour and texture, I'd leave it alone (can you tell I don't like it?); *Gorgonzola* likes Amarone della Valpolicella; *Chashel Blue* needs sweet whites; and *Beenleigh Blue* must have real, cruddy, cloudy, authentic scrumpy cider (what a way to end the chapter!).

THE TOP 250

£5.49 **Prosecco La Marca, NV**, Veneto, Italy (Wai).
La Marca is a perennial favourite – it made the Top 250
last year and has come top in a few consumer tastings I've
organised over the last twelve months. But what makes this
wine so good? It is simply the impeccable balance of fresh,
clean Prosecco fruit and the pure, lively effervescence.
At this price, everyone should keep a bottle in the fridge.

£6.49 **Hardy's Stamp Pinot Noir/Chardonnay,
NV**, Australia (Asd, Saf, Sai, Som and Tes). This is reliable,
fresh, very well made and cheap as chips. It is also sold
everywhere, so you can grab one easily in a thirst attack.

£6.99 **Jacob's Creek, Sparkling Chardonnay/Pinot
Noir, NV**, Australia (Asd, Coo, Mor, Odd, Saf, Sai, Som,
Tes, Thr, Wai, WRa and Unw). I don't care how big or
unbeautiful this company is supposed to be, they still make
cracking wines. Jacob's Creek fizz is phenomenally good.

£6.99 **Banrock Station Sparkling Chardonnay,
NV**, Australia (Asd and Sai). First-class fizz at seven
bangers is hard to come by. Banrock's newly released wine
is a triumph. It is thirst quenching, dry, well balanced and
extremely classy. The packaging is discreet and the overall
impression is of a wine that costs a few pounds more than
its fighting price tag. I shudder to say it but, at this price,
you could even use it for sparkling wine cocktails without
feeling too guilty. I wouldn't, though, I'd just drink it
straight and revel in the great taste.

£7.49 **Sparkling White Burgundy, NV**, France (Wai). This excellent wine is made from Chardonnay and Pinot Noir in the 'traditional method'. So, despite being a two-hour drive south of Champagne, this is a very good substitute. It is particularly dry, tight even, and it is the best wine to use for mixing when making cocktails like Kir Royale (with cassis) or Buck's Fizz (with freshly squeezed orange juice).

£7.99 **Chapel Down Brut, NV**, England (Boo, Saf and Selfridges). Two years in a row in the Top 250 for home-grown talent Chapel Down. This fizz is one of the UK's finest – line them up, I do every year – and it is half the price of most of them. Chapel Down is floral, light, dry and citrusy, and should stop Cava sales in the UK dead in their tracks. Pour this for your friends and spread the word – the English are coming.

£7.99 **Graham Beck Sparkling Brut, NV**, Robertson, South Africa (Bibendum, Luvian's, Philglas & Swiggot, Saf and Sai). This is one of South Africa's best sparkling wines, and it is certainly the best value. Graham Beck has cracked this difficult style of wine in a very short space of time. Four years ago SA was nowhere in the world of fizz, but you'd never know if you tasted this. It is ripe, fleshy and fruit-driven, with a really good lick of luscious Chardonnay fruit. Don't mix it – it's a hedonistic glugger. Also, keep your eyes peeled for a 1998 vintage duo from Graham Beck – the Blanc de Blancs and Blanc de Noirs (Bibendum £10ish) – they are absolutely terrific.

£12.95 Laytons Champagne, Brut, NV, Champagne, France (**Jeroboams**). If you must drink inexpensive Champagne, make it a good one. For years, this has been the best choice of the fine wine merchants' own label fizz. It is elegant, classy and crowd-pleasing, and a must for chic soirées. My advice is to watch out for deals to be had near Christmas – they have been known to knock a few quid off!

£13.75 Clover Hill, 1998, Tasmania, Australia (**deFINE, Inspired, Mayfair, Theatre** and **Helen Verdcourt**). 1998 Clover Hill fizz (60% Chard, 30% Pinot Noir, 10% Pinot Meunier) is fantastic wine. The creamy, complex palate has the most intense, frothy mousse I have ever seen on a bottle of fizz. This wine recently won the Winestate award for best fizz in Australasia, and on a recent trip to Tassie was second only to Pirie in my scores but, interestingly, a fiver cheaper! Well done to this minuscule winery.

£16.99 Le Mesnil Blanc de Blancs Grand Cru Brut, NV, Champagne, France (**Wai**). This is really brilliant Champagne, made from 100% Chardonnay and harvested from the highest quality (Grand Cru) vineyards. The cracking thing about Le Mesnil is its price. You could easily pay ten pounds more for this level of finesse and complexity. Buy yourself one as a Friday night pressie!

£18.95 Pirie, 1998, Pipers Brook, Tasmania, Australia (**Harvey Nichols, Love Saves the Day, Noble Rot, Peckham & Rye, Sommelier Wine** and **Wines of Interest**). OK, listen in. 1996

Pirie made the Top 250 in 2002, and the 1997 was in last year's book, so when I tasted the 1998 in Tassie in March, I was crossing my fingers. Could Dr Andrew Pirie make it three in a row? Of course he could! This beautiful wine is more forward than the classically proportioned 1997, with masses of red fruit nuances (70% Pinot) infiltrating the Chardonnay (30%) creaminess. My advice is to put your 1997 back in the cellar and drink this glorious 1998 vintage first. It tastes like top-flight, prestige cuvée Champagne and sells for less than a shoddy bottle of Mumm Cordon Rouge. Will this be the last Pirie to make the Top 250 now that its creator Andrew has left the company? We shall see...

£18.99 **Fernand Thill, Grand Cru, NV**, Verzy, Champagne, France (**Saf**). Made from 70% Pinot Noir and 30% Chardonnay, Fernand Thill is a rich, full, wild-strawberry-scented wine – just the sort to brighten your winter evenings. This is a classy, rich, ripe, full, tasty Champagne.

£18.99 **D. Henriet-Bazin, Grand Cru, NV**, Champagne, France (**Saf**). This is another blend of 70% Pinot Noir (from Grand Cru village Verzenay) and 30% Chardonnay (from 1er Cru village Villers-Marmery). This cunning blend, from two prime vineyard sites, makes a brilliant, toasty, creamy brew, with considerable weight and enormous length of flavour.

£22.99 **Moët & Chandon, Nectar Impérial, NV**, Champagne, France (**Sai**). This is the most exciting NV Moët I have tasted for ages. The name gives the style away somewhat, as this is a very rich and juicy Champagne. It is smooth, elegant and ever so long on the palate and, with its added degree of fruitiness, it is a definite crowd-pleaser. Nectar is less acidic than the normal bone-dry Brut so it's more conducive to romantic, all-night sipping.

£23.99 **Pol Roger Rich, NV**, Champagne, France (Berry Bros., Castang, Portland, Saf and Valvona & Crolla). Pol Roger makes serious Champagne – the NV Brut White Foil is a cracker. But this wine, the Rich, is a true connoisseur's treat. Like the Moët Nectar, above, it is a fuller, smoother, creamier style, with ample fruit and a succulent yet tangy finish. 'Rich' styles are very much in vogue these days, and you'll see why after just one glass – but, you and I both know you won't be able to stop at one!

£23.99 **R de Ruinart Brut, NV**, Champagne, France (Amps, Eton Vintners, Fortnum & Mason, Hailsham, Harrods, Lea & Sandeman, Luvian's, Philglas & Swiggot, Arthur Rackham and Sai). Ruinart is a small Champagne house with a cult following. It is very well respected in France but has a much quieter image in the UK. You should get to know this wine, as it is ever so classy and fabulously celebratory. Rather than deciding to plump for one of the famous names, why not choose a classic 'house' that flies under the radar?

£25.97 **Delamotte, Blanc de Blancs, 1997**, Champagne, France (Corney & Barrow). This wine is made from 100% Grand Cru Chardonnay vines and it reeks of class. Delamotte is not an everyday name, but it is the sister house of Salon, arguably the most eclectic Champagne producer of all. This is a creamy, rich, persistent, complex Champagne for people who really care about what they drink.

£26.00 **Leasingham Classic Clare Sparkling Shiraz, 1994**, Clare Valley, South Australia (Waitrose Belgravia, Canary Wharf and Kingston branches). This is categorically my favourite sparkling red wine in the world. Believe it or not, the 1995, which follows this, is even better! Classic Clare is crammed with insanely joyful cranberry, raspberry and plum flavours, which seem to boogie around the glass. It is a crying shame that this awesome brew is sold in only three shops – order it for your Christmas feast!

£29.99 **Laurent-Perrier, Ultra Brut, NV**, Champagne, France (Adnams, Corney & Barrow, Fortnum & Mason, Jeroboams, Odd, Terry Platt, Selfridges and Uncorked). Ultra Brut – doesn't that sound hard! There is no 'dosage' (sugar) added to soften the finish, broaden the palate and make this Champagne more commercial, just an arid acidity leaving you gasping for more. Hoorah for rock hard fizz!

£29.99 **Moët & Chandon, Vintage 1996**, Champagne, France (Odd, Sai, Tes, Thr, WRa and Wai). Moët '96 is fast out of the blocks, with an intense whoosh of toasty, ripe fruit on the nose. The palate is equally impressive, with wild strawberry moments and a gorgeous, savoury, long finish. This is the vintage Moët I have been waiting for.

£36.99 **Veuve Clicquot, Vintage Réserve 1996**, Champagne, France (**Asd**, **Bentalls**, **Harrods**, **Lea & Sandeman**, **Maj**, **Odd**, **Sai**, **Selfridges**, Unw and **Valvona & Crolla**). 1947, 1955, 1976, 1982, 1990 and now 1996 – you have to be patient when waiting for truly great Vintage Clicquot. 1996 Veuve Clicquot Vintage Réserve is one of the finest Champagnes I have tasted all year. It is young, granted, but this wine is already showing considerable class.

£38.85 magnum, **Gatinois, Réserve, Grand Cru, NV**, Aÿ, Champagne, France (**Haynes, Hanson & Clark**). Forty quid may be a lot for one bottle of wine, but it isn't for two! This is fabulous value and made from 100% Grand Cru Pinot Noir vines from the best red grape village in Champagne – Aÿ. You will not find better value Champs this year, so grab some of this rich, toasty, full fizz and work those biceps!

£39.95 **Jacquesson, Avize Grand Cru Blanc de Blancs, 1995**, Champagne, France (**Butlers**, **D. Byrne**, **deFINE**, **Direct Wines**, **Edencroft**, **Inspired Wines**, **Mayfair**, **Thomas Panton**, **Stone, Vine & Sun**, **Theatre of Wine** and **Whitebridge**). This extremely dry Champagne is made from a single vineyard plot in the village of Avize. It is a stunning creation, with every facet of elegance and complexity you'd expect from a truly great Champagne house.

£75.00 **Gosset Celébris Rosé, 1998**, Champagne, France (**Corney & Barrow**, Handford, **La Reserve** and **Whitebridge**). Now I'm not usually in favour of this punitively expensive way of drinking pink wine, but I will make an exception for this. I know it is fearsomely dear, but let me tell you, nothing will prepare you for what happens to your palate, sanity, mood and loins when you drink this wine. The nose is nothing short of sensational, with intense cherry/berry fruit. The impact is almost shocking, especially if you are used to limp, damp, strawberry-scented rosé Champagnes that smell more of the punnet than the fruit. The palate is rich and glossy, with pumped up redcurrant and mulberry notes. Just when you're halfway through savouring the layers of ripe red fruit, the palate starts to broaden and lengthen, and it doesn't stop. The intensity of fruit mellows and the core of lean, leggy Chardonnay fruit takes over. This wine is initially the Beast, but halfway through Beauty gets a go. And it goes on and on and on – good job, too, at that price!

£84.99 **Bollinger, RD, 1990**, Champagne, France (**Fortnum & Mason, Harvey Nichols, Lay & Wheeler, Odd, Roberson** and **Wimbledon**). This is a real treat. RD is an iconic wine with a cult following. The 'recently disgorged' phenomenon serves them well, as this awesome 1990 vintage shows with impeccable style, complexity and not a little muscle. It is heroic, there's no other word for it!

£195.00 **Billecart-Salmon, Le Clos Saint-Hilaire, 1995**, Champagne, France (**Berry Bros.**). This is the greatest young Champagne I have ever tasted. Regular readers will know Billecart is my favourite Champagne house. They have outdone themselves with this single vineyard, 100% Pinot Noir, no 'dosage' wine. Only 3,000 bottles were made in 1995. Price is immaterial, buy it if you can and then leave it for at least a decade to age! The 1959 Billecart-Salmon Cuvée Nicolas-François was voted the best Champagne of the twentieth century – these guys really know how to make wine that lives forever.

● ●

£2.99 **Bianco Beneventano, 2002**, Campania, Italy (M&S). This Falanghina/Fiano blend is remarkable value for money. It is fresh, clean, even a little honeyed and floral. If you are on a budget, this wine will give you a lot of pleasure.

£3.19 **Matra Springs, 2002**, Northern Hungary (Wai). Yippee! 2002 Mattress Springs is a winner again. It has gone up 20p on last year's price, but it's still a bargain. Zesty, summery and refreshing, it has tons of fresh fruit under its crunchy exterior. Sealed with a screwcap, this is a perfect apéritif wine. Stock up for unexpected guests.

£3.99 **Lurton Sauvignon Blanc, 2002**, Vin de Pays de Jardin de la France, Loire, France (Sai). This perky little number is a failsafe party wine. Ship it in, in case quantities, as it is bursting with lemon, asparagus, fresh herb and gooseberry nuances. The palate is smooth and ripe and the acidity is nowhere near as lean as most Loire Sauvignons. This is the perfect all-round lunchtime wine.

£3.99 **Waitrose Touraine Sauvignon Blanc, 2002**, Loire, France (**Wai**). This is a cracking price for a crisp, fresh, zippy wine. It is a cheat's Sancerre, made just down the Loire River from Sancerre itself. It has all of the classic hallmarks of the Sauvignon Blanc variety, including rapier-sharp citrus fruit and a zesty finish. This Touraine Sauvignon is the perfect all-purpose food wine and it is half the price of the real thing.

£4.70 **Castillo di Montblanc Viura/Chardonnay, 2002**, Conca de Barberá, Spain (**Jeroboams**). This feisty, herbal Spanish white is ever so refreshing and taste bud tingling. The Viura lends the wine spearmint freshness, while the Chardonnay pads out the palate. The resulting blend is absolutely spot on and this makes Montblanc the perfect starter white.

£4.92 **Vouvray, 2002**, Denis Marchais, Loire, France (**Asd**). This off-dry, smooth, honeyed wine is a dream. It would be perfect for lovers of fruitier whites and also for those gastronomes who want to find the ideal partner for a coarse pâté or luxurious fish main course.

£4.99 **Las Mulas, Verdejo/Sauvignon Blanc, 2002**, Telmo Rodriguez, Rueda, Spain (**M&S**). This budget beauty is simply brilliant. In fact, it is one of the most amazing wines I have tasted this year. It is a blend of Verdejo and Sauvignon Blanc, so I'm sure you can imagine just how clean, crisp, uplifting and zesty it is. There is a lot of Viura

LIGHT, DRY AND UNOAKED

in Rueda, and I'm not a huge fan of this low-quality, bulk wine variety, so if you are snooping around for more Ruedian whites, stick to straight Verdejo or Verdejo/Sauv blends. Telmo Rodriguez is a winemaking wizard, with a magic touch. He has made Las Mulas unmissable, with more complexity and charm than many wines twice the price.

£4.99 **Pinot Blanc, Turckheim, 2002**, Alsace, France (**M&S**). Pinot Blanc is a totally underrated grape variety, as it is so smooth, ripe and enjoyable. Perfect for charming your taste buds, it is also a talented wine when it comes to food matching. Use this as an apéritif wine and serve all manner of spicy nibbles with it and it'll sail through each one.

£4.99 **Tesco Unwind Pinot Grigio, NV**, Friuli Grave, Italy (**Tes**). Tesco has sold squillions of bottles of this screwcap wine. There is nothing fresher than a chilled bottle of PG and Tesco Unwind (better than Unscrew?!) is a stunner. The vibrant acidity coupled with the pear and apple nuances are thirst quenching, uplifting and perfect for a picnic.

£4.99 **Tesco's Finest Chenin Blanc/Forrester's Petit Chenin, 2003**, Stellenbosch, South Africa (**Tes**). The 2002 vintage of this wine was sold as Forrester's Petit Chenin and I declared it the best value South African white wine on the shelves. This year Tesco has dived into the fray and snapped up no less than 15,000 cases of Ken Forrester's 2003 Petit Chenin Blanc and it will appear on the shelves as Tesco's Finest Chenin Blanc. The tank sample I tasted back in April was vibrant, ripe, clean, pineappley, refreshing, uplifting and is sure to be a star. Ken Forrester and Martin Meinert, his winemaking consultant, have the Midas touch with this variety. I suspect you'll find this delicious brew at every smart party this Christmas.

£5.55 **Muscadet de Sèvre et Maine Sur Lie, Domaine de la Quilla, 2002**, Loire, France (**Vine Trail**). I can wholeheartedly say this is the most impressive Muscadet I have tasted in years. Quilla is a big, rich style of Muscadet, crammed full of nervy, tangy, citrus fruit. It has more than enough flavour to cut straight through any fancy fish dish. You couldn't find a more accurate seafood wine if you tasted every one on the shelves.

£5.99 **Dourthe, No. 1 Sauvignon Blanc, 2002**, Bordeaux, France (**Odd**). Crisp, refreshing, cleansing, lively, dry, zesty and fun – well done Dourthe for bringing this cheeky, ripe Sauvignon Blanc to our attention. We need more light-hearted, happy-go-lucky French whites, and this bottle certainly gives cheap Sancerre a good kicking!

£5.99 **Logan Sauvignon Blanc, 2003**, Orange, New South Wales, Australia (**Corks, General Wine, Halifax and Philglas & Swiggot**). Peter Logan has fired this baby Sauv up with more aroma and flavour than many wines twice the price. It is lime-stuffed and so zesty it'd wake the dead. Drink it with Asian fusion cuisine and amaze your chums with the awesome value and mind-blowing flavour!

LIGHT, DRY AND UNOAKED

£5.99 **Pinot Grigio, Podere La Prendina, 2002**,
Veneto, Italy (**M&S**). This is brimming with ripe, pineapple
chunk acidity and floral, thirst-quenching fruit. There are so
many sad, lean PGs out there, but this is the real thing.

£5.99 **Snapper Cove Unwooded Chardonnay, 2002**,
Western Australia (**M&S**). While we all drink tons of New
World Chard, collectively we have moved away from the
heavily oaked styles, in favour of cleaner, refreshing, fruit-
driven wines. This chirpy chappy sees no oak at all, and is
all the better for it. The melon, pear and apple flavours are
silky smooth and the finish is crisp and uplifting.

£5.99 **Stormhoek Sauvignon Blanc, 2003**, Western
Cape, South Africa (**Asd** and **Odd**). This is not South Africa's
finest Sauvignon Blanc but it is definitely the best value.
At £5.99, this is a very significant Sauvignon Blanc indeed.
France can't do it. The Kiwis and the Aussies can't. In fact,
nobody can make this level of quality at the sub-six-pound
mark. This wine is the missing Sauvignon link. In the
international Sauvignon foothills (Touraine, Bulgaria, Pays
d'Oc, Chile) nothing touches this wine. Head up towards a
tenner and you'd still have to pick carefully to find a
competitive bottle. Stormhoek is a controlled explosion of
textured, rich, smooth yet zesty, citrus-bomb fruit – mmmm.

£6.25 **Valdesil Blanco, 2002**, Bodegas Valderroa, Galicia,
Spain (**Laymont & Shaw**). OK, prepare yourself for a bizarre
grape variety – this wine is made from 100% Godello. It

hails from Valdeorras, the easternmost region in Galicia, inland from Rías Baixas (where all of the Albariños are made). It is a fabulous wine with aromatic apricot, peach and honey notes, fine acidity and great length. It is a true bargain. If you are getting bored of international wines, made with international grape varieties, then this bottle will reassure you that, in some parts of the world, people continue to make fantastic handcrafted wines from beguiling indigenous varieties.

£6.29 **Muscadet Côtes de Grandlieu, Sur Lie, 2002**, Domaine des Herbauges, Loire, France (**Laithwaites**). If Quilla (flick back a few pages) is a big style of Muscadet, then this wine is a graceful beauty. It is, as you'd expect, bone dry and extremely refreshing, but there is another dimension to both the nose and palate. It has a lovely, ripe floral aroma, and a very long, balanced finish. Now is the time to reacquaint yourselves with this famous wine region, as two great wines have made the Top 250.

£6.34 **Rueda Superior, José Pariente, 2002**, Bodegas Dos Victorias, Spain (**Georges Barbier**). This glorious white wine is made from 100% Verdejo and is the finest version of this grape I have ever tasted. Two ladies called Victoria are responsible for this beauty and they have totally cracked this style. The mildly tropical nose leads to a tight, clean pineapple and citrus fruit palate, which, in turn, is tracked closely by a refreshing, cool finish. This wine is, not surprisingly, superb with tapas, but you can drink it with almost anything, including spicy food, chilli-laden dishes or even lighter curries. Georges Barbier sells strictly 'by the case' – so grab a few friends and place an order.

£6.59 **Ameztoi Blanco, 2002**, Bodegas Ameztoi, Getariako Txakolina, Spain (**Laymont & Shaw**). Trust Spanish specialists Laymont & Shaw to come up with this outlandish and wonderful white wine. It comes from the rocky Biscay coast, west of San Sebastian, and is made from the Hondarribi Zuri grape variety. Ametzoi has searingly high acidity and an extremely fresh, almost spritzy, fizzing texture. It is a little like glugging bone-dry, light, youthful Muscadet, shot through with a squirt of Perrier bubbles and a few volts of electricity. The flavours are apply, racy, lifted and totally, totally fresh. This is a delicious seafood wine – perfect for *plateau de fruits de mer*.

£6.95 **Bourgogne Aligoté, 2002**, Domaine Vincent Bouzereau, Burgundy, France (**Gunson** and **Haslemere**). Made by Meursault genius Vincent Bouzereau (£19.99, **Wai**, for the real thing), these Aligoté vines are located just south of the village itself, and hit top form in 2002. The creamy, ripe, smooth fruit is sensational. House wine chez moi!

£6.95 **Grüner Veltliner, Hochterrassen, 2002**, Salomon, Krems, Austria (**Lea & Sandeman**). This vibrant GV is full of spritzy, Alpine, cleansing, mildly spicy, floral fruit. Little by little Austrian wines are creeping into our psyche and, if this wine is anything to go by, they are very welcome.

£6.95 **Jurançon Sec, Domaine de Lahargue, 2002**,
South West France (**Vine Trail**). It is ever so hard to find
decent Jurançon in the UK, so snap up this inexpensive,
beguiling wine now. Made from the unusual grapes Gros
and Petit Manseng, it is daring and peachy on the nose. But
don't let that fool you. This is a dry, lean, citrusy wine with
the style and zip to cut through a vast repertoire of dishes.
Start with fish, move through veal and pork to chicken and
game terrines, then head off to spicy food and any salads.

£6.99 **Chapel Hill Unwooded Chardonnay, 2002**,
McLaren Vale, South Australia (**Andrew Chapman** and **Tes**).
Pam Dunsford has made a wonderful unwooded Chard in
2002. Chablis lovers can now afford to start drinking again,
because this wine is more delicious and less expensive than
any 'village' Chablis. Also watch out for 2003 Chapel Hill
Verdelho. Regular readers know I am in love with this wine,
and Pam reports it will be a blinder (£7.49, **Andrew
Chapman**, **Philglas & Swiggot** and **Wai**)!

£6.99 **Gavi Bricco Battistina, 2002**, Araldica, Piemonte,
Italy (**Amps**, **Bacchanalia**, **D. Byrne**, **Halifax**, **Jolly Vintner**,
Noble Rot, **Valvona & Crolla** and **Wai**). This brand new Gavi
is a tremendous wine and a terrific surprise. Normally,
decent examples cost a bomb (see La Giustiniana page 102),
as they are painfully fashionable in Italian restaurants and
this has pushed the price up. Unfortunately, in the wrong
hands the Cortese grape variety can be a little gutless and
dilute. So chances are you'll pay a lot for a dull, thin wine.

LIGHT, DRY AND UNOAKED

Bricco Battistina is, however, a fine, textured wine, with richness, honeyed fruit, nuttiness and a long finish. This is down to the old vines on the Battistina hillside and the small amount of oak aging used to fatten out the palate.

£6.99 **Pinot Grigio, St Michel-Eppan, 2002**, Alto Adige, Italy **(Wai)**. I know there are gallons of cheap Pinot Grigios all over the shelves, but if you spend just a few pounds more, the difference in flavour and depth is amazing. This wine is terrific, loaded with intense apple and pear fruit, and oodles of thirst-quenching acidity. It is the perfect pre-dinner glugger or relaxed lunchtime wine. PG never tasted so good. If you want to taste a ripper of a Sauvignon, 2002 Sanct Valentin (this estate's top label) is also sold by Waitrose from their Inner Cellar Wine List for £12.99.

£7.29 **Pinot Blanc Auxerrois, Albert Mann, 2002**, Alsace, France **(Odd)**. 2002 was a cracking vintage in Alsace and Mann is one of the top winemakers (see Gazetteer). He has managed to turn the often dull and one-dimensional grape Pinot Blanc into a wondrous enchantress. It is honeyed, tropical, golden in colour and ever so sexy and smooth. I have only ever tasted a handful of PBs as good as this, and it is a frighteningly keen price for this level of skill.

£7.95 **Bergerie de l'Hortus Blanc Classique, 2002**, Val de Montferrand, France **(Lea & Sandeman)**. Hortus is really a red wine specialist, but this cunning and unusual blend of Sauvignon Blanc, Chardonnay and heady Viognier

LIGHT, DRY AND UNOAKED

is a joy. The Chardonnay and Viognier tweak the balance of this Sauvignon-based brew, broadening the palate and making it a little more exotically fruity on the nose. This slight shift in flavour gives Bergerie the required aroma and weight to tackle a wide range of dishes. This is an eclectic wine that will stun the adventurous drinker.

£7.95 **Bogle Vineyards Chenin Blanc 2002**, California (Great Western). I bet you didn't expect to find a Californian Chenin in my Top 250! Well, this wine is superb, with a gorgeous honeyed sheen and no oak whatsoever. It is rare to find this grape variety with such charm and texture, but without mouth-searing acidity. Bogle has really triumphed with this unfashionable grape. Drink it with everything since, despite the lack of oak, it has richness, mildly tropical fruit and a long, juicy finish.

£7.95 **La Segreta Bianco, 2002**, Planeta, Sicily, Italy (SWIG and Valvona & Crolla). 2002 was a tricky vintage in Italy, but Sicily had a blinder. La Segreta Bianco is a cunning blend of Grecanico, Chardonnay, Viognier, Sauvignon Blanc and Fiano, and it is made by the coolest winery in Sicily – Planeta. The aromatic Viognier and Fiano lead the way, with a stunning, pineapple, peach and lemon nose. The Chardonnay fattens out the palate and the Grecanico and Sauvignon lift the entire sensation with a herbal, refreshing, invigorating buzz of stylish palate-tweaking acidity. Also, watch out for the briary, glossy, plum and spice-infused 2002 La Segreta Rosso (same price and stockists) – it is a star, too.

£7.99 **Alkoomi Sauvignon Blanc, 2002**, Frankland River, Western Australia (**Saf**). Alkoomi is situated in the far southwestern corner of Australia in a region called Frankland. This area is superb for growing grapes like Sauvignon Blanc, as the climate is sunny during the day, but cool in the evenings – all-important for Sauvignon's crisp, refreshing acidity. Alkoomi is a top-class estate and this wine is buzzing with vitality. It is lively, with citrusy, grassy fruit and a zesty finish – just the sort of wine to get you in the mood for a big evening out.

£7.99 **Stella Bella Sauvignon Blanc, 2002**, Margaret River, Western Australia (**Wai**). Sealed with a screwcap (thank goodness), this wine is a gorgeous creation. The first time I tasted the Stella Bella family of wines my palate was hypnotised. This Sauvignon Blanc is the first of the siblings to find high street stardom. It is fully ripe but grippingly dry, and the counterpoint of luscious lime sherbet and palate-shocking, uvula cryogenics is mind-blowing. I like this wine a lot. Watch out for the equally impressive 2003 following soon – drink it with smart seafood. Also, don't miss Stella Bella's parent label, also from first-class winemaking team Janice McDonald and Stuart Pym – Suckfizzle Augusta. The 2000 Cabernet Sauvignon is £14.99 from Waitrose Canary Wharf and Kingston branches, Noel Young, Peter Green and Great Northern Wine. It is superbly suave Cab with brooding, intense, all-enveloping, dark berry fruit and a minutes-long finish. The 2001, due out in 2004, is even finer!

£7.99 **Wither Hills Sauvignon Blanc, 2003**,
Marlborough, South Island, New Zealand (**Ballantynes**, **Boo**,
Simon Charles, **Great Western**, **Hedley Wright**, **Charles
Hennings**, **Jeroboams**, **Michael Jobling**, **Odd**, **Thos Peatling**,
Edward Sheldon, **Sommelier**, **T&W**, **Wai**, **Villeneuve** and
Wine Society). The stockists mentioned bought the
excellent 2002 vintage of this wine. I am assuming, once
these people get a sniff of the 2003, they will all move straight
on. This is the third vintage in a row for Brent Marris's
awesome value Sauvignon in my Top 250. It is a gorgeous
wine, made in a difficult vintage, and it serves to highlight
just how reliable and skilful this estate is. Vigorous, forward
(there is no need to age it), lemony and lively – hunt down
screwcap-sealed bottles for sheer, unadulterated perfection!

£8.45 **Camel Valley Bacchus, 2002**, Cornwall, England
(**Camel Valley Vineyard** tel. 01208 77959 or wine@camel
valley.com). Where in the world? A boutique vineyard with
a cult following, which sells out of stock before the wine is
even bottled – California maybe? No, Cornwall! The 2002
Seyval Blanc (£8.45) really has already sold out. No matter,
because I prefer the stunning Bacchus with its nettle,
asparagus and gooseberry nose, and smooth, almost creamy
palate punctuated with lime leaf, crunchy pear and green
bean moments. No wonder Cornwall is such a popular
holiday destination with its sun, sea, sand and… wine!

£8.80 **Pinot Blanc, Sand, 2002**, Domaine André Thomas,
Alsace (**Vine Trail**). This is such a treat – the luxurious,

LIGHT, DRY AND UNOAKED

white 97

honeyed, super-smooth, textured fruit bathes the palate as
you sip this stunning wine. Thomas is an excellent producer
and there is a fabulous selection of their wines on the brilliant
Vine Trail wine list. Get yourself on VT's mailing list if you're
serious about small boutique, top-notch French wine.

£8.99 **Curious Grape Bacchus Reserve, 2002**,
England (**Handford**, **Harrods** and **Philglas & Swiggot**).
2002 is the best English vintage in over a decade. 2002
Bacchus Reserve is the finest wine ever made under the
Curious Grape label. I have been banging on about Chapel
Down's wines for years and the Curious Grape range must
surely put them on everyone's hit list. This Bacchus is
elegant, long, classy and impressive – the nettle, herb, lime
and green melon fruit is superb. This is the perfect foody
wine as the crisp acidity is so good at cutting through
creamy sauces, spicy ingredients and fatty recipes. If you
like dry white wines, you'll love this.

£8.99 **Lugana, Ca' dei Frati, 2002**, Dal Cero, Italy
(**Bennetts**, **Harvey Nichols**, **Haynes**, **Hanson & Clark**,
Moriarty, **Tanners**, **Tes** and **Wine Man**). Dal Cero is easily
my favourite producer of Lugana. Year in, year out, this
wine is the model to which all others aspire. The floral,
faintly tropical nose is captivating, as is the sleek, nutty,
honeyed palate and long, dry, tangy finish. This is a classy
Italian white wine that could take the place of Chablis, say,
at the dinner table. It is versatile when matching to food
and is extremely good value.

£9.50 **Falanghina, Di Majo Norante, 2002**, Molise, Italy (**Lea & Sandeman**). Falanghina is a peculiar grape, loaded with white peach, basil, mint and pear flavours. Di Majo Norante is a tremendous operation and they handle this variety with style. It is fairly full on the palate, but at the same time refreshing, zippy and electrifyingly crisp. If you are searching for an interesting dinner party wine then look no further than this beguiling beauty.

£9.99 **The Berrio Sauvignon Blanc, 2002**, Elim, South Africa (**Odd**). This has been one of the most successful wines of the year in my wine-tasting events. I've opened it for loads of people and every time the room grows silent as they fall under its spell. There are very few Sauvignon Blancs in the world as hypnotic as this. It is the epitome of class and elegance, with minutes-long, controlled, zesty, citrusy Sauvignon flavours and a mellow, mildly tropical nose. The 2003 arrives in the autumn and is even more impressive!

£9.99 **Craggy Range, Old Renwick Road Sauvignon Blanc, 2002**, Marlborough, South Island, New Zealand (**Wai**). Steve Smith used to head up Kiwi super winery Villa Maria. He is a top bloke and Craggy Range shows his viticultural and winemaking skills off to perfection. His entire range is a joy, and in some cases a bit of a shock. I prefer this to his other Sauvignon, Avery Vineyards. It has more flesh and intensity and is up there with the very best from NZ. This wine is a great way to get to know Craggy. Watch out for explosive 2003s coming out soon!

LIGHT, DRY AND UNOAKED

£9.99 Puiatti Le Zuccole Chardonnay, 2002, Friuli-Venezia Giulia, Italy (**SWIG** and **Wimbledon**). Le Zuccole is a totally pure, glacially cool wine. Unoaked Chardonnay the world over should take a leaf out of this wine's book. Goodness, I wish more Chablis tasted half as precise as Giovanni Puiatti's creation. Giovanni is a passionate advocate of unoaked wines. He wants his grapes to do the talking – uninterrupted. And that is precisely what they do here. When you drink Le Zuccole it is like giving your olfactory system an aromatherapeutic make over. The floral, lemon and orange blossom notes tweak every nerve ending, leaving you in a state of Zen-like satisfaction.

£10.49 Pouilly-Fumé, Jean-Claude Chatelain, 2002, Loire, France (**Wai**). This is the wine for anyone who has felt, of late, that Pouilly-Fumé has somewhat lost its appeal. Chatelain has hit warp factor five with this classic Sauvignon Blanc. This is ever so aromatic, covering more Sauvignon notes than seem possible – gooseberry, lemon balm, grapefruit, lime zest, elderflower and asparagus. 2002 is a great vintage and this wine is already showing a phenomenal degree of richness and drinkability.

£10.99 Villa Maria Reserve Clifford Bay Sauvignon Blanc, 2002, Marlborough, South Island, New Zealand (**Odd**). This is a pretty big wine, despite being made from the supposedly lean, mean grape variety Sauvignon Blanc. If anything, it is more intense, more focused and more expressive than any Clifford Bay I remember. The good news is it doesn't slip into tinned fruit flavours, like so many Kiwi Sauvignons. It is precise, rapier-like, accurate and phenomenally self-assured.

£11.49 **Iona Sauvignon Blanc, 2003**, Elgin, South Africa (**Peter Green**, **Luvian's**, **Valvona & Crolla**, **Villeneuve** and **Wimbledon**). This is one of the top Sauvignons on the planet and every time I open a bottle, legions of people join the Iona fan club. The nose pole-vaults out of the glass with Olympic precision. The fresh herb, greengage, lime juice, asparagus and pear fruit is sublime. The palate is energetic and the length runs on for minutes. This 2003 turns up in the autumn – I won't be able to control myself!

£11.99 **Ravenswood Lane, The Gathering Sauvignon, 2001**, Adelaide Hills, South Australia (**D. Byrne** and **Noble Rot**). This is one of the classiest wines in the book. There are very few Sauvignons in the world to touch the complexity, elegance and sheer length that this wine offers. Sauvignon devotees will be amazed. Note that this super cuvée, New World Sauv is not from New Zealand! Fans of 2002 Starvedog Lane Sauv (£8.99, **Saf**) will not be surprised, though, as they will already have had a sniff of the excellence that is The Lane – as Ravenswood will be known from now on. Within this illustrious estate's portfolio of gems watch out for 1998 Reunion Shiraz, 2001 Beginning Chardonnay, 1998 Nineteenth Meeting Cabernet and the new vintage of my featured wine, 2002 Gathering, which is a spellbinding Sauv/Sem blend.

£12.15 Chablis, 1er Cru Côte de Léchet, 2002, Domaine Daniel Dampt, Burgundy, France (**Haynes, Hanson & Clark**). This masterful domaine has made the Top 250 three years in a row. 2002 is a lovely Chablis vintage and Dampt thrives in these favourable conditions. This chiselled Chardonnay is so fresh and cool it's the ultimate palate chill-out. Who'd have thought this famous grape could be so mellow and unruffled? You'll forget all of your hassles after half a glass of this.

£14.70 Mâcon-Villages Quintaine, 2002, Domaine Guillemot-Michel, Burgundy, France (**Haynes, Hanson & Clark**). I adore this wine – it is truly astounding and tastes quite some way beyond perfect. The grapes used are grown biodynamically (even more puritanically in touch with Mother Earth than organic!). This wine sees no oak barrels whatsoever, but the colour is golden and the palate intense, luxurious and silky smooth. The Chardonnay fruit is honeyed, floral and succulent, and the finish is never-ending. Guillemot-Michel is an amazing producer and this is a wine that every white Burgundy lover must taste.

£14.95 Gavi di Gavi, Montessora, 2002, La Giustiniana, Piemonte, Italy (**Bennetts**, **Noel Young** and **Valvona & Crolla**). Prior to tasting La Giustiniana's wines I had never really understood the appeal of the Gavi and its grape variety Cortese. But one sniff and sip of this wine and you'll be in no doubt about its style and breeding. The main flavour thrust is the keen citrusy core, enveloped by a rather beautiful aroma of faintly tropical fruit. The entire wine is elongated from tip to toe and is dry, cool and nutty. 2002 was supposedly a shocker in Piemonte but, when your back is against the wall, you sacrifice a lot of sub-standard wine to make a stunner – and that is precisely what Montessora is.

● ●

£4.99 **Domaine Lafage Muscat Sec, 2002**, Vin de Pays des Côtes Catalanes, France (**Wai**). The Muscat grape variety tastes not dissimilar to plump, white, chilled table grapes. This wine is aromatically grapey and also thirst-quenchingly dry. It is perfect for people who like 'medium' whites. By that I mean, it is ripe and fruity, but not sweet! Lafage is stunning with spicy food, as it cools the palate but doesn't get in the way of complex foody flavours.

£4.99 **Casillero del Diablo Viognier, 2003**, Central Valley, Chile (**Saf**). Safeway secured all the stock of the amazing 2002 last Christmas and when I wrote it up in the *Daily Mail* as a Wine of the Week the bottles flew out of the store. My sneak preview of the 2003 back in April was an out-of-body experience. For those of you who grabbed some of the 2002, this wine is, unbelievably, several notches up the ladder. Anyone who missed this phenomenal experience must be satisfied with the bold but true statement that this is the finest value Viognier in the world. Winemaker Marcelo Papa puts 60% of the fruit in stainless steel tanks to straightjacket the peachy, almond

LIGHT, DRY AND UNOAKED/AROMATIC

and nutmeg fruit. Then a daring 40% is flung into sexy, praline and vanilla-kissed barrels to do its erotic, exotic thing. The result is jaw-droppingly brilliant. The UK will receive a little over 5,000 cases, so hurry along – it won't last long.

£4.99 **Inycon Fiano, 2002**, Sicily, Italy (**Sai** and **Valvona & Crolla**). Sicily had a phenomenal vintage in 2002 and the entire Inycon varietal range is a joy – do track down the juicy, rich Merlot (£4.99, **Coo**, **Mor**, **Saf** and **Tes**) and spicy, robust Syrah (£4.99, **Sai**). But my chosen wine for this year's Top 250 is the Fiano. Very few people have tasted this unusual variety. It has an aromatic nose not dissimilar to Viognier and a zesty finish not unlike Albariño. It can sometimes handle oak well, but this wine steers clear of costly barrels. Inycon Fiano has a pretty, rich, golden colour for a young wine, with a heady, peachy nose and full palate. It finishes well with trademark clean, perkily refreshing acidity. The remarkable thing is that it is under a fiver. Not a huge price to pay for a wine that is long, smooth, supple, classy and, most importantly, eclectic, unique, quirky and thought-provoking – which is the whole point about wine in the first place.

£5.49 **Jacob's Creek, Dry Riesling, 2002**, South Eastern Australia (**Asd**, **Coo**, **Sai**, **Tes** and **Wai**). This wine is available in both screwcap and cork-sealed versions. If it were a car, the standard model would be the cork and having a screwcap (guaranteeing a perfect flavour) would be an optional extra, like, say, aircon (is this all a little too Top

AROMATIC

Gear and not enough Top 250?!). They are, however, the same price. My advice is to buy the one that cracks open, not pops. It is a delicious wine and one of the best value New World Rieslings available. One quick twist of the wrist and you will be bathed in crisp, lime-juice-infused, mildly tropical, dry wine – I'm thirsty just writing this.

£5.99 **Dr L. Riesling, 2002**, Dr Loosen, Mosel-Saar-Ruwer, Germany (**Boo** and **Sai**). This is a fabulous, fruit salady Riesling from master craftsman Ernie Loosen. It is 'off dry' and welcoming, and one of the very few wines that you and your granny would enjoy in equal measure!

£5.99 **Dürkheimer Michelsberg Riesling, 2002**, Helmut Darting, Pfalz, Germany (**M&S**). Everyone should taste this perfect, inexpensive bottle of German Riesling. We've all forgotten just how stunning and uplifting this style of wine can be. It is fresh, clean and vibrant, and should be poured as an apéritif. There is a juicy core of rhubarb, fruit salad and lime fruit tucked away like a soft centre in the middle, and it sneakily reveals itself on the palate. It is a surprise, and a lovely one at that. This style of wine is faithful to the German classic Riesling model but zesty enough to appeal to our modern palates.

£5.99 **Torres Viña Esmeralda, 2002**, Penedès, Spain (**Boo**, **Odd**, **Tes**, **Thr**, **Unw**, **Wai** and **WRa**). Three years in a row for Esmeralda in the Top 250 (congrats), and this wine just gets better and better. One of the many reasons for its inclusion this year is that some of the stock is screwcap-sealed. The result is surely one of the greatest Asian and Indian food wines of all time, let alone the fact that it has divine right to tapas and apéritif drinking. The aromatic, floral, mildly tropical nose is sublime and the palate is bracing, firm, cheerily uplifting and wickedly addictive.

£6.99 **Bonterra Tri-Varietal White, 2002**, California (**Boo** and **Sai**). 2002 Tri-Varietal White is a brand new project for Bonterra. This is a new price point for them as well – the brilliant '01 Roussanne is £10.99 (**Odd**) and the '00 Zinfandel is £8.99 (**Maj**, **Odd**, **Saf** and **Wai**) – since organically grown grapes command a premium. But, as more grapes are being planted and tended in this way, prices are starting to come down. Made from Chardonnay, Sauvignon Blanc and Muscat, it is the Muscat element that really gets me going. It spikes the wine with juicy, summery, perfumed flavours and lifts the entire balance to a new dimension. This is a superb debut for Bonterra and a wine that will be drunk by the gallon by organic wine fans.

£6.99 **The Hermit Crab Marsanne/Viognier, d'Arenberg, 2002**, McLaren Vale, South Australia (**Bibendum**, **Boo**, **Great Gaddesden**, **Odd** and **Philglas & Swiggot**). d'Arenberg is a Rhône grape variety expert, and it shows in this cheeky, perky wine. Hermit Crab is singing in 2002 as the Viognier glides around on the surface, flinging out apricot and honeysuckle, while underneath the Marsanne offers us bright lime and waxy honeyed notes. All of this is mopped up with a pinpoint accurate, acidic finish, which leaves you smacking your lips and wanting more.

£6.99 **Tokay Pinot Gris, Cuvée Réserve, 2001**, Turckheim, Alsace, France (**Booths of Stockport, D. Byrne, Classic Wines, Corkscrew Wines, Inspired Wines, Jolly Vintner, Magnum, Noble Rot, Odd, Premier Cru, Thr, Helen Verdcourt, Wadebridge, Wine Society** and **WRa**). The ripe, floral fruit on this Tokay Pinot-Gris is heavenly. It is not an intense, oily style, just a mildly tropical wine with a touch of spice and a gorgeous thirst-quenching finish. You can match this wine to any fish, chicken or vegetable dish, particularly if you are cooking with Asian spices, ginger or chilli. The 2002 is another winner that will zoom into view in the autumn.

£6.99 **Yalumba Y Viognier, 2002**, South Australia (**Maj, Philglas & Swiggot, Sai, Selfridges, Tes, Unw, Wai** and **Noel Young**). Yalumba's well-priced Y range is a great way to get into Aussie varietal wines, particularly Viognier, as Yalumba is such a committed fan of this tricky grape. This exudes peach, apricot and honeysuckle and manages it without getting too big and alcohol-heavy. It is perfect with fish and chicken. Watch out for the fresh new 2003 arriving soon.

£7.49 **Chapoutier Ardèche Viognier, 2002**, France (**Avery's** and **Wadebridge**). Chapoutier has seemingly made this wine with the lightest, fairy-dust-scented grapes and bottled them at a canter to retain all of the perfume

AROMATIC

and charm that Viognier possesses. It is the gustatory version of the Alexander Technique. It primps and tweaks the taste buds, realigning your senses and doing it with a smile and a curtsey. It has apricot blossom, peach kernel and a light dusting of nutmeg. Open, drink and savour this pretty little wine.

£7.49 **Tim Adams Riesling, 2003**, Clare Valley, South Australia (**Booths of Stockport**, **Ozwines** tel. 0845 450 1261 and **Tes**). Is it too early to have another best vintage in living memory? Tim's 2002 was a cosmic creation but my problem is that the 2003 is, if anything, its equal and in a few years might even have the edge. The main difference between the two years is that the 2003 is lusciously forward, juicy and textured. It is not as highly strung as last year's splendid wine and, for that reason, you can drink it soon. There is, of course, a magnificent wall of acidity confirming the ageability of this wine (a decade at least), but it has kicked off early, with extraordinary waves of lemon and lime fruit. This is one of the most amazing value wines in the world and it will make you really smile – miles wide.

£7.99 **Alkoomi Riesling, 2002**, Frankland River, Western Australia (**Saf**). Alkoomi Riesling is a supremely classy wine. The trademark tropical fruit oozes guava, pineapple, honey and mandarin, and it is all underpinned with a glacially cool palate and a bone-dry, minutes-long finish. This is an excellent wine for spicy food or classy aperitifs.

AROMATIC

£7.99 **Gewürztraminer, Paul Zinck, 2001**, Alsace, France (**Maj**). Zinck is a small producer with big wines. This Gewürz is pinpoint accurate with lychee, rose petal and honeysuckle on the nose and a luscious, ripe but dry finish.

£8.39 **Domaine Gerovassiliou Malagousia, 2002**, Epanomi, Greece (**Odd**). This is a funny one, made from Malagousia and Assyrtico. It is, to my palate, along the same lines as a warm climate Viognier, since there is a definite peach, lime and orange zest theme running through it. Drink it with fish stews and saffron rice.

£8.99 **Albariño, Pazo de Señorans, 2002**, Rias Baixas, Galicia, Spain (**Boo**). I love drinking this estate's wines when I'm on hols in Spain, and I am delighted to see that the ever-vigilant Sally Holloway, buyer at Booths, has grabbed some cases to sell in the UK. This is a sensational wine, which counterpoints exotic fruit and flower nuances on the nose, with a peachy, honeyed palate and a gorgeous, dry finish. The result is a phenomenal wine at a stunning price.

£8.99 **Graacher Himmelreich Riesling Kabinett, 2002**, Dr Loosen, Mosel-Saar-Ruwer, Germany (**Sai**). Oh my God, this is sensational wine. I gave it a near perfect score in my notes and I pray you get the chance to taste it because it is the definition of fine German Riesling and the model on which every Riesling in the world should be based. If you like this wine then try another stunner – 2002 Urziger Würzgarten Riesling, Dr Loosen (£9.99, **M&S**).

AROMATIC

white 109

£8.99 **Nepenthe Riesling, 2002**, Adelaide Hills, South Australia (Odd and Wai). This is the best Riesling Nepenthe has made since I first discovered this estate back in 1999. It is absolutely wonderful and everything a bottle of wine should be – elegant, fresh, balanced, thought-provoking and, most importantly, downright delicious.

£8.99 **Pewsey Vale, Eden Valley Riesling, 2000**, South Australia (Thr and WRa). Pewsey Vale makes legendary Riesling and this 2000 is no exception. It is robust, rich and creamy, with lime and rhubarb fruit, and a minutes-long finish. The perfect wine to have with a Thai dinner.

£9.99 **Isabel Dry Riesling, 2002**, Marlborough, South Island, New Zealand (**Bennetts, Harrods, Inspired Wines and Morris & Verdin**). This estate produces wonderful wines. You cannot go wrong with their Sauvignon Blanc. The Pinot Noir has recently hit the heights required of it and the Chardonnay is not too shabby either. But this year I felt that the Riesling was the star. It hasn't a trace of lard on its gloriously sexy chassis. It is cool and nervy, with honey and lime juice in equal measure. It is not as aromatic as others in this book, but it has a terrifically long palate.

£9.99 **Pinot Gris, Josmeyer Estate, 2001**, Alsace, France (M&S). I have followed this wine for nearly eighteen months and it is developing more intriguing nuances and gaining more complexity every day. It is cool, calm, honeyed and spicy, with fresh fruit salad aromas, and,

AROMATIC

curiously, white pepper moments popping in and out of my taste radar. This is a refined bottle, with perfect balance and excellent depth. You should grab a bottle as it is an elegant dinner party companion. The excellent 2002 will behave the same way when it arrives later in the year!

£11.49 **Matakana Pinot Gris, 2002**, Matakana, North Island, New Zealand (**Berkmann**). 2000 Matakana PG is a delicious bottle of wine but it is running out and, as there was no 2001 made, I headed straight for the 2002. What a gem! 2002 is twice the wine, with gorgeous, rich, sassy, juicy, tropical, fully ripe, exotic fruit. This wine is bulging out all over the place and, were it not for the acidity, would be in danger of toppling over chest first. The glossy, oleaginous texture is kept in check perfectly by the neat rear end – it is truly balanced despite its initial palm-sweatingly heady proportions. You can tackle an enormous range of dishes with Matakana PG – rich fish main courses, roast chicken, veal, sweetbreads, wild mushroom risotto, buffalo (joke), roast pork and on and on…

£12.99 **Grosset Hill-Smith, Mesh Riesling, 2002**, Eden Valley, South Australia (**Bennetts**, **Philglas & Swiggot**, **La Reserve**, **Roberson**, **Vin de Van** and **Noel Young**). Mesh was the most highly anticipated new Riesling in Oz – made by Robert Hill-Smith of Yalumba fame and the eponymous Jeffrey Grosset. It is a tremendous inaugural vintage, which is summed up by its restraint more than anything else, and it's easily one of the best 250 wines I've tasted in the last year!

AROMATIC

£12.78 **Craigow Riesling, 2002**, Coal River Valley, Tasmania, Australia (**Bacchanalia** and **Bibendum**). After blazing a trail last year with the 2001 vintage, I simply had to head down to Tassie to check this estate and its wines out for myself. The new vintage of Craigow Riesling is in perfect condition. The texture, fruit, balance and depth of flavour are simply superb. It is even a step up on last year's wine. If you want to find out more about the wine world's still-hidden secret – Tasmania – you must taste this wine. The Pinot from this estate is also fantastic and Bibendum have a small amount (£15ish). Who knows, we may even get a go at the celestial Gewürz soon, when this estate and Tasmania's reputation gathers well-overdue momentum in the UK.

£13.95 **Manna Cru, Franz Haas, 2001**, Alto Adige, Italy (**Bennetts**, **Fortnum & Mason**, **Philglas & Swiggot**, **Reid Wines** and **Villeneuve Wines**). The Italians are the masters of the universe at complex white grape blends. Not the obvious or tried-and-tested Marsanne/Roussanne or Sauv/Sem style blends, but crazy stuff where taste, not tradition, leads the way. Manna is a blend of Riesling, Sauv Blanc, Traminer and a portion of barrel-fermented Chardonnay. Phew! Don't panic, just wallow in this oily, rich, tropical temptress of a wine. It is a simply superb bottle of wine. I have followed Manna for years and I reckon this is the best vintage to date. So, if you fancy skiing off the wine piste, head for this quirky, talented, silky smooth fruit bomb of a white.

AROMATIC

£14.99 **Leasingham Classic Clare Riesling, 1998**, Clare Valley, South Australia (**Tes**). It is a travesty that Leasingham's wines are not better known in the UK. Every self-respecting wine merchant in the country should taste their recent range. Granted this historic estate in Clare was in the wilderness for a while, but it has found its feet over the last few years, thanks to Kerri Thompson's magical winemaking. Leasingham Classic Clare Riesling does just what it says on the tin! It is a classic, it is from Clare and, judging by the vintage, Leasingham has been kind enough to keep it in the cellar for you for a few years, so some sexy aromas have crept out of the woodwork. This wine is balanced and rich, and has years ahead of it. But what has happened in the last five years is remarkable – it is hypnotic and spicy, with lemon balm, brioche, orange blossom, lime twists and showy moments of mango, quince and white flowers. If you have a Riesling bone in your body (every one does), you should try to buy this wine. I've already seen a sample of the CC 2002 wine and it is so sensational you will want to start your vertical tasting collection immediately! If you want to get in the mood for this heroic brew, watch out for 2002 Leasingham Bin 7 Riesling (£8.99, **Wai**), and the new label Magnus Riesling (£6.99), which should kick off with the 2003 sublime vintage.

£16.99 **Gewurztraminer, Herrenweg de Turckheim, 2000**, Domaine Zind-Humbrecht, Alsace, France (**Wai**). This stunning wine is limited in stock but it has to make the Top 250, even if only a few hundred quick-off-the-mark

AROMATIC

readers have the pleasure of drinking it. It is a debauched mouthful of intense, oily, creamy, tropical fruit, with a touch of spice and a ridiculous level of sweetness on the mid-palate. This wine is made by one of the most revered estates in Alsace – Zind-Humbrecht has won every award going and this wine is one of the reasons why. The balance between fruit intensity and cleansing acidity is staggering. Either pitch this bottle against any tricky dish you care to think of, or just sink into the sofa and sip away.

£17.00 **Colli di Lapio, Fiano di Avellino, 2002**, Clelia Romano, Campania, Italy (**SWIG** and **Wimbledon**). This is one of the most enchanting wines I have ever tasted. I couldn't believe it when Clelia poured me a tasting glass back in April in Verona. I was immediately struck dumb and then grinned like a fool for at least half an hour. The nose was fabulous, flamboyant, lush and aromatic, reeking of peaches and honeysuckle. But Fiano is a strange variety and, despite the extraordinary exuberance on the nose, the palate was classically buttoned up, with a lithe, sleek frame and extremely tight, refreshing acidity on the finish. I cannot recommend this wine enough.

£17.95 **Felton Road Riesling, 2002**, Central Otago, South Island, New Zealand (**Avery's**, **Berry Bros.**, **Haynes**, **Hanson & Clark**, **Jeroboams**, **Lay & Wheeler**, **Lea & Sandeman**, **Raeburn** and **Reid Wines**). Felton Road wines are very hard to find – you'll have to badger all the merchants above to get a bottle. But if there is a wine worth hunting for, this is

AROMATIC

it. My chosen Riesling is one of three made at Felton Road. Their 2002 Dry Riesling is just that – dry, never ending, fine and zesty. This is nowhere near dry, as it has 25gm residual sugar to heighten the flavour and texture. It is by far and away the finest NZ Riesling I have ever tasted. The smooth, cultured, luxurious palate is creamy, exotic, dreamy, tropical and ever so long. This is up there with the finest Alsatian or German creations. There is another Riesling at Felton Road, with even more richness, but if you are reading this far, you're already hooked!

● ●

£6.99 **Rio Azul Chardonnay, 2001**, Michel Laroche/Jorge Coderch, Casablanca Valley, Chile (**Bibendum**, **Great Gaddesden** and **Sai**). This is a stupendous achievement, and a wonderful marriage between Chablis guru Laroche and Valdivieso boss Coderch. These cross-continent partnership programmes rarely add up to the sum of their parts, but Rio Azul Chard has far surpassed even my wildest hopes for quality. If you like classy French, Australia, Californian… or even Chilean Chard, then this is a bargain wine for you.

£7.99 **Tim Adams Semillon, 2001**, Clare Valley, South Australia (**Maj** and **Tes**). Three years in a row for this King of Sémillons. Just as last year, two vintages will appear during the calendar year in which this book is out, so grab the 2000 and my featured 2001, and conduct a mini vertical tasting. I am amazed at how reliable this wine is year in, year out. It is one of Australia's hidden gems and more people should give it a whirl. The flavours in this honeyed, hazelnut and lemon balm wine are nothing short of hypnotic.

£8.49 **Jordan Chardonnay, 2002**, Stellenbosch, South Africa (**Boo**, **Cairns & Hickey**, **Connollys**, **Peter Graham**, **Great Gaddesden**, **George Hill**, **Jeroboams**, **Christopher Piper**, **St Martin**, **Frank Stainton**, **Unw**, **Wai** and **Wright Wine Co.**). Welcome back Jordan Chard. Make yourself at home. The 2000 vintage won a place in TWL02, but last year's 2001 vintage was just too oaky and sinewy – the balance was out – sorry Gary & Cathy J! But, I was terribly excited about the 2002 vintage sneak preview I tasted back in January. Yum. It was open, fruit-driven and expressive, and the shiny, neon/gold Chardonnay fruit slid down a treat. This wine only spent nine months in oak barrels and the balance between oak and fruit is spot on. This wine is back to being one of South Africa's finest value Chardonnays – hurrah! It is available all over the country so there is no excuse not to taste it. And, if this wine grabs your palate and doesn't let go, find 2000 Jordan Cab (£9.99), it is a stunning wine and one of the best vintages ever made.

£8.99 **Neil Ellis Chardonnay, 2002**, Stellenbosch, South Africa (**Tes**). Neil makes taut, lime juice-driven Chardonnays, in direct contrast to the more relaxed Jordan Chard (above). But, I love this nervy, edgy, linear style as it opens gradually over time and is great for matching to food. Global Chardonnay competition at this price point is

OAKED

intense (Oz is the main rival), but I can safely say that this is one of the finest sub-tenner Chardonnays around. It has plenty of oak and fruit in perfect balance, which is why this wine tastes so fit. The finish is a gustatory firework display of grapefruit and lemon acidity – I'm getting thirsty...

£8.99 **Penfolds Thomas Hyland Chardonnay, 2002**, South Australia (**Maj**, **Tes**, **Thr** and **WRa**). Winemaker Peter Gago has fantastic taste and he has finessed the oak so well on this brand new Chardonnay. It sees half-new, half-used French oak barrels for only seven months, and that is the key. The lemony, honeyed flavours are cut with lime, hazelnut and brioche notes. This is one of the most significant wines to come out of the Penfolds stable since 1998 St Henri – from which I'm still reeling.

£8.99 **Wither Hills Chardonnay, 2002**, Marlborough, South Island, New Zealand (**Boo**, **Simon Charles**, **Great Western**, **Hedley Wright**, **Charles Hennings**, **Jeroboams**, **Michael Jobling**, **Odd**, **Thos Peatling**, **Edward Sheldon**, **Sommelier Wine**, **Wai** and **Wine Society**). Winemaker Brent Marris has sealed half of his '02 Chardonnay with screwcaps. This is a good move since, aside from the obvious and immediate obliteration of the incidence of 'corked' bottles, it will also slow the ageing of this wine. WH Chard does need time to develop, but I suspect it never gets it, as we all drink it the second we get it home. Perhaps this year we will all slow down and give it a chance to unwind? Each year this wine is tweaked a little and in 2002 it is the

OAKED

texture that has received a fine tune. It is now gloriously smooth and honeyed. The palate is a little fuller than the excellent 2001, and the balance is in check. Also, don't forget WH Pinot Noir (£14.99). The 2002 is the best ever, with sexy, fleshy fruit and a totally beautiful oaky veneer. Try Oddbins or Waitrose for a screwcapped version!

£9.99 **Penley Estate Chardonnay, 2001**, Coonawarra, South Australia (**Lay & Wheeler** and **Maj**). Winemaker Kym Tolley is a perfectionist and this wine shows why. It is a full, even masculine style of wine with considerable weight and yet, it is not overly alcoholic, just remarkably persistent on the palate. The mint and green leaf nuances break down the orange peel and honey Chardonnay power, and the sappy oak cages the wine in, keeping it under control. This is an awful lot of wine for a tenner. Treat it like Premier Cru white Burgundy and you'll be impressed. It will age gracefully and must be matched to big main courses – I would head to roast chicken territory, with fat chips and tarragon *jus*.

£9.99 **Raats Chenin Blanc, 2002**, Stellenbosch, South Africa (**Odd**). Raats make a mini, unoaked version of this wine, which is keen, lean and racy (£6.99, **Odd**), but it was their other two wines that caught my attention. Firstly, the oaked Chenin, which is a lovely, praline and wild flower imbued creature. Its richness and texture is cut with Chenin's naturally high, refreshing acidity so, while this is a big wine, it is also curiously refreshing. South Africa was always going to make great Chenin to rival even the Loire Valley, as there are some amazing, old vines out there. The second wine is the incredible 2001 Raats Cabernet Franc (£14.99, **Odd**). It is pure, turbo-purple and gorgeously aromatic, with violets, plum and pencil lead notes – a mini-Cheval Blanc.

£10.65 **St Véran, Cuvée Béatrice, Orchys, 2001**, Collovray & Terrier, Burgundy, France (**Jeroboams**). 2001 was a cracking vintage for white wines from Burgundy's Mâcon region. Jean-Luc Terrier and Christian Collovray, from Domaine des Deux Roches, have pulled out all the stops for this special cuvée St Véran. Bottled under their own names, rather than that of their domaine, it is a celestial glass of Chardonnay. I suppose, when you put your name on the label, you make certain that it's a first-class offering. The honey, oak, richness and texture are in perfect harmony. It is difficult to think of a more precise bottle of ten-pound white wine.

£11.16 **Montagny, 1er Cru, 2001**, Jean-Marc Boillot, Burgundy, France (**Domaine Direct**). Jean-Marc's 2000 made last year's book and this 2001 is even better. It is a serious bottle that I have road-tested on hundreds of tasters this year and, on every occasion, they were mightily impressed. At just over ten quid this is stunning 1er Cru white Burgundy made by the Prince of Puligny-Montrachet!

£14.59 **Lynmar Russian River Chardonnay, 2000**, California (**Vineyard Cellars**). Lynmar has a brilliant range of wines – phone Vineyard Cellars for a copy of their

OAKED

tremendous Californian wine list. 2000 Lynmar Russian River Chard is cheaper than many boutique, cult, collectors' item Californian Chardonnays, but it could kick most of their arses in a blind tasting! It is smooth, classy, stylish and balanced. The fruit is polished and ripe with fabulous, controlled oak and a gorgeous, savoury finish. This is a globally brilliant bottle of wine. Despite what everyone says, California can make great value wine.

£15.99 **Hardy's Eileen Hardy Chardonnay, 2001**, Australia (**Mor** and **Philglas & Swiggot**). Eileen always used to be a bit of a fatty but nowadays she's slimmed down and is looking trim and sexy. Rather than sourcing hot, fully ripe Chardonnay grapes, Eileen is now made from cool climate, edgy, tangy Chardonnay fruit and it's made all the difference. In fact, the grapes come from as far afield as Tasmania, the Yarra Valley and Tumbarumba (where?). The oak is less aggressive and really suits this new zesty, lithe, lemony, tight chassis. It is a crime that only a few merchants in the UK stock this wine. Times change and Eileen deserves a much wider audience. Remember, this is the top white wine that Hardy's makes – and IT IS ONLY £16!

£19.99 **Chablis 1er Cru Fourchaume, 2000**, Vignoble de Vaulorent, William Fèvre, Burgundy, France (**Saf**). This is a brilliant bottle of top Chardonnay – 2000 was a phenomenal vintage in Chablis. The honeyed, creamy, mildly oaked fruit is perfectly balanced and it is drinking beautifully now. This is posh wine for special Sunday lunch feasts.

OAKED

£4.90 **Les Grès Rosé, 2002**, Coteaux du Languedoc, France (**Jeroboams**). Last year's Grès Rosé was a massive hit in my Top 250. This winemaker Xavier Luc has refined the blend of Syrah and Grenache, and made another cracker. It is an elegant, pale salmon colour, with light, slightly spicy wildberry fruit and a whoosh of cleansing acidity, skilfully countered by the faintest touch of raspberry-juice residual sugar. Yum – this can match virtually any dish. When you pick up your rosé, grab a few bottles of the stunning Grès Syrah and Viognier – they are also truly amazing.

£5.49 **Abbaye de Sylva Plana Rosé, 2002**, Faugères, France (**Maj**). This is a meaty, dry rosé for foody consumption. Treat it like a red wine – give it some air and watch it unwind. The red fruit flavours will emerge and bring with them intriguing nuances of liquorice and five-spice. It is particularly good with Indian lamb dishes.

£5.49 **Mount Hurtle Grenache Rosé, 2003**, Geoff Merrill, McLaren Vale, South Australia (**Odd**). This brand-new 2003, which I tasted less than a week after it was bottled in June, is amazing (due to the UK in the autumn under Mount Hurtle and Geoff Merrill labels). And why? It is sealed with a screwcap – it looks cute, it is dry, it is crammed with red berry fruit, it is an Indian, Mexican and BBQ food superstar, it has a whopping 14 degrees of alcohol behind its unassuming label, and, lastly and perhaps most importantly, it tastes grrrrreat. Spicy, summer pudding flavours are followed by a wallop of yummy residual sugar and crunchy acidity, and end with that all-important afterburn of Grenache power. Just remember to ration granny or she'll get competitive!

£5.69 **Torres Santa Digna Cabernet Sauvignon Rosé, 2002**, Curicó Valley, Chile (**Ameys, Amps, Peter Graham, Charles Hennings, Hoults, Oxford Wine Co., Roberts & Speight, Selfridges, Tanners**). Santa Digna is one of the smoothest, most cherry-stuffed rosés on the shelves. It is made from Cab Sauv, which in itself is pretty strange, but the classic cassis, cherry and berry aromas and flavours are all there. This is a phenomenally well-made wine (from Spanish genius Miguel Torres' stable) and one that is guaranteed to please everyone you know.

£7.99 **Château de Sours Rosé, 2002**, Bordeaux, France (**Corney & Barrow, Goedhuis & Co., Maj, Playford Ros** and **Tanners**). This is my favourite rosé of the year and a wine that I have a case of in my cellar and a further two, no make that one bottle of in the fridge! Two years in a row for talented Scot Esme Johnstone and his team. More please – I can't live without Sours rosé now!

£9.95 **Sancerre Rosé, Domaine Serge Laloue, 2002**, Loire, France (**Jeroboams**). So much Sancerre rosé is hollow and tasteless these days, and I suspect that hollow, tasteless trendies drink it. This wine, however, is fabulous. It is beautiful to look at – the colour is the palest pink, the label design and capsule are chic, and the whole aura surrounding this bottle is seriously attractive. Sancerre rosé occasionally has this allure but is a huge let down on the nose and palate. Laloue's rosé, though, is absolutely brilliant. The nose of wild strawberries and redcurrants is gorgeous, and the palate is dry, long and satisfying.

● ●

£2.99 **Marks & Spencer Gamay, 2002**, Vin de Pays de L'Ardèche, France (**M&S**). Lighter than the Garnacha (below), this is the most impressive sub-three-pound red wine of the year. It is not dissimilar to a fresh, strawberry-juice-scented Beaujolais, but without any of the off-putting, bubblegum and banana nuances so often associated with the Gamay grape variety. Chill it a touch for parties and you'll be amazed at how easily and smoothly it slips down.

£3.03 **Gran Garnacha, 2002**, Cariñena, Spain (**Sai**). This is an all-purpose, fresh, cheeky, quirky, little red. The fruit flavours sit at the red end of the spectrum, with cranberry, cherry and mulberry notes bouncing around gleefully on the palate. It is designed to be drunk with simple, red-friendly dishes, like pizza. At three quid, this is one wine that is definitely worthy of its place in this illustrious roll call.

£3.99 **El Furioso Tempranillo, 2002**, Castilla y Léon, Spain (**Odd**). This wine and its creamy white Albillo sister (£3.99, **Odd**) make a handsome duo on the shelves. Both are cool gluggers, unencumbered by complexity and layers

LIGHT AND FRUITY

rosé/red   123

of fruit. They are just one dimensional, thirsty people's wines for parties and mind-switched-off drinking. We all need a little of that now and then.

£3.99 **Lavila, 2002**, Vin de Pays d'Oc, France (**Wai**). Made from a cocktail of Carignan, Grenache and Merlot, this is the velvetiest, juiciest and most cultured inexpensive red of the year. It has intensity, integrity and structure, so will not disappoint wine bores, while, on the other hand, novices will fall for its blackberry-themed charms. It has virtually no tannin so is perfect for drinking with or without food.

£3.99 **Tesco Californian Merlot, 2002**, USA (**Tes**). The new Californian range at Tesco is looking good, and this jammy, smooth Merlot is the pick of the bunch. Anyone who can produce good, cheap Californian wine is clearly doing the right thing. This wine is a perfect place to start for novice red wine drinkers. It is stuffed with sweet, red cherry and strawberry fruit flavours and there is a generous lick of juicy, ripe fruit on the finish.

£4.99 **Lafayette, Merlot, NV**, Bordeaux, France (**Tes**). This wine's *raison d'être* is to introduce Bordeaux to a new, youthful audience. It is packaged beautifully in a heavy glass bottle with a classically designed, 'spirit of freedom' label. The Merlot fruit is smooth, pure and Ribena-flavoured. The Marquis de Lafayette was a great revolutionary and this wine is, too. It is a triumphant effort and one that has started to make me change my mind about cheap claret.

a *favourite tipple*

£4.99 **Peter Lehmann Grenache, 2002**, Barossa Valley, South Australia (**Boo**, **Odd**, **Sai** and **Tes**). PL's Grenache is fast becoming a favourite tipple of mine. The new 2002 with its screwcap aloft (**Odd** and **Tes**) is a fantastic creation. It is rammed with loganberry, plum, mulberry and black cherry fruit, and, once you twist off the cap, it explodes in the glass. This wine also chills well and is great with spicy food – try crispy aromatic duck for an epic combo!

£5.99 **Simon Gilbert Barbera, 2002**, Mudgee, New South Wales, Australia (**Amps**, **Corks**, **Philglas & Swiggot** and **Saf**). I doubt there is a fruitier, fleshier, shinier Italian Barbera on the shelves at £5.99 than this awesome offering from the perennial overachiever Simon Gilbert. Nobody would ever expect Piemonte's juice bomb of a grape Barbera to be grown in New South Wales's high altitude region Mudgee – but it works really, really well! Tell everyone you know and give Simon a fright!

£6.00 **Mâcon Rouge, 2001**, Louis Jadot, Burgundy, France (**Asd**). Joyous, ripe, red juice from this cunning 90% Gamay/10% Pinot Noir blend. Drink with charcuterie and cheese – or posh ploughman's, if you wish.

£6.21 **Beaujolais-Villages, Jean-Charles Pivot, 2002**, Burgundy, France (**Domaine Direct**). This is the Beaujolais producer that I have followed every year for the past decade. Pivot's 2002 is a joy, with lifted, aromatic, wild strawberry flavours and a delightful, refreshing finish.

LIGHT AND FRUITY

£7.99 **Ninth Island Pinot Noir, 2002**, Pipers Brook, Tasmania, Australia (Boo, D. Byrne, Connollys, Constantine, Corkscrew, Harvey Nichols, Hoults, Nicholls & Perks, Noble Rot, Portland, Premier Cru, Roberson, Sommelier, Tes and Wai). Three years in a row and this wine is still the finest sub-tenner Pinot Noir on the market. 2002 was a stunning vintage in Tasmania's Tamar Valley, where these grapes are grown. It was such an excellent crop that some fruit from this wine was used to prop up Pipers Brook's Estate Pinot Noir (sold for £20)! If I was given this to drink at a dinner party, I would be in heaven – it is cool and smooth, with strawberry, red cherry and redcurrant aromas, and darker plum and briary flavours on the palate. The length of finish and silky texture are amazing. This is class in a glass.

£13.95 **Chassagne-Montrachet, 2001**, Domaine Marc Morey, Burgundy, France (**Haynes, Hanson & Clark**). This is at the upper end of 'Light and Fruity', but it will amaze you with its cherry bomb fruit and silky texture. Everyone thinks Chassagne is a white grape village, but over half is planted with Pinot Noir. Morey is a first-class producer and this is a phenomenal bargain for a wine with this degree of skill.

• •

£3.99 **Cortello, 2001**, Estremadura, Portugal, (**Saf**). This is a cracking red. It is so cheap and yet has masses of briary, spicy, red fruit. I still can't really believe it! Buy it – you know it makes sense.

LIGHT AND FRUITY/MEDIUM WEIGHT

£3.99 **Viña Fuerte Garnacha, 2002**, Calatayud, Spain (**Wai**). I went nuts on this wine last year and I am happy to report to Viña Fuerte fans (and there is a veritable army of you), that the new vintage is every bit as mighty as last year's wine. It still has pretty pokey alcohol (14 degrees) and a full-bodied approach, but the power is tempered and the trademark herbal ciggie nuances are still there to take your mind off the wine's brawn. At four quid this is a no-brainer.

£4.49 **Banrock Station Shiraz/Mataro, 2002**, South Eastern Australia (**Asd, Coo, Mor, Saf, Sai, Som, Tes** and **Wai**). If you are rushing out to a party and need a failsafe bottle, this is it and it's available virtually everywhere. The new vintage of Banrock's inexpensive red blend is the best they have ever made. It is briary, smooth, spicy and plummy, and the value for money will amaze you.

£4.49 **Santa Julia, Bonarda/Sangiovese, 2002**, Mendoza, Argentina (**Mor** and **Wai**). These guys make seriously chunky, plummy wines and this funky blend of strangely herbal, blueberry-stuffed Bonarda and Tuscany's Chianti variety Sangiovese is an autumnal must. It is a teeny price for this degree of skill. Also, try Santa Julia's epic take on Rioja, with their 2002 Tempranillo (£4.99, **Som** and **Tes**).

£4.99 **Aradon Rioja, 2002**, Spain (**Odd**). This smooth, sexy, youthful brew is already drinking well despite its youth. It is perfumed and balanced, and would suit medium-weight main course dishes. Cheap Rioja has never looked so good.

MEDIUM WEIGHT

£4.99 **Château Beau Mayne, 2001**, Bordeaux, France (**Tes**). Good balance, screwcap, classy flavours… red Bordeaux? Yes, and it is a very good example of the progress made in this massive wine region. The screwcap, by the way, helps keep the dark fruit in place and will enable this wine to develop well for a year or two.

£4.99 **First Step Merlot, 2002**, Step Road Winery, Langhorne Creek, South Australia (**Wai**). With pure unadulterated Merlot fruit, this is velvety smooth and totally juicy. Cherry, plum, raspberry and cranberry flavours all jostle for attention. Very few sub-fiver Merlots work, but this one shines with polished fruit and super-sexy appeal.

£4.99 **La Riada, Old Vines Garnacha, 2002**, Campo de Borja, Spain (**Thr** and **WRa**). This wine blew me away when I tasted the very first UK sample in June. It is a storming bottle of wine that tastes every inch a tenner. The raspberry, vanilla and sweet oak nuances float around on the surface, while underneath there are black cherries and plums bouncing around. I cannot recommend this wine enough.

£4.99 **Magnolie, Brindisi Rosso, 2001**, Puglia, Italy (**Saf**). This wine is made under the expert guidance of consultant supremo Ricardo Cotarella. It is a blinding blend of 80% Negroamaro and 20% Montepulciano, and then 10% of the wine sees six months in oak. This serves to season the liquorice, plum, bitter dark chocolate and blackberry flavours with a warm cinnamon spice veneer.

MEDIUM WEIGHT

£4.99 Portada, 2001, José Neiva, Estremadura, Portugal (Saf). This wine tastes like an asteroid collision between a spice container and a ton of plump, red and purple berries. It is dark and brooding in the glass, but the nose and palate, from the 50% Castelão and 50% Tinta Roriz, are extraordinary. Cherries, sweet plums and strawberries are all over the place. It is intense on the palate and there is some sneaky black fruit on the finish but, the overall balance is remarkable.

£4.99 Seventh Moon Winery Cabernet Sauvignon, 2001, California (Asd, Mor and Wai). Strike up the band! At last, a £5 Californian Cabernet that doesn't taste like Ben & Jerry's Chunky Monkey. OK, it took an Aussie winemaker under the Hardy's umbrella to do it, but I'm not quibbling. The lack of jammy, confected, supposedly consumer-friendly flavours is a shock. What you actually experience is a frighteningly good bottle of calm, almost restrained New World Cabernet. If you like claret but wisely avoid dipping below a fiver, then this will make your decade. It is fabulously well balanced, with ripe, blackcurrant-driven fruit and a wonderfully lively finish.

£4.99 Tempus Two, Lisa McGuigan Shiraz, 2002, South Eastern Australia (Tes). This stunning wine is full of tangy, ripe, smoky, herbal Shiraz fruit, and there is more than a passing whiff of Frazzles, which I love! Tempus Two is savoury and refreshing, despite its size, and the balance is spot on. If you love meaty, wintry reds, this gives you buckets of flavour for under a fiver.

MEDIUM WEIGHT

£5.00 **Valpolicella, Sagramosa, 1999**, Pasqua, Veneto, Italy (**Asd**). This superb Valpol must be half price! It is totally packed with juicy, black-wine-gum fruit and the finish is sublime. I love it. You should load up – Sagramosa will disappear quickly, as it is the ultimate Italian spag bol wine! ●

£5.15 **Monasterio de Santa Ana Monastrell, 2002**, Jumilla, Spain (**Wai**). Monastrell is a synonym for France's Mourvèdre and the New World's Mataro – so, in theory, this is a meaty, robust fellow. The vines used are very old and this concentrates the flavour of the finished wine. It also spends a brief spell in oak barrels, which seasons the dark fruit and adds spice and vanilla notes. I know what you're thinking – how can all of this be done for a fiver? Well, I have no bloody idea! The resulting wine is astonishing. It is incredibly smooth, with an espresso coffee aroma, liquorice, spice, deep, dark, black plum and berry fruit and a dusty, earthy finish. This is a mightily impressive wine.

£5.49 **Miranda Merlot, 2002**, South Eastern Australia (**Bibendum**). The new screwcapped varietal series of wines from Miranda is a winner. The best two are the Cabernet and my chosen Merlot, which both have fantastic concentration and accurate varietal appeal. Nobody had stuck their hand up for them when I wrote this note back in July, but you can always contact shippers Bibendum Wine and they'll let you know where to find them. Miranda is set for a storming return to the high street.

MEDIUM WEIGHT

£5.99 **Marqués de Griñon Tempranillo, 2001**, Rioja, Spain (Maj, Mor, Sai, Tes, Thr, Unw and WRa). Marqués de Griñon has stated that they will do whatever it takes to make the best Rioja around. If that is the case, then they don't have to do an awful lot more to improve this tremendous 2001 vintage. The purity of strawberry, plum and vanilla-kissed fruit is captivating as it glides across the palate. If you want to get back into Rioja after losing your way, then start here. This wine is phenomenally well made and terrific value. Also, watch out for 2000 Marqués de la Concordia Crianza, Hacienda Concordia, Rioja (£7.99, Odd and Unw are likely to stock it), which is a 'reserve' level – one step above my featured wine. It is absolutely brilliant – stuffed with pristine, concentrated fruit, excellent sweetness and ripeness, and superb balance. It is destined to arrive in the autumn.

£5.99 **Mas Collet, 2001**, Montsant, Celler de Capçanes, Tarragona, Spain (Boo and Wai). High up in the hills, to the southwest of Barcelona, is the wine region of Tarragona. This Garnacha, Tempranillo, Carineña, Cabernet Sauvignon blend spends a brief spell in oak barrels and then it is ready to go. The juicy cranberry and mulberry fruit explosion is remarkable. This is just the sort of red wine to accompany stews and hotpots, as it has tremendous spice and acidity. The excellent 2000 gives way to my fiery 2001 in the autumn. Make sure you decant this wine, as it will open up and reveal a multitude of layers of plummy fruit and spice.

MEDIUM WEIGHT

£5.99 **The Wolftrap, 2002**, Boekenhoutskloof, Western Cape, South Africa (**Asd** and **Odd**). If you are a true wine lover (and/or buy this book each year!), you will have drunk Marc Kent's wines on many occasions. He is the genius behind Porcupine Ridge and Boekenhoutskloof wines. But, what should Marc do for his next trick? Well, if at the end of the harvest, you have a few Cabernet Sauvignon, Syrah, Merlot and Pinotage grapes hanging around, why not whisk them together and magic up a cheeky, briary, chunky red blend? Hurrah, The Wolftrap is born and it doesn't half taste terrific. It is predictably spicy, intense, well balanced and rich, and it oozes devilish charm.

£6.49 **Ancien Comté, Corbières Réserve, 2001**, Languedoc, France (**Tes**). This wine even smells like the south of France with its wild, lavender, herb and rosemary scents. It is dark, meaty and packed with briary notes. This is a superb red that will keep you warm on a cold night.

£6.49 **Commanderie, 2000**, Côtes de Castillon, Bordeaux, France (**Tes**). I always bang on about how disappointing inexpensive red Bordeaux is, but this wine really surprised me. It is a chunky, brooding, spicy, powerful red, with lashings of blackcurrant aromas and flavours. It needs decanting and would be a mighty wine for roast beef.

£6.49 **Vinsobres Les Cornuds, 2001**, Côtes-du-Rhône-Villages, Perrin & Fils, France (**Tes**). This is a totally classy bottle of wine from the little known Rhône village of

MEDIUM WEIGHT

Vinsobres, situated at the northern end of the southern Rhône region. It is a straight 50/50 blend of southern Rhône stalwart Grenache and northern Rhône mainstay Syrah. There is a whisper of oak but the driving force is one of dark, dense, black fruit with a fine dusting of white pepper and spice. I taste hundreds of Côtes-du-Rhônes a year and I would be surprised if there were a better bottle at this cracking price.

£6.50 **Pirque Estate Cabernet Sauvignon, 2001**, Chile (**M&S**). Alvaro Espinoza, the man behind this wine, is a magician. There is so much going on in the glass, it totally belies its price. I am so impressed with Pirque and I reckon it will age really well for another four or five years. You should buy some of this and some Gallais Bellevue below and hold comparative tastings over the next few years.

£6.99 **Château Gallais Bellevue, 2000**, Cru Bourgeois, Médoc, Bordeaux, France (**M&S**). Made by the team at Ch. Potensac (see Gazetteer), this is a terrific bottle of wine. 2000 is an awesome vintage and, if you give it some air, it will open up into a cracker. It is phenomenally under priced so grab some if you have a roast beef and claret habit on Sundays. Serve this in a decanter and you could easily trick wine snobs into thinking they were drinking seriously expensive claret!

£6.99 **Durius Tinto, 2001**, Marques de Griñon, Arribes del Duero, Spain (**Maj**, **Mor**, **Sai**, **Thr**, **Unw** and **WRa**). Durius is the Latin name for the mighty Duero/Douro River that flows from Spain into Portugal and on the banks of which dwell the great vineyards that make Port. The Arribes del Duero region is a relatively new one and it is found on the Spanish/Portuguese border. Durius is made from Tempranillo, the noble grape that makes Rioja, so from the outset this wine has elegance and breeding. But, what differentiates it from other Spanish wines is the glossy, blackcurrant fruit intensity, the dark chocolate and tobacco moments, and its velvety smooth palate. The silky texture is simply stunning and makes you crave more. I get the feeling that this wine is not only breaking the mould but recasting a new one to which all other estates must now aspire. I can't believe that this wine is only seven pounds.

£6.99 **Pepi Merlot, 2000**, California (**Tes**). This is a cracking and highly juicy bottle of inexpensive USA Merlot. It has blueberry, plum, mint, chocolate and cranberry notes, and is so slippery smooth it will disappear in a trice.

£6.99 **Porcupine Ridge Syrah, 2002**, Coastal Region, South Africa (**SWIG**, **Wai** and **Wine Society**). To be fair to Porky Pie and its creator Marc Kent, they should have won three places in this year's Top 250. The Cabernet (£6.99, **Som** and **Stokes**) and the Merlot (£6.99, **Ballantynes**, **Odd** and **SWIG**) are both monumentally serious wines but, hey, life isn't fair! So, I picked my favourite of the new 2002s and the Syrah won by a nose. It is hard to put into words (but I'll try) just how much integrity and complexity dwells in this seven-pound wine. If you consider that its direct bloodline is Marc's other label Boekenhoutskloof Syrah (my favourite South African wine), perhaps you will start to see what I mean. This wine is quite simply the best-balanced and best-value Syrah I have tasted this year.

£6.99 **Rutherglen Estates Durif, 2002**, Victoria, Australia (**Wai**). Goodness me, this is a superbly fat, plump, chunky, juicy wine. It is made from the weird grape variety Durif and it also has a smidgen of aromatic Viognier (yes, the white grape) thrown in to lift the nose. The result is a sensational, rich, dark, chocolaty, plummy wine, with absolutely no tannin whatsoever. This is liquid velvet and a guaranteed bodice ripper if ever there was one.

£7.49 **Château La Raze Beauvallet, 2001**, Bordeaux, France (**Tes**). Tesco is leading the way with screwcaps and they are to be applauded since, thanks to them, fewer people in the UK have to put up with drinking corked bottles of wine. La Raze is a really classy, full, balanced bottle of claret, destined to be drunk with Sunday lunch.

£7.49 **Ravenswood Vintners Blend Zinfandel, 2001**, California (**Boo**, **Saf**, **Som** and **Tes**). 2000 Ravenswood Zin is a roller coaster of a wine, but I have already sniffed and slurped the 2001 and it is even more exhilarating. There are tons of Zinfandels out there and, despite being one of the cheapest, it is right up there quality-wise. Ravenswood Zin has masses of super-smooth, ripe fruit. There are some flashy moments of dark chocolate

MEDIUM WEIGHT

with sweet, heady spices to balance the plump, juicy blueberry and black cherry fruit flavours, and the sheer size and length of this wine is worth the price alone.

£7.99 **Brookland Valley Verse 1 Shiraz, 2001**, Margaret River, Western Australia (**Berry Bros. and Odd**). Margaret River Shiraz is not big and rich like the porty Barossa Valley wines, but cool, medium-weight, peppery, intense and blackberry-driven – it's like turbo-charged Crozes-Hermitage. Watch out for the amazing 2002 as well, it is even finer than the 2001 and is due in around Christmas.

£7.99 **Leasingham Magnus Shiraz Cabernet, 2001**, Clare Valley, South Australia (**Saf**). Safeway currently sell 2000 Leasingham Bastion Shiraz Cab, which is due to undergo a name and vintage change to become the spectacular 2001 Magnus. 2001 is not only a better vintage but these two super red grapes are really beginning to relish their respective jobs in the partnership. The Shiraz brings sweet, blackberry-driven spice and allure, while the Cabernet weighs in with muscle and the firm, mouth-watering finish. This wine will surely put Leasingham reds on the map since, at eight quid, there is little to touch this wine.

£7.99 **Regolo, Sartori, 1999**, Veneto, Italy (**Thr** and **WRa**). This fabulous super-Valpolicella is fermented on Amarone lees and, therefore, picks up tremendous richness of fruit. It also has four years under its belt, so it's at the peak of its powers. This is a very classy wine for an Italian feast.

£8.00 **Frankland Estate Rivermist Shiraz, 2001**, Frankland, Western Australia (**Bennetts, Morris & Verdin** and **Philglas & Swiggot**). Rivermist is the baby red from the top class Frankland Estate and it is a veritable bargain. It is an inky black beauty, stuffed with cherries, plums and peppery nuances. This is a superb bottle of red that will work equally well with barbecued food or Sunday lunch. When the 2002 arrives in due course, grab a case, as it is a blinder. Also, watch out for 2002 Isolation Ridge Riesling from Frankland Estate (£10ish) – it is a sensational wine and awesome value.

£8.99 **Château Amarande, 1998**, Bordeaux, France (**Odd**). This Merlot-dominant stunner is a gorgeous antidote if you are (and who isn't?) suffering from the Bordeaux blues. This bottle is a shining light in a sea of dreary reds – I have to taste hundreds of poor bottles to find a star like Amarande. It is silky smooth, ripe and juicy, and has benefited from two years slumbering in spanky oak barrels. This is a classy wine, indeed, and one that, I'm sure, will amaze even the most reluctant of claret drinkers.

£8.99 **Rioja Crianza, Viñas de Gain, 2000**, Artadi, Spain (**Boo**). I was totally gob-smacked when I went around the Booths press tasting back in June. I thought that, after writing up the 1998 in TWL03, I'd never see Viñas del Gain at £8.99 again. This tastes like twenty-five quid's worth of wine. I don't care whether you live near Booths in the north of England or not, get on the dog and bone now! You'll thank me – I promise. Feel free to send flowers! This is – and I have to be so careful not to swear – a perfect bottle of wine. It is so pumped up, bright, powerful and imposing but, at the same time, it is drinking marvellously now. Remember where you read it and spread the word!

£8.99 **Rosso di Montepulciano, Poliziano, 2001**, Tuscany, Italy (**Boo** and **Sai**). Poliziano is an amazing and historic estate in the legendary Montepulciano area. This Sangiovese is vivid purple, spicy, tangy, dense and loaded with blackberry fruit. It is the perfect wine for wintry game or beef dishes and is a bargain at nine quid. Just to prove how amazing Poliziano is, the 2002 (which was supposedly a poor vintage) is absolutely sublime. Keep your eyes peeled, it's due out at Christmas.

£8.99 **Tim Adams Shiraz, 2001**, Clare Valley, South Australia (**Tes**). I have been waiting an age for this wine to realise its full potential and, in 2001, it has done just that. This is an incredible effort. The fruit is so focused and stylish, you must track some down. It's only nine pounds, will live for a decade and will only get better. If you want a brother for it, then have a go at TA's phenomenal Grenache-based red – 2000 Fergus (£9.99, **Booths of Stockport**, **Andrew Chapman**, **Maj** and **Portland**). It gained the exact same points out of twenty in my notes as the 2001 Shiraz but, as I don't publish my scores, you'll never know what they got. I can, however, tell you that they only dropped four points between them!

£9.95 **Cullen, Ellen Bussell Cabernets, 2002**, Margaret River, Western Australia (**Bennetts, Liberty** and **Noel Young**). Vanya Cullen has launched a fantastic new range of wines this year – called Ellen Bussell. The red is bright, lifted and already drinking. It is lighter than many Cabernet blends and is stuffed with blueberry, loganberry and blackberry fruit. For a tenner, this is a spectacular effort, as I gave it a near perfect score when I tasted it back in March. This is their very first write up in the UK, so make the most of it! The Cullen portfolio is a dream, but special mention should go to 2001 Diana Madeline Cabernet Sauvignon, named after Vanya's much-loved mum and Margaret River pioneer, who died earlier this year. It is a fitting tribute.

£9.99 **Avila Pinot Noir, 2001**, San Luis Obispo County, California (**Berry Bros.** and **Odd**). California is a fine place to look for smart, glossy, fruit-driven, velvety-smooth Pinot Noirs. The problem is that they inevitably cost a fortune. This wine is the exception. It is liquid velvet, with plum and red cherry flavours running the full length of the palate. It even has some darker elements of chocolate and sweet spices woven into the mix.

£10.95 **Château La Branne, 2000**, Médoc, Bordeaux, France (**Lea & Sandeman**). Inexpensive claret is the most difficult sector in the entire world of wine. Most efforts are either feeble or brutally tannic. L&S have reversed this trend and sourced some fine wines for their adoring

MEDIUM WEIGHT

customers. La Branne is one of them – it is half Cab Sauv and half Merlot, it is stuffed with ripe blackcurrant fruit and has a lovely smooth, savoury finish. L&S have two other noteworthy clarets – 2000 Château du Maine, Graves (£9.95) is a little lighter than La Branne and 2000 Château Comte, Canon Fronsac (£13.95) is a bit bigger and more intense!

£10.95 **Dolcetto d'Alba La Lepre, 2002**, Fontanafredda, Piemonte, Italy (**Handford**, **Valvona & Crolla** and **Wimbledon**). Despite being a very difficult vintage in Piemonte, winemaker Danilo Drocco has pulled the rabbit out of the hat. Does Lepre mean hare? If it doesn't, it should – look at the furry label! It is attractively packaged (I know that shouldn't sway me), and the crunchy, black cherry and blackcurrant fruit, with the lashings of green, perky acidity blew my palate away. Dolcetto should drink well young, so get drinking and cooking – wild boar or venison should do it!

£10.95 **Moulin-à-Vent, Château des Jacques, 2001**, Louis Jadot, Beaujolais, France (**D. Byrne**, **Luvian's**, **Vicki's**, **Wai** and **Wimbledon**). Isn't it bizarre that top notch Beaune-based Burgundy specialists Jadot are now better known on the high street for their celestial Beaujolais? The main reason for this is their more expensive Côte d'Or wines are primarily drunk in restaurants, or are so smart they head straight into private collections. No matter – this stunning, organic wine benefits from the centuries of Jadot expertise and is terrific value for one of the best Beaujolais you will find anywhere. If you have been unlucky enough

MEDIUM WEIGHT

to taste the farcical annual November release of Beaujolais Nouveau, then you might be itching to skip this wine and move on. But wait! This is serious and could knock many a red Burgundy from an esteemed village into a cocked hat. Trust me on this one – it is a spectacular wine.

£12.95 **Saint-Joseph, Domaine Pierre Gonon, 2000**, Northern Rhône, France (**Vine Trail**). This vintage and the 2001 that follows are superb examples of Syrah at its peak. The northern Rhône is the spiritual home of this grape variety and it still makes some of the most complex red wines in the world. This is not a heavy wine, but is an intense one, with wild mushrooms, herbs and spices on the nose, and a super-smooth palate. It is drinking perfectly now and would be a treat with any beef, lamb or game main course.

£17.95 **Keith Tulloch, Kester Shiraz, 2000**, Hunter Valley, New South Wales, Australia (**Ballantynes**, **Love Saves the Day**, **La Reserve** and **Vin du Van**). This wine is so relaxed and moreish it's like rhythmic waves of Côte-Rôtie washing over your palate. Hang on – it is also fully ripe, deep and textured, elegantly peppery and seriously brilliant value. I bet most Côte-Rôtie wishes it was as good as this at romancing your taste buds and making you feel like you've just drunk one of the most profound wines of the year!

£19.99 **Knappstein Lenswood, Pinot Noir, 2000**, Adelaide Hills, South Australia (**Handford**, **Harrods** and **Uncorked**). Tim and Annie Knappstein have made a blinding

Pinot in 2000. This is a textured beauty, with mellow, all-enveloping brambly flavours and a tremendous finish. This is the top-of-the-tree Aussie Pinot.

£22.95 **Chambolle-Musigny, Domaine Virgile Lignier, 2000**, Burgundy, France (**Wai**). This is a spectacular bottle of sultry, smooth Pinot Noir. Virgile Lignier is a mere lad, but he has shown remarkable maturity by handling his 40-year-old vines with respect and encouraging them to give their best. He dunks the pristine fruit into French oak barrels for a year and this seasons the recipe to perfection. Every wild strawberry and black cherry flavour you could expect from a top Chambolle is here. It is not cheap, but then red Burgundy of this quality never is.

● ●

£3.99 **Conde de Navasqüés Tempranillo, 2002**, Navarra, Spain (**Saf**). This unoaked, inexpensive Tempranillo is mind-blowing value for money. It is dense, dark and ever so juicy, and with an inky colour and glossy sheen, it is surprisingly ready to go. I really can't quite believe the price.

£4.99 **Casillero del Diablo Cabernet Sauvignon, 2002**, Maipo Valley, Chile (**Odd**, **Saf**, **Sai**, **Tes**, **Thr**, **Wai** and **WRa**). There are very few New World Cabernets that have made my Top 250. But, don't worry, you only really need one for everyday drinking – this one! Casillero Cab is a monumental effort at this price, with every nuance and flavour box ticked. This is one of the classic ranges of all time, so look out for a superb 2002 Chard (£4.99, **Maj**, **Odd**, **Thr** and **Wai**), and the spanky, oak-tweaked 2001 Marques de Casa Concha Cabernet (£6.99, **Saf**).

£4.99 **Castillos Volandos, Old Block Garnacha/ Tempranillo, 2002**, Campo di Borja, Spain (**Odd**). Oof, this is a big boy. It is dark, rich and packs a meaty punch. There is a lot of wine here for a fiver. Drink it with earthy, rustic stews and country cooking.

£4.99 **Da Luca Primitivo-Merlot, 2002**, Puglia, Italy (**Wai**). This wine packs one hell of a punch for its diminutive price tag. The intensity of raisin, plum, liquorice and blackberry fruit is amazing. It is a fairly big wine – so do give it some air to allow it to unwind before you drink it. The two red grapes work well together, with the Merlot being the good cop and Primitivo the bad. This is a winner with wintry dishes and chargrilled steaks.

£4.99 **Grenache Noir Old Vines, 2001**, Vin de Pays Catalan, France (**M&S**). This is the second vintage in a row in my Top 250 for this rather blandly named wine. And I am delighted to report that this 2001 has even more earth and spice and brooding power than the 2000. It is still the same price and looks great in the smart, heavy glass bottle, so don't delay. For goodness sake, some of the Grenache vines in this wine are over 100 years old!

BLOCKBUSTER

£5.99 **DFJ Touriga Nacional/Touriga Franca, 2001**, Estremadura, Portugal (**Saf**). This wine is stunning value and shows how amazing Portuguese reds have become in the last few years. It is deep, dense and stylish, with tar, dark choccie, plum and blackcurrant flavours all folded into the mix. It spends a brief three months in oak, which adds toasty, spicy elements. All in all, this is a serious wine that would amaze a wine connoisseur. I bet they'd say it was well over a tenner, if you asked for a guestimate price!

£5.99 **Fitou, Les Douze, 2001**, Languedoc-Roussillon, France (**Asd** and **Sai**). Thank goodness Fitou has had a makeover of late (remember the eighties versions?). This wine is made from the grapes harvested by twelve winemakers (hence the name) in the village of Tuchan. It is a classic blend of Carignan, Syrah and Grenache, and the result is one of the most juicy, rich, accurate and delicious Fitous around. The blackberry, leather and spice flavours coat the palate, and make you crave wintry, robust meaty dishes. At six quid, this is a bargain – so raise twelve glasses to Michael, Philippe, Nicolas, Vincent, Josie, François, Eric, Didier, Jean-Luc, Patrick, Yannick and Lionel.

£5.99 **Simon Gilbert Card Series Shiraz, 2001**, Mudgee, New South Wales, Australia (**Butlers, deFINE, Saf** and **Scatchards**). Whenever I taste Simon Gilbert wines I am always left wondering how they do it for the money. They certainly look the part, and one sniff and you're sold. This dense, lusty Shiraz is crammed full of blackberry fruit, smoky bacon, cracked pepper, charred wood, eucalyptus and warm leather (mmm). Until I stop scoring these wines in the high teens out of twenty they will keep appearing in the Top 250. Let's hope they stay at this ridiculously low price.

£6.29 **Fairview Malbec, 2001**, Paarl, South Africa (**Mor** and **Saf**). Crash helmets on – this is a big, inky black wine, drenched in spicy, roasted plum and black cherry fruit. Decant it, as it is a little brutish on first taste and needs air to calm it down. Once relaxed (the wine, not you!) it will unroll like a very dark red carpet across your palate. Treat it to some carnivorous fare (the more rustic the better) and you'll be amazed by how genial it becomes at the table.

£6.49 **Hardy's Varietal Range Reserve Shiraz, 2001**, South Eastern Australia (**Tes**). Hardy's VR is the perfect introduction to Aussie wine and, more importantly, a superb lesson in the differences in flavour between grape varieties. The VR Reserve, however, is a whole new ballgame. The quality of fruit is staggering. The pure, slick, brambly fruit is pumped up and laden with plum, cherry, spice, ground pepper and dark cassis flavours. The colour is black and the texture silky smooth, and all of this class and complexity is kept in place with a screwcap – thank goodness. If you love this, and you will, taste the 2001 Cabernet (£6.49 **Tes**).

£6.95 **Heartland Wirrega Vineyard Shiraz, 2001**, Limestone Coast, South Australia (**Compendium**, **Great Western** and **Odd**). Heartland is made by one of Australia's

BLOCKBUSTER

best young winemakers Ben Glaetzer – a dead ringer for Ben Affleck (hey girls!). Wirrega is a meaty number, with broad, brooding power and spicy oak. This is an excellent wine destined to be drunk with macho meat feasts – so get cracking and knock the horns off a steer.

£6.99 **Concha y Toro, Lot Vic 3 Syrah, 2002**, Rapel Valley, Chile (**Odd**). I did back flips about Marcelo Papa's 2001 'Lot' Series last year and, after tasting a sneak preview of the entire range of 2002s, I am certain he has done the impossible and improved them. There are five wines in the line-up – from a £5.99 Malbec to a £9.99 Cabernet – and every wine shows an unwavering commitment to supreme fruit, deft use of oak, sumptuous texture and a complete finish. The Syrah nudged the others out of the top spot because it is a difficult variety to crack and Marcelo has imbued this wine with style, aroma and true intensity.

£6.99 **Diemersfontein Pinotage, 2003**, Wellington, South Africa (**Wai**). Every year there is a very special day in December. No, not when Santa gets wedged in your chimney but the day when the new vintage of Diemers Pinotage hits the shelves at Waitrose. It may seem bizarre to be talking about '03 reds so soon, but I've already dipped my hooter in a menacing preview of this wine and it is a beast. It delivers on every level and I defy any lover of balls-out reds not to fall head over heels for this wine. They've even made an eye-watering Petit Verdot this year – keep your eyes peeled and I'll see you in the stampede.

£7.49 **MontGras, Limited Edition Cabernet Sauvignon/Merlot, 2000**, Colchagua Valley, Chile (**Wai**). 2000 Ninquén (£15.99, **Sai**), Chile's finest red, made TWL02 and MontGras is made from the declassified grapes that didn't quite make the grade for Ninquén. It is extraordinarily good value and one of the finest wines they have ever made, but hurry, it is in very short supply.

£7.49 **Peter Lehmann, Clancy's, 2001**, Barossa Valley, South Australia (**Asd**, **Boo**, **Odd**, **Sai**, **Unw** and **Wai**). I went bonkers last year about 2000 Clancy's, the superb, macho red blend from Peter Lehmann's formidable cellar, but this wine is even better. If you tasted Clancy's at one of my book signings or on last year's road show, then I promised you even more power and style in 2001. I know it's hard to believe, but it's there! Yippee! I was right!

£7.99 **St Hallett Faith Shiraz, 2001**, Barossa Valley, South Australia (**Tes**). Faith is still a superb example of Barossa Valley Shiraz, despite the fact that Captain Bob (McLean) has left the building. It is plump, glossy and stuffed with inky blackberry and black cherry fruit flavours. The nose is classically spicy and peppery, and the finish is savoury and lip-smackingly long. You could also trade up and track down the glorious and historic 2001 St Hallett Old Block Shiraz (£14.99, **Tes**), made from 100-year-old vines. You will taste the relationship between them in their flavour. Which proves that Faith is very much a chip off the Old Block.

BLOCKBUSTER

red 147

£7.99 **Wynns Shiraz, 2001**, Coonawarra, South Australia (**Thr** and **WRa**). This sappy, eucalyptus-imbued Shiraz is the epitome of Coonawarra winemaking. It is stunning value, as there is a magnum's worth of flavour in this bottle. It is powerful, teeth-stainingly black and oh so peppery – yum.

£8.60 **Rasteau Domaine du Trapadis, 2000**, Southern Rhone, France (**Vine Trail**). This Grenache/Carignan/Syrah blend is midnight black in colour and inundated with charcoal and black cherry flavours. The surprise is that this wine doesn't see any oak barrels in the course of its production. It is just pure, unadulterated, massive, inky fruit.

£8.99 **Canale, Black River Reserve Malbec, 2001**, Patagonia, Argentina (**Sai**). This wine is so big, black and scary it's the creature from the black lagoon. It is impenetrably black in colour, frighteningly tannic and monstrously heavy, so do put on your seatbelt and drink with caveman-sized carnivorous fare!

£8.99 **Fairview Peg Leg Carignan, 2001**, Paarl, South Africa (**Great Western**, **Simon Charles** and **Wine Society**). Wow, the swarthy red grape Carignan gets a chance to do its thing without being swamped by its usual Rhône-blend companions, Syrah, Grenache and Mourvèdre. Charles Back – the Willy Wonka of SA with his cheeky Goats do Roam wines – is the brain behind this creation. He has perfected the knack of turning all sorts of underrated varieties into classic wines. The black fruit intensity and spicy, earthy aromas are reminiscent of some of his other gorgeous wines, but it is the smoothness and intensity of the dark plum and bitter chocolate fruit that I like so much.

£9.95 Avila Zinfandel, 2000, Santa Barbara County, California (**Berry Bros.**). Avila Pinot is in my Top 250 and is easier to get hold of, but do pay attention to this stunning Zin. It is every barbecued steak's dream date. It is plummy (even pruney), smooth, sophisticated and luxurious. The juicy, black fruit keep coming in waves, counterpointed by spicy moments and stunning savoury oak nuances. This is not a high-alcohol, headachy wine, as so many other Zins seem to be, but a cultured, complex, elegant thoroughbred.

£9.99 Côtes-du-Rhône-Villages, Les Echalas, 2001, Clos Petite Bellane, France (**Odd**). Aaarrrgghh – big wine alert! Echalas is a Shrek of a wine, with brooding, meaty, spicy, densely packed black fruit. It is crammed with fat blackberry flavours and liberally dusted with ground white pepper nuances. There are smoky bonfire night snorts and the scent of freshly cut timber takes to the air when you uncork this wine. Despite the fact that the price has crept up over the years, Echalas is still one of the benchmark red Rhônes – it would give an Aussie Shiraz a fright, believe me!

£9.99 Heritage Shiraz, 2001, Barossa Valley, South Australia (**Booths of Stockport**, **Andrew Chapman**, **Moriarty**, **Ozwines** tel. 0845 450 1261, **Philglas & Swiggot** and **Portland**). I have waited for fifteen years for Steve Hoff

BLOCKBUSTER

to make this wine. Heritage is a great operation, making manly, hairy Barossa reds and leesy, ripe, limey whites, and I have been buying them for years. But when I first tasted Steve's 2001 reds, I had an out-of-body experience. 2001 was a top vintage in Barossa, but nothing prepared me for the sappy, dark core of explosive Shiraz fruit. It is nothing short of (and I rarely use the word) perfect. In fact, I'll say it louder – this is a PERFECT bottle of Aussie Shiraz. Everyone should do everything in their power to drink a glass of this wine, it could even be a life-changing moment – it was for me.

£9.99 **Peter Lehmann Futures Shiraz, 2001**, Barossa Valley, South Australia (**Boo** and **Odd**). Futures is a new wine from top geezer PL, filling the gap between his stalwart, award-winning £7.99 Barossa Shiraz and his brutal, unforgiving, forever-young £30 Stonewell Shiraz. The question is, why should you trade up a few quid to Futures from the Barossa? Well, you get a stellar grape variety, a rock-hard winemaker (Ian Wigan), a colossal vintage and a wine that tastes like it's fifteen quid's worth of fruit – which, by all accounts, it probably is.

£9.99 **Rustenberg John X Merriman, 2001**, Stellenbosch, South Africa (**S.H. Jones**, **Lea & Sandeman**, **James Nicholson**, **La Reserve** and **Weavers**). John X is a big old fella, with deep, dark fruit and a spicy, intense nose. This is a complex Bordeaux blend (Merlot/Cab Sauv/Cab Franc) that sees some top-class French oak and is truly magnificent value. Any Bordeaux producers reading this can start weeping now. Also, watch out for the sexy 2002 Rustenberg Chard (£9.99, same stockists) and a tidy range of wines from the second label Brampton (£6.99).

£10.99 **Graham Beck The Ridge Syrah, 2000**, Robertson, South Africa (**Bibendum**, **Luvian's** and **Maj**). This is Graham Beck's top red. It is a lesson in oak barrels and how they affect the flavour of a big, rich red wine. The sweet, juicy, super-ripe black fruit comes from the American oak-aged part and the savoury, spicy, peppery part comes from the expensive French barrels. This is a very well-priced wine for the class and power in the glass, and it is guaranteed to blow your dinner party guests away.

£11.99 **d'Arenberg Galvo Garage, 2001**, McLaren Vale, South Australia (**Odd**). Even committed Rhône lovers d'Arenberg couldn't resist cracking the Bordeaux combination with a classic blend of 66% Cabernet Sauvignon, 20% Merlot and 14% Cabernet Franc. It is a muscular style of red, to be drunk with big, meaty main courses. Also, grab some 2002 Laughing Magpie (£11.99, **Bibendum**, **Great Gaddesden**, **Odd**, **Philglas & Swiggot** and **Noel Young**) – it's Côte-Rôtie on acid! These wines both show that there is much more to d'Arenberg than just silly names.

£11.99 **Koltz, The Carbine, 2001**, McLaren Vale, South Australia (**Saf**). The Carbine is made from Shiraz, Cab Sauv and Merlot, and it's given 13 months in French and American oak barrels. This recipe is benchmark for

Australia's idyllic McLaren Vale reds, and yet the flavour is truly astounding and puts it way ahead of its peers. It is packed with smoky, intense, liquorice, plum, blackberry and black cherry flavours. The texture is velvety smooth and minutes long on the palate.

£12.50 **Chianti Classico, Brolio, 2001**, Tuscany, Italy (**SWIG** and **Wimbledon**). After winning 'Winery of the Year 2002' in the Gambero Rosso Italian wine guide, Brolio hasn't let up on its quest to make awesome Chianti. The 2000 made TWL02 and this 2001 is even better. The intensity of herb, spice, smoky oak and plum and blackcurrant fruit is all there in the 2000, but the 2001 has the X factor – all of these flavours plus a magical, super-smooth texture. By Christmas this wine will be ready to go, and you'll be amazed by the style and panache shown on the nose and palate.

£12.95 **Crozes-Hermitage, Cuvée Alberic Bouvet, 2001**, Domaine Gilles Robin, Northern Rhône, France (**Lea & Sandeman**). This is the most impressive Crozes I have tasted in years! The clever smattering of new oak has lifted this wine and it is in a class of its own. Make an orderly queue and ask L&S if they have any half bots – they are pocket rockets.

£12.99 **Marqués de Griñon, Dominio de Valdepusa Syrah, 2000**, Spain (**Wai**). This is a stunning wine, full to the brim with spice, power, depth and colour. It shows that Syrah is going to be one of the most important grapes on the Spanish wine scene in the near future. This is a wine that always wins blind tastings. On one level, it is just downright delicious but, on another, it is technically brilliant and awesomely complex. Hurry – minuscule stocks!

£13.95 **Henschke Henry's Seven, 2001**, Eden Valley, South Australia (**Lay & Wheeler**). This wine won a 100-bottle blind tasting I did in Australia in January 2003. It is a Shiraz, Grenache and Viognier blend, and is sheer perfection. Henschke is one of the top estates in Australia and they could easily have a handful of wines in this list but I have picked the best for you. Phone L&W for a full list.

£14.99 **The Chocolate Block, 2002**, Boekenhoutskloof, South Africa (**Handford**, **Odd** and **Wai** Canary Wharf and Kingston branches). Brand new, forward and seriously cool, and with only fifteen barrels made, Chocolate Block will disappear fast. Made by superstar Marc Kent and designed to fit the Boekenhoutskloof wines but with more breeding than the chunky, sturdy Porcupine range. Bring it on!

£14.99 **Houghton, Margaret River Cabernet Sauvignon, 2001**, Western Australia (**Fenwicks**, **The Vineyard** and **Wine Society**). This terrific Cabernet from the ten-out-of-ten 2001 vintage is an absolute dream. It would blow any Napa Cab at twice (or even three times!) the price, away. As would the 2001 Shiraz and 2002 Sauv, Chard and Riesling from Larry Cherubino's awesome WA range, which should all be in store by October. The prices

BLOCKBUSTER

range between £8.99 and £15 for these cosmic wines so, for sheer bravado and out-and-out quality, they are unbeatable. It is a travesty that these Houghton wines haven't got a larger audience, as they are truly mind-blowing.

£16.50 **Châteauneuf-du-Pape, 2000**, Domaine de Ferrand, Southern Rhone, France (**Vine Trail**). If you like Châteauneuf-du-Pape but often find it disappointing, look no further than this wine. It is simply brilliant and stupendous value for money. Those of you who follow my recommendations closely will have already picked up the phone! While you are ordering your CdP, grab some 2001 Côtes-du-Rhône Cuvée Antique, Ferrand (£7.65) – it is an heroic effort and not far off the real thing!

£18.99 **Amarone della Valpolicella Classico, 1999**, Brigaldara, Veneto, Italy (**Boo**). This is the greatest Amarone I have tasted in ages. It is balanced, drinking well, full-bodied, extremely complex and loaded with chocolate, plum, liquorice and tar flavours. It is no surprise that this estate has won three glasses (a prestigious accolade) in the Gambero Rosso Italian wine guide for each of its last few vintages of Amarone. If I had to guess the price of this wine blind, I'd have said north of £30, not south of £20!

£19.85 **Gran Elías Mora, 2000**, Bodegas Dos Victorias, Toro, Spain (**Georges Barbier**). Toro is a totally underrated region in northeast Spain, very near the world-famous region Ribera del Duero. The two Victorias make mind-blowing wine in Toro (and Rueda, see page 91), which overshadows just about everything I have tasted from Ribera. Only 36 barrels of their entire 2000 harvest made the grade for Gran Elías Mora. It also received 17 months in top French oak barrels. Made from Tinta de Toro, a local variant of Tempranillo, with a dribble of Garnacha, this 'Gran' wine only appears in the best vintages. The texture and layers of subtle oak lift the violet, raspberry and liquorice notes, which overlay the deep, dark blackberry core and the palate is liquid velvet. Crack one open and wallow in Toro.

£23.95 **Ulithorne, Frux Frugis Shiraz, 2001**, McLaren Vale, South Australia (**Haslemere** and **Vin du Van**). I tasted the very first bottled sample of Frux Frugis back in November '02 and was mightily impressed. It shows remarkable restraint and control for such a big wine, and the balance throughout is near perfect. This is one of the most complete wines I have tasted this year.

£23.99 **Boekenhoutskloof Syrah, 2000**, Franschhoek, South Africa (**Ballantynes**, **Handford**, **Jeroboams**, **Milton Sandford**, **Odd**, **Stokes**, **SWIG**, **Wai** Canary Wharf and Kingston branches, and **Wine Soc**). This is *the* wine – 20 out of 20! Any of the Boekenhoutskloof range are worth grabbing with both hands – whether it be the explosive Cabernet (£19.99), my chosen Syrah or the neon, lime juice Sémillon (£13.49). I have tasted every wine ever made at this estate and not one of them is anything less than mesmerising. Try any of the merchants listed and, if they

BLOCKBUSTER

have sold out, put your name down for some 2001. Also, watch out for a bizarre 2002 Noble Late Harvested Sémillon, codenamed 'The Bitch' bottled in halves. It will be shipped in the autumn and when I tasted it out of barrel back in January it was sensational. I reckon it will be blindingly expensive, though! Oh well, that's what credit cards are for.

● ● ● ● ● ● ● ● ● ● ● ● ● ● ● ● ● ● ● ●

£3.29 **Villa Jolanda Moscato d'Asti, NV**, Piemonte, Italy (**Tes**). There is no finer, inexpensive pudding wine than this brilliant, frothy Moscato. It is the perfect fizz to enjoy with strawberries, fruity tarts or chocolate puddings. Fizzy, grapey, juicy and sweet – just what the doctor ordered.

£4.49 half bottle **Miranda The Pioneers, 2002**, Raisined Muscat, Australia (**Maj**). This cheeky, little sweetie is made from partially dried Muscat grapes which focus the sugars and produce a sumptuous, honeyed, hypnotic wine. A half bottle will easily pour six glasses, so this is an inexpensive and delicious accompaniment to a fruity or chocolate pudding. ●

£5.81 **Moscatell de Tarragona, 2001**, Vino Dulce, Cellers de Montbrió del Camp, Tarragona, Spain (**Georges Barbier**). Remember this is a full bottle of wine (75cl), not a half, so it is seriously good value. This is not a soapy, bubble-bath-scented Moscatell, but a glorious, rose petal, caramel, honey and gardenia-scented wine. The grapes are picked very late, partially fermented and then fortified, much in the same way as the French classic Muscat de Beaumes-de-Venise. The cool thing is you'll never find a cheaper, better Muscat than this – believe me, I've looked for sixteen years.

£6.99 **Clairette de Die, Jaillance, NV**, Rhône, France (**Wai**). Three years in a row in the Top 250 for this elegant, French substitute for Asti. This sparkling Muscat is vibrant, grapey and uplifting. Jaillance is the best Clairette de Die I have ever tasted and, given its lowish alcohol (7.5%) and the fact that the grapes are organic, it should have a wide audience. You'll get six or seven good glasses from a bottle, so it works out to a quid a pop. A small price to pay for an enlivening, juicy, fizzy, perfect match for any dish.

£6.99 50cl bottle, **Torres Muscatel Oro, NV**, Penedès, Spain (**Sai**). This stunningly designed wine tastes like a million dollars. It is liquid honey, nuts and caramel – yum. You will adore this creation, particularly with Christmas cake!

£7.49 half bottle, **Dindarello, 2001**, Maculan, Breganze, Veneto, Italy (**Odd** and **Valvona & Crolla**). Dindarello is mildly sweet, tropical and honeyed, and not too sticky and oily, so it will not overshadow delicately flavoured puddings. This is an extremely beautiful and elegant wine.

£7.99 half bottle, **Sainsbury's Classic Selection Sauternes, 2001**, Bordeaux, France (**Sai**). Smooth, sweet, honeyed fruit, with lovely nutty aroma and exotic, floral palate – a lovely wine for fruity puds.

£8.49　50cl bottle, **Visanto Boutari, 1997**, Santorini, Greece (**Odd**). This is wickedly dark in colour – almost burnt amber – and it tastes like liquidised Christmas pudding, Cadbury's Caramel and rose petals. The grapes are dried to concentrate the sugars, then fermented and matured in oak barrels. The result is, pound for pound, the most impressive sweetie in the book! It is awesomely heady, delightfully rich, sinfully marmaladey and gorgeously smooth. Drink with chocolate, fruitcake or someone you love.

£9.70　50cl bottle, **Château Salitis, Ultime Vendange, 1999**, Vin de Pays d'Oc Doux, France (**Jeroboams**). Salitis is a very rare wine indeed. It is made from the Sauv Blanc grape variety, which rarely makes sweet wines without the help of other varieties. This odd wine came about thanks to some freak weather conditions late in the 1999 ripening season. The winemaking team behind this estate noticed that the grapes were on tip-top form and were starting to be affected by 'noble rot'. In the end the grapes were harvested in November, some two whole months later than normal! The rot had done its magical trick of turning a light, dry style of white grape into something more suitable for an unctuous sweet wine. Ultime Vendange (the ultimate harvest) is spectacular, overflowing with dribbly honey, praline, marmalade and tropical fruit. Do not miss it.

£9.99　half bottle, **Brown Brothers Noble Riesling, 1999**, King Valley, Victoria, Australia (**Rodney Densem, Noble Rot, Christopher Piper** and **Stevens Garnier**). This intensely rich, tropical Riesling is a fantastic tipple. It is deep coloured, violet and exotic-fruit scented and totally syrupy! You will only need a thimbleful to get you going!

£10.95 50cl bottle, **Coteaux du Layon Beaulieu, Les Rouannières, 2001**, Château de Pierre Bise, Loire, France (**Lea & Sandeman**). This wine is so special – it is mouth-coatingly exotic, tropically fruity, long, smooth and honeyed, with a glorious finish and a last lick of acidity to freshen the palate. Château de Pierre Bise is an exemplary estate, making some of the finest sweet wines in the entire Loire Valley. Get in quick, as stocks are very limited.

£11.99 50cl bottle, **Pansal de Calàs, 2000**, Cellers Capçanes, Montsant-Tarragona, Spain (**Boo** and **Georges Barbier**). This is a Garnacha/Cariñena blend, which is made into a sweet, rich red in the same style as a Banyuls or Maury from the South of France. It tastes like a rum and raisin, dark chocolate, prune, fig and burnt toffee concoction. Pansal is amazing because it can be drunk instead of a pud wine or port, as it presses both buttons. I would have it after dinner with choccies and an espresso coffee.

£20.99 50cl bottle, **Tokaji Aszú, 5 Puttonyos, 1993** Domaine Disznókó, Hungary (**Odd**). Shh! Don't tell anyone but this wine made my Top 250 in 2002. I can't believe it but Oddbins found more stock! It is now ten full years old and looking better than ever, so wade in for this honey, praline, orange zest and old-fashioned toffee-flavoured wine.

£24.95 **Chateau Bastor-Lamontagne, 1999**, Sauternes, France (**Wai**). If you're into sweet wines, then stock up on a few bottles of this celestial Sauternes. A 'full' bottle will easily serve twelve thirsty guests and provide them with a cosmic, tropical, palate-titillating treat. This is not a sickly sweet pudding wine, but an elegant, smooth, classy wine, with oodles of finesse and breeding.

• •

£5.99 **La Gitana Manzanilla, Hidalgo, Sherry, NV**, Spain (**Laymont & Shaw, Lay & Wheeler, Maj, Sai, Tanners** and **Wai**). Gitana is a fresh, clean, tangy, apéritif-glugging Manzanilla at a fabulous price. If you fancy a 50cl bottle (£4.50), try **Lea & Sandeman, Lay & Wheeler** or **Tanners**.

£5.99 **Pellegrino Marsala Superiore, NV**, Sicily, Italy (**Saf, Sai, Tes** and **Wai**). This may be an unfashionable style of wine, but by God it's a great drink. This is superb value (it's a full bottle) and it keeps for ages, so you can sip away without a worry. Make sure you chill this Marsala down to fridge temperature since this will make the finish taste refreshing and not too cloying. The flavours you can expect are along the rum and raisin spectrum, coupled with toffee, plum, Demerara sugar and dark chocolate – yum.

£5.99 **Waitrose Solera Jerezana Dry Amontillado Sherry, NV**, Spain (**Wai**). Waitrose own-label sherries are among the best in the country. For the last three years no less than two have made my Top 250 each year. This is because they offer unbeatable value for money. My chosen pair possess grown-up flavours, with fresh, classy elegance and depth. Crucially, they are also only six pounds for a full bottle! This Dry Amontillado is raisiny, full, intense and dry, with nutty richness and a lush caramel aroma.

£5.99 **Waitrose Solera Jerezana Rich Cream Sherry, NV**, Spain (**Wai**). See above. This stunning Cream Sherry is the ideal glass with cakes and steamed puds. Stay ahead of the pack by checking out my Food and Wine chapter (page 9) for ideas on what to drink with it.

£8.49 **Warre's Warrior Special Reserve Port, NV**, Douro, Portugal (**Asd**, **Coo**, **Mor**, **Odd**, **Saf**, **Sai**, **Tes**, **Thr**, **Unw**, **Wai** and **WRa**). Three years in a row for the port to beat at the fighting end of the price spectrum. Warrior is such a brilliant name for this meaty, muscular wine. I suppose you feel a little like a warrior after a few sips, as it is heady, packed with plummy fruit and it warms you through from the tips of your toes to the edge of your eyebrows, leaving an inch or two on the top of your head to let off steam. This is the ideal port for sofa sipping, as it is not too expensive but has all of the richness and festive charm you could be searching for.

£8.99 50cl bottle, **Blandy's Alvada, 5-year-old Rich Madeira** (**Sai** and **Stevens Garnier**). This is a stunning, plump raisin, burnt toffee and almond-scented Madeira.

There is no better wine to go with your Christmas pud, so you must buy a bottle at Christmas! Everybody loves its heady, smooth, nutty flavour, so chill it a touch, uncork it on Christmas Eve, and it will still be fresh and zesty on New Year's Day (having said that you'll probably finish it sooner!).

£9.99 half bottle, **Brown Brothers Liqueur Muscat, NV**, Victoria, Australia (Boo, Rodney Densem, Victor Hugo, Maj, Noble Rot, Oxford Wines, Christopher Piper and Stevens Garnier). Everyone needs a bottle of Aussie liqueur Muscat in the drinks cabinet. It is the most heavenly brew – reminiscent of raisins, burnt toffee, nuts, mocha and molasses. This is what you should be sipping in front of the TV at Christmas.

£9.99 **Taylor's LBV Port, 1998**, Douro, Portugal (Maj, Mor, Odd, Saf, Sai, Thr, Wai and WRa). Every bottle of Taylor's LBV is a triumph, so when the 1998 is launched in September, I'll be there with a glass in hand for a taste. If you want to be certain of drinking a great wine then buy a bottle of the awesome 1997, which will still be all over the place until Christmas. But if, like me, you fancy a gamble, then head for the 1998. It should be a monster!

£9.99 **Warre's Otima, 10-year-old Tawny Port, NV**, Douro, Portugal (Asd, Coo, Odd, Saf, Sai, Tes and Wai). There is only one other bottle of port that looks as arty as this trailblazer (and it is in the Top 250). It is a banker as a Christmas pressie (after you've bought this book for everyone you know, of course). Sip this stunning tawny port chilled after dinner and watch your guests melt with smug satisfaction. They may even start daydreaming – don't interrupt them, they are enjoying themselves! If you want to serve this with food, try ginger cake, nuts or toffee puds. Mmm.

£10.69 half bottle, **Noé, Pedro Ximénez, Muy Viejo, Sherry, NV**, González Byass, Spain (Fortnum & Mason and Sainsbury's Fine Wine Shops). Only 2,000 bottles of this bizarre wine are produced annually. It is a 30-year-old, super-sweet sherry, made from the deliriously yummy grape variety Pedro Ximénex (otherwise known as PX). The resulting flavour is totally luxurious, with moments of raisin, espresso coffee, toffee, Brazil nuts and plums. Serve it chilled and this rich, heady concoction will hypnotise your taste buds. It is expensive, but you only need a tiny glass, as the flavour lasts forever and, once uncorked, the wine can survive for a month.

£12.99 **Dow's Crusted Port, 1998**, Douro, Portugal (Odd, Sai, Tes and Wai). Golly, watch out for this bruiser – it's a port for true aficionados. When you get it home, you need to stand it up for a few days to let the 'crust' or heavy sediment fall to the bottom of the bottle. Then decant it carefully. It will have a ton of sediment which will have given this wine more weight, colour, tannin, muscle and grip than usual, making it a real mouthful! Good luck, this is a serious bottle of wine.

£16.49 **Taylor's 10-year-old Tawny Port**, Douro, Portugal (**Asd**, **Boo**, **Maj**, **Saf**, **Sai** and **Selfridges**). This is the guv'nor – really juicy, rich and raisiny. It is not a bottle to give away, as it's not as pretty as Otima (see page 162). This is one to keep for yourself!

£16.99 5ocl bottle, **Henriques and Henriques 15-year-old Malmsey Madeira** (**Lea & Sandeman**, **Harrods** and **Wai**). Three words only – Christmas pressie list please! Sorry, that's four.

£19.99 **Fonseca Guimaraens, 1987**, Port, Douro, Portugal (**D. Byrne**, **Corney & Barrow**, **Fortnum & Mason**, **Sai** and **Wimbledon**). This old bottle is creamy and smooth and ever so gentlemanly. It is now sixteen years old and at its peak, so mellow out and snuggle down on the sofa for a long night.

£21.99 **Taylor's Quinta de Vargellas, 1988**, Port, Douro, Portugal (**Fortnum & Mason**, **Sai**, **Selfridges**, **Tes** and **Wai**). This majestic port is spicy, dense and dark, and packed with muscular, full-on, smoky, pruney juice. It is a brilliant bottle that is great value considering its age.

£22.00 **Graham's Malvedos, 1995**, Port, Douro, Portugal (**Odd** and **Sai**). This is about as serious as it gets – classy, minutes long, brooding, dreamy and totally satiating. It is incredible that, for the most amazing Single Quinta port you can buy, Champagne prices haven't really kicked in. This proves that port is one of the best value wines in the world.

GAZETTEER

GRAPE VARIETIES

Before I kick off with my hot list of favourite world wineries, I have compiled a short Albariño-Zinfandel of the most important white and red grape varieties. These tasting notes should give you an idea of some of the flavours in the wines mentioned.

WHITES

Albariño/Alvarinho (Al-ba-reen-yo/Al-va-reen-yo)

A particularly good example can have a peachy aroma like Viognier, and a flowery, spicy palate like Riesling. They always have a very dry, refreshing finish, often with a touch of spritz.

Aligoté (Alee-got-ay)

Aligoté produces dry, lean apéritif styles of wine designed for drinking within the first year of release.

Chardonnay (Shar-dun-ay)

Ranging in style from fairly colourless, neutral and characterless to wildly exotic, rich and golden – you can find honey, butter, freshly baked patisserie, hazelnuts, vanilla, butterscotch, orange blossom and fresh meadow flowers in top Chardonnays.

Chenin Blanc (Shun-nan Blon)

Chenin is an underrated grape that makes zippy, dry, apéritif wines, medium-dry, food-friendly styles and full-on, honey and succulent peach sweeties, dripping in unctuous, mouth-filling richness.

Gewürztraminer (Guh-vurz-tram-inner)

'Gewürz' has the most distinctive aroma of any grape variety. Pungent lychee, spice and rose petal cavort on the nose, and are often accompanied by oiliness on the palate and a long, ripe finish. This grape often has the unusual knack of smelling sweet, and then surprising you by tasting much drier than you'd imagine.

Manseng (Man-seng)

Both Gros and Petit Manseng wines have a complex nose of quince, peach and lemon curd and a citrusy, floral palate accompanied by a firm, crisp finish. Although pretty rare, they are also used to make celestial sweet wines.

Marsanne (Marce-ann)

Plump, rich, vaguely floral and peachy and always oily, Marsanne makes rather hefty foody wines and likes to be blended with the more elegant grape Roussanne.

Muscat (Mus-cat)

Muscat wines vary from the lightest, fizziest soda-siphon of grape juice, to the deepest, darkest, headiest liqueur, like a rugby player's liniment. Muscat is the only grape variety that actually smells and tastes 'grapey'.

Pinot Blanc/Pinot Bianco (Pee-no Blon/Pee-no Be-ancko)

Almost all Pinot Blanc made worldwide is unoaked, dry and relatively inexpensive, tasting vaguely appley, creamy and nutty. Most PB is dull, but occasionally a delicious one comes along (see Top 250).

Riesling (Rees-ling)

One of the truly great white varieties, Riesling produces an array of wine styles, from bone-dry apéritifs, through structured, foody beauties, via long-lived, complex and off-dry stunners and ending up at heart-achingly beautiful sweeties. Rhubarb, petrol, honey, honeysuckle and spice are there in varying degrees throughout this cornucopia of guises.

Roussanne (Roo-sann)

Generally lean, leggy and hauntingly aromatic, with hints of apricot and honey. When on top form, Roussanne takes well to oak barrels and can provide a welcome change of direction for Chardonnay drinkers.

Sauvignon Blanc (So-veen-yon Blon)

'Sauv' Blanc is an up-front, brazen, aromatic, happy-go-lucky style, with an asparagus and elderflower scent and refreshing, zesty, dry, citrusy fruit. Sauvignon is the definitive apéritif grape variety.

Sémillon (Sem-ee-yon)

The dominant aromas in dry Sémillon are honey and lime juice, and sometimes creamy vanilla and toasty oak elements creep in, depending on style. But Sémillon also makes incredible, unctuous sweet wines, tasting of honey, honey and more honey.

Tokay-Pinot Gris/Pinot Gris/Pinot Grigio (Tock-eye Pee-no Gree/Pee-no Gree/Pee-no Gridge-eeo)

The flavour of Tokay-Pinot Gris is somewhere between Pinot Blanc and Gewürztraminer. The distinctive nose of this grape is one of spice, fruit and honey. It does not have the rose-petal-perfumed element of Gewürz, and tends to be drier, like Pinot Blanc. Italy's Pinot Grigio is more akin to Aligoté, as it usually makes a light, dry, apéritif style of wine.

Viognier (Vee-yon-yay)

In the best examples, Viognier offers a mind-blowing perfume of peach kernels, wild honey and apricot blossom, followed by an ample, curvaceous body with plenty of charm and a lingering, dry aftertaste.

REDS
Cabernet Franc (Cab-er-nay Fronk)

Often used in a blend with Cabernet Sauvignon, Cabernet Franc lends a certain aromatic quality to a red wine. It has firm acidity, oodles of black fruit flavours and usually sports violets and green, leafy notes on the nose.

Cabernet Sauvignon (Cab-er-nay So-veen-yon)

Age-worthy Cabernet Sauvignon forms the backbone of many sturdy, lusty red wines. Its hallmarks are a deep colour, blackcurrant flavour, with occasional cigar-box or cedarwood notes and, when on top form, has a smooth, velvety, dark-chocolate texture and flavour.

Gamay (Ga-may)

Gamay is a jolly fellow, that makes underrated, early drinking wines ranging in taste from frivolous, summery, strawberry juice concoctions to wintry, black cherry and pepper styles.

Grenache/Garnacha (Gre-nash/Gar-natch-ah)

Grenache is usually blended, often with Syrah (Shiraz) among others. It is a meaty, earthy, red- and black-fruit-drenched variety, often with high-ish alcohol and a garnet hue. It sometimes picks up a wild herbal scent not dissimilar to aromatic pipe smoke.

Malbec (Mal-beck)

This brutish grape is inky black in colour and loaded with macerated black fruit flavours and earthy spice, often enhanced by a dollop of well-seasoned oak. Malbec is one of the biggest, brawniest red varieties on the block.

Merlot (Mer-low)

Merlot is a juicy grape, with supple, smooth, silky, blackberry, plum, red wine gum and fruitcake flavours. It happily flies solo, but loves the company of Cabernet Sauvignon in a blend. As Merlot is usually oak aged the fruit flavours are often accompanied by a touch of sweet wood-smoke barrel nuances.

Mourvèdre/Monastrell/Mataro (More-veh-dr/Mon-ah-strell/Mat-are-oh)

This rich, plum and damson-flavoured variety is often made into powerful, earthy, long-lived wines. It is not the most charming variety in its youth, but ages gracefully, picking up more complex aromas and flavours along the way.

Nebbiolo (Neb-ee-olo)

A tough grape that often needs five years in the bottle to soften to drinkability. A great Nebbiolo can conjure up intense plummy flavours with leathery, spicy, gamey overtones and a firm, dry finish.

Pinotage (Pee-no-tahge)

Pinotage is an earthy, spicy, deeply coloured grape with tobacco and plums on the nose, crushed blackberry fruit on the palate and a hearty, full, savoury finish.

Pinot Noir (Pee-no Nw-ar)

When on form, the Pinot Noir nose is often reminiscent of wild strawberries, violets and redcurrants, with a black cherry flavour on the palate. There is usually a degree of oakiness apparent, depending on the style. As these wines age, they can take on a slightly farmyardy character as the colour fades from dark to pale brick red.

Sangiovese (San-geeo-vay-zee)

This grape has red and black fruit flavours (mulberry, cherry, plum, blackcurrant and cranberry) on the nose with a whiff of fresh-cut herbs and leather for good measure. There is usually an oaky element tucked into the wine, and Sangiovese always has an acidic kick on the finish.

Syrah/Shiraz (Sirrah/Shirraz)

Syrah invokes explosive blackberry and ground pepper aromas with vanilla, smoke and charred oak nuances. In the New World, big, inky-black Shiraz (the Syrah synonym) has high alcohol and a mouth-filling prune, chocolate, raisin and spice palate.

Tempranillo (Temp-ra-nee-yo)

Ranging in flavour from vanilla and strawberry, early drinking styles, to dark, brooding, black cherry reds, Tempranillo is Spain's most noble red grape, and the main variety in Rioja and countless other noble Spanish wines.

Zinfandel (Zin-fan-dell)

'Zin' tastes like a flavour collision between turbo-charged blackberries and plums, a vanilla pod convention and a fully stocked spice warehouse. These wines generally have luxurious, mouth-filling texture and pretty high alcohol.

WINE REGIONS OF THE WORLD

In this crucial chapter I have taken my lifetime's tasting notes and whittled them down to just the very best Domaines, Châteaux, Wineries, Tenutas, Bodegas and Estates. Each year this list is completely overhauled, and every entry is made to fight for its place in this elite list of the world's best wine producers.

If a favourite winery of yours is missing, it is either because I haven't yet tasted their wines or, sadly, they have not quite made the cut. Please do drop me a line to the address at the end of the book (see page 233) if you have a hot tip and I will track the wines down in time for next year's edition. Every year I start off with a huge list of estates and then ruthlessly prune it down to a more manageable size of epic wineries. This year is no exception – it is about half its original size. I have avoided wineries that churn out so-so, average wines and also any who have made one-hit-wonder wines, in favour of focusing on the top quality, talent-soaked, hard-working wineries whose wines have set my palate alight with wonder and enthusiasm. These are the producers who you can rely on day in day out when you are out shopping for home drinking, eating out in a restaurant, travelling the globe on business or holiday, or when buying a gift for a wine-smart friend. Once in a while you'll spot a producer or winery whose name is in **bold**. I have specially selected these estates as they are truly outstanding and their entire portfolio of wines is top-notch. If a producer is both in **bold** and has a **£**, it means that its wines are on the expensive side (£25 plus). These plutonium-plated names are the money-no-object, lottery-win wines, for those of you with a no-upper-limit mentality. This doesn't mean that every wine they make is out of reach, far from it. Their flagship wine may be dizzily dear, but their other labels may still be brilliant and significantly cheaper, so do take note of these wineries. Those **bold** estates without a **£** make eminently more affordable wines (somewhere between £5 to £25), so keep an eye out for them – this is where I do virtually all of my everyday drinking.

AUSTRALIA

Australia is continuing to make wine waves globally. The UK is Australia's most important market and we are lucky enough to get the widest range of Aussie wines in the world to savour. Make the most of it, as Australia is hitting the quality and value nail squarely on the head. France has recently been wounded below the water line with reports that their position at the top of the world wine ladder is not only under threat, but has fallen, and they have to take a step down in favour of this New World usurper. This is terrific news, as all of the hard work in the vineyards and know-how in the winery is finally paying off for Australia. This news will surely make the Old World pull its collective socks up, and we can only expect to see better, more professional European wines in the future.

We have fallen in love with Australian wine in a very short period of time. The once one-dimensional, cheap, varietal wines, with catchy names and jazzy labels have given way to a new school of thought. Now Australia's viticultural diversity is celebrated with strong regional wines with distinct characteristics and carefully chosen grape varieties. It is about time we realised that Australia is not one huge homogenous vineyard, but an infinite number of sites and microclimates, with dramatic variations in soil, temperature, altitude and rainfall – Tasmanian sparklers, Margaret River Cabernets, Clare Valley Riesling and McLaren Vale Shiraz have all firmly established their credentials Down Under. We are catching up fast and will soon experience tailor-made wines from all corners of Australia.

These days I unscrew (and uncork) a huge number of Aussie bottles chez Jukesy. I am enormously excited about wines from all over the globe, but for sheer value for money and guaranteed crowd-pleasing, the Aussies rule. It is no surprise that Australia has a huge slice of my Top 250. I have a varied wine diet, but I feel that giving up Aussie wine now would be the gastronomic equivalent of forgoing freshly baked bread or farmhouse cheeses, so crucial is my dependency on this country's wines.

As I wrote last year – no other New World country is even close to offering the cornucopia of terrific wines hailing from the sunny shores of Oz. This statement is unlikely to change for a decade.

WESTERN AUSTRALIA
The top producers are – **Alkoomi**, Amberley, Ashbrook Estate, **Brookland Valley**, **Cape Mentelle**, **Cullen**, **Devil's Lair**, Evans & Tate, **Frankland Estate**, **Houghton**, Howard Park, **Juniper Estate**, **Leeuwin Estate**, Millbrook, **Moss Wood**, **Picardy**, Pierro, Plantagenet, **Suckfizzle Augusta (Stella Bella)**, **Vasse Felix**, Voyager, West Cape Howe, Wignalls and Xanadu.

SOUTH AUSTRALIA

The top producers in each region are:

Clare Valley – **Tim Adams**, Jim Barry, Crabtree, **Grosset**, Knappstein, **Leasingham**, Mitchell, **Mount Horrocks**, Neagles Rock, Pikes, Sevenhill, Wakefield (Taylors) and **Wendouree £**.

Barossa Valley – Burge Family Winemakers, Grant Burge, Charles Cimicky, Craneford, Elderton, **Glaetzer**, **Greenock Creek**, **Haan**, **Heritage**, **Peter Lehmann**, **Charlie Melton**, **Penfolds**, Rockford, **St Hallett**, Seppelt, **Torbreck £**, Turkey Flat, **Two Hands**, **Veritas**, The Willows and **Yalumba**.

Adelaide Hills – **Ashton Hills**, **Barratt**, Chain of Ponds, Hillstowe, **Knappstein Lenswood**, **The Lane**, **Nepenthe**, **Petaluma**, Shaw & Smith, **Starve Dog Lane** and **Geoff Weaver**.

Eden Valley – **Henschke**, **Irvine**, **Mesh** and Pewsey Vale.

Coonawarra – Balnaves, **Bowen**, **Hollick**, **Katnook**, Lindemans, Majella, **Parker**, **Penley** and Wynns.

McLaren Vale – d'Arenberg, Chalk Hill, **Chapel Hill**, Clarendon Hills, Coriole, Fox Creek, Richard Hamilton, **Hardys**, Kangarilla Road, **Kay Brothers Amery**, Maglieri, Geoff Merrill, **Mitolo**, Noon, Pertaringa, Pirramimma, Rosemount (McLaren Vale), Tatachilla, **Wirra Wirra** and Woodstock.

Adelaide Plains – **Primo Estate**.

NEW SOUTH WALES

The top producers are – Allandale, Arrowfield, De Bortoli (Riverina), **Brokenwood**, **Clonakilla**, **Simon Gilbert**, **Lake's Folly**, Lindemans, **Logan Wines**, Meerea Park, Mount Pleasant, Rosemount (Hunter Valley), Rothbury Estate, **Tower Estate**, **Keith Tulloch** and Tyrrell's.

VICTORIA
The top producers are – Baileys of Glenrowan, Bannockburn, Best's, Bleasdale, De Bortoli (Yarra Valley), Brown Brothers, **Campbells, Chambers Rosewood,** Coldstream Hills, **Craiglee, Crawford River, Dalwhinnie, Diamond Valley Vineyards, Domaine Chandon (Green Point), Gembrook Hill, Giaconda £,** Jasper Hill, Métier Wines, **Morris,** Mount Langi Ghiran, **Mount Mary,** Phillip Island Vineyard, Redbank, **Scotchmans Hill,** Seppelt Great Western, Stonier, **Tallarook,** Taltarni, T'Gallant, David Traeger, Virgin Hills, Wild Duck Creek, Yarra Burn, **Yarra Yering** and **Yeringberg.**

TASMANIA
The top producers are – Clover Hill, Craigow, Domaine A (Stoney Vineyard), Elsewhere, Freycinet, Grey Sands, **Jansz, Stefano Lubiana,** No Regrets, **Pipers Brook (Ninth Island),** Providence, Spring Vale, Tamar Ridge and Touchwood.

AUSTRIA
I've worked hard on Austria this year and tasted a lot of impressive wines. On the whole they are still expensive but, if you are into top Chardonnay, Riesling or Grüner Veltliner, find some of these. We do not get a very big selection of producers in the UK, but here is an essential list of wineries making stylish dry whites, interesting, if quirky reds and stunning sweeties – Paul Achs, **Bründlmayer, Feiler-Artinger, Freie Weingärtner Wachau,** Graf Hardegg, G & H Heinrich, Hiedler, **Franz Hirtzberger,** Höpler, Jurtschitsch, **Emmerich Knoll, Alois Kracher,** Helmut Lang, Sepp Moser, Willi Opitz, **F.X. Pichler,** Josef Pöckl, Polz, **Prager,** Schloss Gobelsburg, **Manfred Tement,** Dr Wolfgang Unger, Velich and Wieninger.

CANADA

It is taking an eternity for the Canadians to get their wines over to the UK, but whenever they do they are guaranteed a warm welcome, especially for their stunning Icewines. **The best estates are – Burrowing Owl**, **Cave Springs**, **Château des Charmes**, Henry of Pelham, **Inniskillin**, Daniel Lenko, **Mission Hill**, Paradise Ranch, Quails' Gate, Southbrook Farms, Sumac Ridge and Tinhorn Creek.

CHILE AND ARGENTINA

Chile and Argentina kindly provide us with worthy, meaty reds and clean, vibrant whites at around the seven-pound price point. Above this level most wines seem to get a nosebleed. There are one or two exceptions, but just whacking a wine into even more new oak for longer is not the answer to making a super-cuvée. Thankfully some properties continue to impress, but there needs to be an awful lot more team-playing to start to challenge the street cred and breadth of excellence of Australia. Choose inexpensive South American wines carefully, as most Chardonnays continue to be sloppy, Sauvignon Blancs lack fruit and reds are usually overly earthy and bitter.

The best Chilean estates are – Alvaro Espinoza, **Casa Lapostolle**, **Concha y Toro**, Cousiño Macul, Errázuriz, Montes, **MontGras**, Viña San Pedro, **Miguel Torres**, Valdivieso and **Veramonte**.

The best Argentinian estates are – Argento, **Catena Zapata**, Familia Zuccardi (La Agricola), **Finca El Retiro**, **Norton**, **Santa Julia**, Terrazas, Valentin Bianchi and Weinert.

FRANCE
BORDEAUX

Unfortunately, most decent Bordeaux reds (clarets) fall into the super-scary price band. They also generally have to be at least ten years old to really start drinking. When compiling this list I was very hard on the region and have culled a large, sprawling list down to a core of superb châteaux. Bordeaux is the home of the majestic red grapes Cabernet Sauvignon, Merlot and Cabernet Franc. The percentages of each grape variety in the final blend vary from château to château, but you can be sure that whatever the outcome, the brew will have spent eighteen months or so maturing in spanky oak barrels. This recipe is the model for red wines around the globe. Tread carefully and then go for it, when you are feeling flush, patient or both.

RED WINES
THE LEFT BANK

Graves Bahans-Haut-Brion £, Les Carmes-Haut-Brion, Chantegrive, Domaine de Chevalier, de Fieuzal, Haut-Bailly, **Haut-Brion £**, La Louvière, **La Mission-Haut-Brion £**, **Pape-Clément** and **Smith-Haut-Lafitte**.

Haut-Médoc and (Bas) Médoc Arnauld, de Lamarque, Malescasse, Patache d'Aux, Potensac, Rollan de By, **Sociando-Mallet**, Tour du Haut-Moulin and Villegeorge.

Margaux d'Angludet, Cantemerle, Durfort-Vivens, Ferrière, d'Issan, La Lagune, **Margaux £**, **Palmer £** and Rausan-Ségla.

Moulis and Listrac Chasse-Spleen, Clarke, Fourcas Loubaney and **Poujeaux**.

Pauillac Batailley, Les Forts de Latour, Grand-Puy-Lacoste, **Haut-Bages-Libéral**, Haut-Batailley, **Lafite-Rothschild £**, **Latour £**, Lynch-Bages, **Mouton-Rothschild £**, **Pichon-Longueville Baron £**, **Pichon-Longueville-Comtesse de Lalande £** and Pontet-Canet.

St-Estèphe Beau-Site, Le Boscq, Calon-Ségur, **Cos d'Estournel £**,

Haut-Marbuzet, La Haye, Lafon-Rochet, **Montrose £**, Les-Ormes-de-Pez and de Pez.
St-Julien Clos du Marquis, **Ducru-Beaucaillou £,** Gruaud-Larose, Lagrange, **Léoville-Barton £**, **Léoville-Las-Cases £**, **Léoville-Poyferré £**, St-Pierre and Talbot.

THE RIGHT BANK
Canon-Fronsac and Fronsac Canon-Moueix, Fontenil, du Gaby, Hervé-Laroque, Mazeris, Moulin-Haut-Laroque and La Vieille-Cure.
Côtes de Bourg and Blaye Haut-Sociando, **Roc des Cambes** and Tayac.
Lalande-de-Pomerol Bel-Air, Belles-Graves, La Fleur de Boüard and Laborde.
Pomerol Beauregard, Bon Pasteur, Certan-Giraud, Certan-de-May, **Clinet £**, Clos de Litanies, Clos du Clocher, Clos René, **La Conseillante £**, La Croix-St Georges, Domaine de l'Eglise, **l'Eglise-Clinet £**, l'Enclos, **l'Evangile £**, La Fleur de Gay, La Fleur-Pétrus, Le Gay, Gazin, **Lafleur £**, Latour à Pomerol, **Pétrus £**, Le Pin, **Trotanoy £** and **Vieux-Château-Certan £**.
St-Emilion **Angélus £**, L'Arrosée, **Ausone £**, Beau-Séjour Bécot, **Canon-La-Gaffelière £**, Le Castelot, **Cheval Blanc £**, Clos Fourtet, Dassault, La Dominique, Figeac, Larmande, Monbousquet, **Tertre-Rôteboeuf £**, La Tour-du-Pin-Figeac, **Troplong-Mondot £** and Valandraud.

DRY WHITE WINES
Graves Carbonnieux, **Domaine de Chevalier £**, de Fieuzal, **Haut-Brion £**, **Laville-Haut-Brion £**, Pavillon Blanc de Château Margaux, **Smith-Haut-Lafitte** and La Tour Martillac.

SWEET WHITE WINES

Sauternes and Barsac d'Arche, Bastor-Lamontagne, Broustet, **Climens £**, **Coutet £**, Doisy-Daëne, Doisy-Dubroca, Doisy-Védrines, de Fargues, Filhot, Gilette, Guiraud, Les Justices, **Lafaurie-Peyraguey £**, Liot, de Malle, Nairac, Rabaud-Promis, **Raymond-Lafon £**, Rayne-Vigneau, **Rieussec £**, **Suduiraut £**, **La Tour Blanche £** and **d'Yquem £**.

BURGUNDY

I visit Burgundy more than any other wine region in the world because I love the wines, the food and the people. Burgundy also happens to be my favourite wine region in the world. But unless you arm yourself with this list of top Domaines, you could lose your way, and be ripped off in the process, as Burgundy is a veritable minefield of tiny vineyards and artisan producers. And, despite the views, not everything made in these stunning vineyards is up to scratch. Burgundy is the home of the world-famous white grape Chardonnay and its eclectic, elegant and occasionally flamboyant red companion, Pinot Noir. The greatest Chardonnays and Pinot Noirs in the world are produced here – categorically. Everyone else tries to reach these heights of perfection, and some come close, but these vineyards are very special and, in my opinion, Burgundy will always be top of the pile. The zippy white grape Aligoté, and much-derided red variety Gamay (Beaujolais), ably support the two aforementioned super-grapes. So you can eat and drink without busting the bank if you stick to these last two varieties – only for lunch, though, then it's back to Pinot and Chardonnay for dinner! What follows is worth its weight in Grand Cru Pinot – the ultimate list of Domaines, which will, I hope, unlock the code to the most enigmatic region of all.

CHABLIS
Chablis (white) **Billaud-Simon**, A & F Boudin, Daniel Dampt, **René & Vincent Dauvissat**, **Jean-Paul Droin**, Jean Durup, William Fèvre, des Genèves, Louis Michel, **Raveneau £** and Laurent Tribut. St-Bris-le-Vineux and **Chitry** (white) Jean-Hugues Goisot.

CÔTE DE NUITS
Marsannay-la-Côte and Fixin (mainly red) Charles Audoin, René Bouvier, Bruno Clair and Fougeray de Beauclair.
Gevrey-Chambertin (red) **Claude Dugat**, Bernard Dugat-Py, **Géantet-Pansiot**, **Denis Mortet**, **Joseph Roty**, **Armand Rousseau** and **Serafin**.
Morey-St-Denis (red) des Beaumont, **Dujac**, **des Lambrays**, Hubert Lignier, Virgile Lignier and **Ponsot**.
Chambolle-Musigny (red) **Ghislaine Barthod**, Pierre Bertheau, **Christian Clerget,** Jacques-Frédéric Mugnier, **G. Roumier** and **Comte de Vogüé**.
Vosne-Romanée and Flagey-Echézeaux (red) **Robert Arnoux**, Sylvain Cathiard, René Engel, **Jean Grivot**, **Anne Gros**, Lamarche, **Leroy £**, **Méo-Camuzet**, Mongeard-Mugneret, **de la Romanée-Conti £** and **Emanuel Rouget**.
Nuits-St-Georges (red) Bertrand Ambroise, Jean Chauvenet, **Robert Chevillon**, Daniel Chopin-Groffier, Jean-Jacques Confuron, Faiveley, **Dominique Laurent**, Lécheneaut, Alain Michelot, **Nicolas Potel** and Daniel Rion.

CÔTE DE BEAUNE
Ladoix (mainly red) Edmond Cornu.
Aloxe-Corton and **Ladoix-Serrigny** (mainly red) Michel Voarick.
Pernand-Vergelesses (red and white) **Bonneau du Martray**

(Corton-Charlemagne) **£**, Dubreuil-Fontaine and Maurice Rollin.

Savigny-lès-Beaune (red and white) Chandon de Briailles, Maurice Ecard and **Jean-Marc Pavelot**.

Chorey-lès-Beaune (red) Germain and **Tollot-Beaut**.

Beaune (mainly red) Bouchard Père et Fils, Maison Champy, Joseph Drouhin and **Louis Jadot**.

Pommard (red) Comte Armand, **Jean-Marc Boillot** and **de Courcel**.

Volnay (red) **Marquis d'Angerville**, Coste Caumartin, **Michel Lafarge**, **Hubert de Montille** and **Roblet-Monnot**.

Monthelie (red and white) Denis Boussey.

Auxey-Duresses (red and white) Jean-Pierre Diconne and Claude Maréchal.

St-Romain (mainly white) d'Auvenay and Christophe Buisson.

Meursault (white) **Vincent Bouzereau**, **Jean-François Coche-Dury £**, Vincent Dancer, Jean-Philippe Fichet, Jean-Michel Gaunoux, **Patrick Javillier**, **des Comtes Lafon £**, Marc Rougeot, **Roulot** and Michel Tessier.

Puligny-Montrachet (white) **Louis Carillon**, Chartron & Trébuchet, **Domaine Leflaive £**, Olivier Leflaive, Paul Pernot and **Etienne Sauzet £**.

Chassagne-Montrachet (white) Guy Amiot, Blain-Gagnard, Michel Colin-Deléger, Duperrier-Adam, Fontaine-Gagnard, **Jean-Noël Gagnard**, Gagnard-Delagrange, **Bernard Morey**, **Marc Morey**, **Michel Niellon** and **Ramonet £**.

St-Aubin (red and white) Marc Colin, Henri Prudhon and Gérard Thomas.

Santenay (red and white) Vincent Girardin.

CÔTE CHALONNAISE

Rully (red and white) Vincent Dureuil-Janthial, de la Folie and Eric de Suremain.

Montagny (white) Stéphane Aladame.

Mercurey (red and white) **Michel & Laurent Juillot**, **Bruno Lorenzon**, J. & F. Raquillet and Antonin Rodet.

Givry (red and white) Joblot and François Lumpp.

MÂCONNAIS

Mâcon, Pouilly-Fuissé, St-Véran and Viré-Clessé (mainly white) Daniel Barraud, **Château de Beauregard**, **André Bonhomme**, **des Deux Roches**, Michel Forest, **Château Fuissé (Jean-Jacques Vincent)**, Goyard, **Guillemot-Michel**, Robert-Denogent, Talmard, **Jean Thévenet** and Verget (Guffens-Heynen).

BEAUJOLAIS

Producing mainly red, the most highly regarded sub-regions are the ten Cru Villages: Brouilly, Chénas, Chiroubles, Côte de Brouilly, Fleurie, Juliénas, Morgon, Moulin-à-Vent, Régnié and St-Amour. **The top producers are** – Aucoeur, Hélène & Denis Barbelet, **F & J Calot**, Champagnon, Michel Chignard, André Cologne, **Coudert**, Georges Duboeuf (domaine-bottled wines only), **J.-L. Dutraive**, J.-F. Echallier (des Pins), **Henry Fessy**, Jean Foillard, Maurice Gaget, **Pascal Granger**, **Louis Jadot (Château des Jacques)**, **Paul Janin**, Jacky Janodet, **Marcel Lapierre**, Bernard Mélinand, **Alain Passot**, **Jean-Charles Pivot** and Vissoux.

CHAMPAGNE

I try not to put too many non-vintage Champagnes in my Top 250 as they tend to vary so much in flavour with bottle age and storage conditions. So use this list as a guide to the consistently best suppliers of NV and Vintage Champagne. This year I have also included a few brilliant, smaller houses for you to track down when you are on holiday in France. They are all particularly good value.

FAMOUS NAMES

Billecart-Salmon *NV* Brut Réserve, Brut Rosé, Blanc de Blancs and Demi-Sec. *Vintage* Le Clos Saint-Hilaire, Cuvée Nicolas-François Billecart, Elisabeth Salmon Rosé, Grande Cuvée and Blanc de Blancs.
Bollinger *NV* Special Cuvée. *Vintage* Grande Année, RD and Vieilles Vignes Françaises Blanc de Noirs.
Deutz *Vintage* Blanc de Blancs and Cuvée William Deutz.
Gosset *NV* Brut Excellence and Grande Réserve Brut. *Vintage* Grande Millésime Brut.
Alfred Gratien *Vintage* Brut
Charles Heidsieck *Vintage* Brut Millésime.
Jacquesson *Vintage* Blanc de Blancs, Dégorgement Tardive and Signature.
Krug £ *NV* Grande Cuvée. *Vintage* Vintage and Clos du Mesnil.
Laurent-Perrier *NV* Cuvée Rosé Brut, Grand Siècle 'La Cuvée' and Ultra Brut.
Moët & Chandon *Vintage* Brut Impérial and Cuvée Dom Pérignon Brut.
Pol Roger *NV* Brut 'White Foil'. *Vintage* Brut Vintage, Brut Chardonnay, Brut Rosé and Cuvée Sir Winston Churchill.
Louis Roederer *NV* Brut Premier. *Vintage* Blanc de Blancs, Brut Millésime, Cristal and Cristal Rosé.
Ruinart *Vintage* 'R' de Ruinart Brut and Dom Ruinart Blanc de Blancs.
Salon £ *Vintage* Blanc de Blancs.

Taittinger *NV* Brut Réserve. *Vintage* Comtes de Champagne Blanc de Blancs.
Alain Thiénot *Vintage* Brut and Grande Cuvée.
Veuve Clicquot *NV* Brut 'Yellow Label' and Demi-Sec. *Vintage* Vintage Réserve, La Grande Dame Brut and La Grande Dame Rosé.

SMALLER HOUSES
Albert Beerens, Château de Boursault, Edouard Brun, Claude Carré, Paul Déthune, Egly-Ouriet, Gatinois, Pierre Gimonnet, J-M Gobillard, D. Henriet-Bazin, André Jacquart, Larmandier-Bernier, Leclerc Briant, Legras, A. Margaine, Pierre Moncuit, Pertois-Moriset, Bertrand Robert, Jacques Selosse, Fernand Thill, G. Tribaut and **Vilmart.**

ALSACE
We still have yet to really discover Alsace wines in the UK. But with the awesome 2001 vintage on the shelves, we should all try to support this underrated wine region. These under-priced, over-performing wines provide us with some of the best foody, apéritif, decadently sweet and casual-drinking wines in the world. You will have to look to the smaller, independent wine merchants for most of these names. Grape varieties to seek out are Gewürztraminer, Riesling, Tokay-Pinot Gris, Muscat, Pinot Blanc and Sylvaner. It is still worth avoiding the reds and fizzies!
The best producers are – Paul Blanck, Bott-Geyl, Albert Boxler, Ernest Brun, **Marcel Deiss**, Hugel, **Marc Kreydenweiss**, Albert Mann, Mittnacht-Klack, **Ostertag**, Rolly Gassmann, Schlumberger, **Schoffit**, André Thomas, **Trimbach**, **Weinbach** and **Zind-Humbrecht**.

THE LOIRE VALLEY

My list of wines follows the Loire river inland from the Atlantic, picking out the greatest estates in this elongated, inexpensive river region. Sauvignon Blanc and Chenin Blanc are the main white grapes grown here. Sauvignons are nearly always dry, whereas the Chenins can be fizzy, dry, medium-sweet or full-on sweeties. The majority of serious reds are made from Cabernet Franc, with Gamay and Pinot Noir stepping in for lighter styles.

Muscadet (white) Château de Chasseloir, **Chéreau**, de la Mortaine and **de la Quilla**.

Savennières (white) **des Baumard**, **Clos de la Coulée de Serrant** and **La Roche-aux-Moines**.

Coteaux du Layon, Coteaux de l'Aubance, Bonnezeaux and **Quarts de Chaume** (white sweeties) **des Baumard**, Château de Fesles, **Château Pierre-Bise**, Vincent Lecointre, Didier Richou and de la Roulierie.

Saumur (sparkling) Bouvet-Ladubay.

Saumur and **Saumur Champigny** (red and white) **du Hureau**, **Filliatreau**, Langlois-Château and **Nerleux**.

Chinon (mainly red) **Bernard Baudry**, Couly-Dutheil, **Desbourdes** and **Charles Joguet**.

St-Nicolas de Bourgueil (red) Max & Lydie Cognard-Taluau and Jean-Paul Mabileau.

Bourgueil (red) **Pierre-Jacques Druet, Lamé-Delille-Boucard, de la Lande (Delaunay)** and Joël Taluau.

Vouvray (white) Bourillon-Dorléans, Philippe Foreau and **Gaston Huet**.

Sauvignon de Touraine (white) **Alain Marcadet**.

Gamay de Touraine (red) Henry Marionnet.

Jasnières (white) Joël Gigou and Jean-Baptiste Pinon.
Cheverny (white) Salvard.
Sancerre (white, rosé and red) **Sylvain Bailly**, Bailly-Reverdy, Philippe de Benoist, **Henri Bourgeois**, **Cotat**, Daulny, **Vincent Delaporte**, André Dézat, Alain Gueneau, Serge Laloue, Christian Lauverjat, **Alphonse Mellot**, Henri Natter, **Pascal & Nicolas Reverdy**, Vacheron and **André Vatan**.
Pouilly-Fumé (white) Jean-Claude Chatelain, **Didier Dagueneau**, Serge Dagueneau, André Dézat (Domaine Thibault), Château du Nozet (de Ladoucette), **Michel Redde**, Hervé Seguin, Tabordet and **Château de Tracy**.
Menetou-Salon (mainly white) de Chatenoy, **Henry Pellé** and **Jean Teiller**.
Quincy (white) **Jacques Rouzé**.

THE RHÔNE VALLEY

The Rhône is a powerhouse of great French wines. It makes some of the most spectacular reds and whites on the planet, while at the same time giving us some amazing bargains. It is here that Syrah, Grenache and Mourvèdre rule the reds. And Viognier commands the whites in the north, while Roussanne and Marsanne are in charge in the south. Get to know this region as well as you can, because there is so much quality and value to be found. This is the home of Syrah, so nail this taste and then look at what the New World has done with it, with their Shiraz (Syrah on holiday) incarnations. For me Syrah is one of the top three red grapes in the world (along with Pinot Noir and Cabernet). There is no doubt the Rhône provides us with wines that embody power, majesty and poise.

THE NORTHERN RHÔNE
FROM NORTH TO SOUTH

Côte Rôtie (red) Guy Bernard, Bernard Burgaud, Chapoutier, **Clusel-Roch £**, **Yves Cuilleron**, **Pierre Gaillard**, **Yves Gangloff £**, Marius Gentaz-Dervieux, Jean-Michel Gerin, **E. Guigal (Château d'Ampuis) £**, **Jamet** and René Rostaing.

Condrieu (white) Louis Cheze, **Yves Cuilleron £**, Christian Facchin, Robert Niero, **André Perret**, **Georges Vernay** and **François Villard £**.

St-Joseph (red and white) **Jean-Louis Chave**, Delas, Bernard Faurie, **Pierre Gonon** and Jean-Louis Grippat.

Hermitage (red and white) **Chapoutier £**, **Jean-Louis Chave £**, **Delas**, **Michel Ferraton**, Grippat, **Paul Jaboulet Aîné £**, Sorrel and **Tardieu-Laurent £**.

Crozes-Hermitage (mainly red) **Albert Belle**, du Colombier, Olivier Dumaine, **Alain Graillot**, Domaine Pochon and **Gilles Robin**.

Cornas (red) **Thierry Allemand**, **Auguste Clape**, Jean Lionnet, Robert Michel, **du Tunnel (Stéphane Robert)**, Noël Verset and **Alain Voge**.

THE SOUTHERN RHÔNE

Côtes-du-Rhône (and -Villages) (red) **Brusset**, **Clos Petite Bellane**, **Coudoulet de Beaucastel**, **Domaine Gramenon**, E. Guigal, Piaugier, Rayas (Fonsalette), Marcel Richaud, **Tardieu-Laurent** and Château du Trignon.

Lirac, Rasteau, Tavel and Vacqueyras (red) Clos des Cazaux, des Espiers, **de la Mordorée**, La Soumade, **Château des Tours** and **du Trapadis**.

Gigondas (red) Font-Sane, R. & J.-P. Meffre (Saint-Gayan), **Saint-Cosme**, **Santa-Duc** and Château du Trignon.

Châteauneuf-du-Pape (red and white) **de Beaucastel**, Les Cailloux, Chapoutier, de la Charbonnière, **Charvin, Clos du Caillou, Clos des Papes**, de Ferrand, Fortia, **de la Janasse**, de Marcoux, **de la Mordorée, du Pegaü, Rayas**, Versino and Le Vieux Donjon. **Muscat de Beaumes-de-Venise** (sweet white) Chapoutier, **Domaine de Durban** and Paul Jaboulet Ainé.

FRENCH COUNTRY

This may be a difficult section to read, as it is so bitty and broken up, but take it slowly and you'll find some amazing, handcrafted wines that don't cost a bomb and deliver amazing amounts of flavour impact. French Country means 'the rest of France's southerly wine regions'. Here I have picked out my favourite dry white, sweet white, red and fortified estates.

Miscellaneous estates of excellence (and where to find them): de l'Aigle – Limoux; **Mas Amiel** – Maury; **Domaine de Baruel** – Cévennes; **Cazes** – Rivesaltes; **Clos de Fées** – Côtes de Roussillon-Villages; **Mas de Daumas Gassac** – l'Hérault; **Domaine Gardiès** – Côtes de Roussillon-Villages; **de la Granges des Pères** – l'Hérault; **Domaine des Ravanès** – Coteaux de Murveil; **Elian da Ros** – Côtes du Marmandais.

SOUTHWEST FRANCE

Bergerac (red and white) de la Jaubertie, **Moulin des Dames** and **La Tour des Gendres**.
Cahors (reds) **du Cédre, Clos Triguedina** and Lagrezette.
Jurançon (dry and sweet whites) Bellegarde, **Cauhapé**, Clos Guirouilh, Clos Lapeyre, **Clos Uroulat**, Charles Hours and de Lahargue.

Madiran (reds) d'Aydie, **Alain Brumont (Bouscassé and Montus)** and Domaine Pichard.

Monbazillac (sweet white) de l'Ancienne Cure, la Borderie and **Tirecul La Gravière**.

Saussignac (sweet white) Château Richard and Clos d'Yvigne.

LANGUEDOC-ROUSSILLON

Banyuls (fortified) and **Collioure** (red) **de la Casa Blanca**, Château de Jau, **du Mas Blanc** and de la Rectoire.

La Clape (red and white) **Camplazens, de l'Hospitalet** and Pech-Redon.

Corbières (mainly red) **La Baronne**, Etang des Colombes, de Lastours, **Meunier St. Louis**, Château les Palais, Pech-Latt and Château Vaugélas.

Costières de Nîmes (red, white and rosé) **des Aveylans**, de Belle-Coste, Grande-Cassagne, Mourgues-du-Grès and **de Nages**.

Coteaux du Languedoc (red and white) **Les Aurelles, Font Caude**, Mas Jullien, **Mas Mortiès**, Puech-Haut, **Roc d'Anglade**, La Sauvageónne and Abbaye de Valmagne.

Faugères (mainly red) **Alquier**, des Estanilles and **Moulin de Ciffre**.

Minervois (red and white) **Borie de Maurel, Le Cazal, Clos Centeilles**, Fabas, de Gourgazaud and d'Oupia.

Pic St-Loup (mainly red) Mas Bruguière, Cazeneuve, Ermitage du Pic St-Loup, **de l'Hortus**, de Lascaux and Lascours.

St-Chinian (red and white) Cazal-Viel, Coujan, des Jougla and Mas Champart.

PROVENCE

Bandol (red) Pradeaux, **de la Bégude**, Château Jean-Pierre Gaussen,

Lafran-Veyrolles, de Pibarnon, Pradeaux, Mas de la Rouvière, **La Suffrène** and **Tempier**.
Les Baux-de-Provence (mainly red) Hauvette, des Terres Blanches and **de Trévallon £**.
Bellet (red, white and rosé) Château de Crémat.
Cassis (mainly white) Clos Ste-Madeleine.
Côtes de Provence (mainly red) **de la Courtade**, Gavoty, de Rimauresq and de St-Baillon.
Palette (red, white and rosé) **Château Simone**.

GERMANY

Apparently the Riesling revolution is about to happen. Any second now… I have been waiting for a decade for this great day! I am writing up more Rieslings than ever before, so I hope you'll join me in celebrating this spectacular grape. Below is a list of some of the finest exponents of this grape variety on the planet. It is as simple as that. All you have to do is find them and drink them. Then you'll see what I'm talking about.

The best producers are – J.B. Becker, Dr Bürklin-Wolf, J.J. Cristoffel, **Fritz Haag**, Weingut Kerpen, **von Kesselstatt**, Koehler-Ruprecht, **Franz Künstler**, H. & R. Lingenfelder, Schloss Lieser, **Dr Loosen**, **Egon Müller**, Müller-Cattoir, **J.J. Prüm**, Schloss Reinhartshausen, Willi Schaefer, **von Schubert-Maximin Grünhaus**, **Selbach-Oster**, Dr H. Thanisch and **Robert Weil**.

GREAT BRITAIN

Once again, I haven't let patriotism get the better of me and, after tasting every bottle of wine I could get my hands on, I have recommended only the most reliable, professional, homegrown talent. Most UK wine drinkers haven't bothered to taste English wine and I bet if they did they'd get a pleasant surprise. Almost all UK wineries also welcome visitors – see www.englishwineproducers.com. Remember prices are lowest if you buy direct from the winery. **The chosen few are** – Biddenden, **Camel Valley**, **Chapel Down (Curious Grape)**, **Davenport**, Nyetimber, **RidgeView** and Shawsgate.

ITALY

Italy has really got its act together in the last few years. Let me guide you through the thousands of grape varieties, regions and wine styles with my succinct list of the best Italian producers. Italy still makes some of the best-value wines on the shelves, and if you are tempted to venture up the price ladder, you'll find they also make some seriously brilliant wines around the ten to fifteen pound mark. You will probably have to go to top quality independent wine merchants to find the majority of the estates listed below.

NORTHWEST
PIEDMONT

Barolo, Barbaresco, Barbera, Dolcetto and other reds – **Elio Altare**, **Ascheri**, **Ca' Rossa**, Ceretto, **Cigliuti**, Domenico Clerico, **Aldo Conterno**, Giacomo Conterno, **Conterno Fantino**, **Fontanafredda**, **Angelo Gaja £**, Giuseppe Mascarello, **Parusso**, E. Pira, **Bruno Rocca**, **Luciano Sandrone**, **Paolo Scavino**, **La Spinetta**, Aldo Vajra and **Roberto Voerzio**.

Moscato (fizzy, sweet white) **Fontanafredda** and La Spinetta **£**.
Gavi (dry white) Nicola Bergaglio, **La Giustiniana** and **La Scolca**.
Arneis (dry white) **Bric Cenciurio** and **Carlo Deltetto**.

LOMBARDY
Red and white – Bellavista (Franciacorta), Ca' del Bosco (Franciacorta), Ca' dei Frati (Lugana) and Nino Negri (Valtellina).

NORTHEAST
TRENTINO
All styles – Vigneto Dalzocchio, Bossi Fedrigotti, **Ferrari**, **Foradori**, Letrari, Pojer & Sandri and **San Leonardo**.
ALTO ADIGE
All styles – **Colterenzio**, **Franz Haas**, Hofstätter, Alois Lageder and San Michele Appiano.
VENETO
Soave (white) **Roberto Anselmi**, Ca' Rugate, Gini, **Pieropan** and Prà.
Valpolicella (red) **Allegrini**, Ca' del Pipa, Dal Forno, Masi and Giuseppe Quintarelli £.
Miscellaneous estates of excellence – (fizz) **Ruggeri** (Valdobbiadene); (reds and sweeties) **Maculan** (Breganze).
FRIULI-VENEZIA GIULIA
Mainly white – Girolamo Dorigo, Livio Felluga, **Vinnaioli Jermann**, Miani, Davide Moschioni, **Lis Neris (Alvararo Pecorari)**, **Giovanni Puiatti**, **Dario Raccaro**, Ronco del Gnemiz, Roncùs, **Mario Schiopetto**, Tercic and Villa Russiz.

CENTRAL
TUSCANY
Chianti (red) P. Antinori, **Castello di Brolio**, Villa Caffagio, Carobbio, **Castello di Fonterutoli**, Isole e Olena, **Felsina Berardenga**, Le Filigare, Fontodi, **La Massa**, Poggerino, Querciabella and Selvapiana.
Brunello di Montalcino (red) Altesino, **Argiano**, Case Basse,

Costanti, Fanti San Filippo, **Fuligni**, La Gerla, Lisini, **Mastrojanni**, Silvio Nardi, Pietroso and Sesti.

Vino Nobile di Montepulciano (red) **Dei**, Il Macchione, **Poliziano** and Villa Sant'Anna.

Carmignano (red) Ambra and **Tenuta di Capezzana**.

Super-Tuscans (red) Ardingo (Calbello), **Il Borro**, Il Bosco (Manzano), **Brancaia**, Camartina (Querciabella) **£**, Campora (Falchini), Il Carbonaione (Poggio Scalette), **Casalfero** (Barone Ricasoli), Cepparello (Isole e Olena) **£**, Cortaccio (Villa Caffagio), Flaccianello della Pieve (Fontodi), Fontalloro (Felsina Berardenga), Ghiaie della Furba (Capezzana), **Lupicaia (Tenuta del Terricio) £**, **Nambrot (Tenuta di Ghizzano) £**, **Ornellaia (Mondavi/L. Antinori)** **£**, Palazzo Altesi (Altesino), Paleo Rosso (Le Macchiole), Le Pergole Torte (Montevertine), Saffredi (Le Pupille) **£**, Sammarco (Castello dei Rampolla), **Sassicaia (Marchesi Incisa della Rochetta) £**, **Siepi (Fonterutoli) £**, **Solaia (P. Antinori) £**, **Solengo (Argiano) £**, Tassinaia (Tenuta del Terriccio) and Tignanello (P. Antinori).

Maremma and Morellino di Scansano (mainly red) **Lohsa** (Poliziano), Costanza Malfatti, Le Pupille and **Tenuta di Belguardo & Poggio Bronzone (Mazzei)**.

Vernaccia di San Gimignano (white) Montenidoli, **Panizzi** and Pietraserena.

Vin Santo (sweetie) **Avignonesi £**, **Isole e Olena £**, Selvapiana and Villa Branca.

MARCHE

Red and white – **Coroncino**, Saladini Pilastri, Le Terrazze and **Umani Ronchi**.

UMBRIA

Red and white – Luigi Bigi, **Arnaldo Caprai**, La Carraia, **Castello della**

Sala, **La Fiorita Lamborghini**, Lungarotti, **Palazzone** and **Sportoletti**.
LAZIO
Red and white – **Castel De Paolis**, **Falesco** and Pallavincini.
ABRUZZO AND MOLISE
Red and white – **Di Majo Norante** and **Edoardo Valentini**.

SOUTHERN AND ISLANDS – ALL STYLES
PUGLIA
Botromagno, Francesco Candido, **Tenuta Rubino**, **Cosimo Taurino** and Vallone.
CAMPANIA
Colli di Lapio, Feudi di San Gregorio, **Luigi Maffini**, **Mastroberardino**, **Montevetrano** and **Taburno**.
BASILICATA
D'Angelo, Basilisco and **Paternoster**.
CALABRIA
Librandi and San Francesco.
SICILY AND PANTELLERIA
Abraxas, De Bartoli, Calatrasi, **Inycon**, **Maurigi**, Morgante, Salvatore Murana, **Planeta** and Abbazia Santa Anastasia.
SARDINIA
Argiolas, Giovanni Cherchi, **Gallura**, **Santadi** and Sella & Mosca.

NEW ZEALAND
New Zealand is a country that has seemed to tread water in the last year, not improving enormously, but not slipping either. Each year I add a handful of names to this list as we in the UK continue to drink more and more Kiwi wine. There is no doubt New Zealand winemakers are continuing to move in the right direction, but it is taking a long

time to reach the sort of potential that this country must have hidden somewhere. This frustrates me, as in South Africa and Australia they make quantum leaps each year. I hope New Zealand is aware that they are a sitting duck at the moment and with useful Sauvignon Blanc coming out of the Cape, Casablanca and cooler Aussie regions they might not have it all their way for very much longer.

The top producers are – **Alana Estate**, **Ata Rangi**, **Cloudy Bay**, **Craggy Range**, Kim Crawford, **Dry River**, Esk Valley, **Felton Road**, **Forrest Estate**, Goldwater Estate, Grove Mill, Hawkesbridge, Huia, **Hunter's**, **Isabel Estate**, **Jackson Estate**, **Kumeu River**, Lawson's Dry Hills, Martinborough Vineyard, Matakana, Mount Difficulty, **Mountford**, **Palliser Estate**, Rippon Vineyard, Saint Clair, Selaks, Seresin, Stonecroft, **Stonyridge**, Te Mata, Tohu, Unison, Vavasour, Vidal, **Villa Maria** and **Wither Hills**.

PORTUGAL

Portugal makes two of the finest fortified wines in the world – port and Madeira. These two creations are staggeringly fine in the right hands. I have the gold-plated list of producers for you. In addition I have also compiled a list of the top producers of non-fortified wines. I must admit that I don't drink much Portuguese wine, but things are improving rapidly and there are encouraging signs for the future.

PORT

The best special-occasion port houses are – Dow, Fonseca, **Graham**, **Quinta do Noval Nacional**, **Taylor** and **Warre**.
The less famous overachievers are – Churchill, **Quinto do Infantado**, **Niepoort**, Quinta do Portal, **Ramos-Pinto**, **Senhora da Ribeira** and **Quinta do Vesuvio**.

MADEIRA
The top producers are – Blandy's, **Cossart Gordon** and Henriques & Henriques.

THE REST OF PORTUGAL
Here's a short hit list of commendable winemakers in the better regions.

Alentejo Quinta do Carmo, Cortes de Cima, **João Portugal Ramos** and **Segada**.

Bairrada Caves São João and **Luis Pato**.

Beiras Caves Aliança.

Dão Quinta da Carbiz, **Quinta dos Roques** and Conde de Santar.

Douro Quinta do Crasto, Quinta da Gaivosa, **Niepoort**, **Quinta do Portal**, Quinta de Roriz, Quinta de la Rosa and Quinta do Vale da Raposa.

Estremadura Quinta da Boavista, Palha Canas and Quinta de Pancas.

Ribatejo Bright Brothers and **Quinta da Lagoalva**.

Terras do Sado Quinta de Camarate, **José-Maria da Fonseca**, Pasmados, Periquita and **João Pires**.

Vinho Verde Quinta do Ameal and Palácio da Brejoeira.

SOUTH AFRICA
South Africa has finally started to perform at all price points. I was always happy with the top end stuff and, interestingly, cheap whites. But, now that most of the old virussed vines are being ripped out, cheap reds are looking good. I took a trip to the Cape this year and saw some staggeringly good wines and this has re-ignited my enthusiasm. There is also a non-stop supply of new and

interesting estates, so this list has expanded a lot since last year. And, once again, it is worth pointing out that one of the great things about South Africa is that none of the estates below has a wine over £25. My problem (and it is a real brain ache) has been choosing favourites, as I think they are nearly all worthy of bold type. Go for any of the wines made by these estates and you should, I hope, be impressed at not only the taste, but also the value for money.

The top producers are – Avondale, Beaumont, **Graham Beck**, Beyerskloof, **Boekenhoutskloof (Porcupine Ridge)**, **Bouchard Finlayson**, **Columella (Sadie Family)**, **Jean Daneel**, De Trafford, **Diemersfontein**, Neil Ellis, **Fairview**, **Ken Forrester**, Glen Carlou, Grangehurst, **Hamilton Russell**, Hartenberg, **Iona**, **Jordan**, Kanonkop, Klein Constantia, Linton Park, Longridge, Meinert, Mont du Toit, Morgenhof, **Phileo**, **Raats**, **Rustenberg (Brampton)**, Simonsig, Southern Right, **Spice Route**, **Springfield**, Stellenzicht, **Thelema**, **Veenwouden**, **Vergelegen**, Villiera, **Warwick Estate**, Waterford, WhaleHaven and Wildekrans.

SPAIN

I have only noted my favourite regions and, within each, my top producers. Spain is still woefully underrated, but bit by bit the Spanish machine is getting into its stride. There are some super bargains to be had, but for every great value bottle there are ten stinkers, so stick to my list for safety. Almost all of the wineries below make great red wines, only a handful make whites to match.

ANDALUCÍA

Jerez (sherry) **González Byass**, Hidalgo, **Emilio Lustau**, Osborne and **Valdespino**.

ARAGÓN
Calatayud Marqués de Aragón and San Gregorio.
Campo de Borja Bodegas Borsao.
Somontano Blecua (Viñas del Vero) and Enate.

CASTILLA Y LEÓN
Bierzo Descendientes de J. Palacios.
Ribera del Duero Alión, Cillar de Silos, Condado de Haza,
Pago de Carraovejas, **Pesquera, Dominio de Pingus,** Tarsus,
Valduero and **Vega Sicilia £.**
Valladolid Mauro.
Rueda Agrícola Castellana and **Bodegas Dos Victorias.**
Toro Alquiriz (Vega Sicilia) and Viña Bajoz.
Arribes del Duero Durius Alto Duero (Marqués de Griñon).

CATALUÑA
Conca de Barberá Josep Foraster and **Miguel Torres.**
Empordà-Costa Brava Mas Estela.
Penedès Can Ràfols dels Caus, **Jean Léon,** Puig i Roca and **Miguel
Torres.**
Tarragona-Montsant and **Priorat Celler de Capçanes, Clos Mogador
£, Clos de L'Obac,** Mas d'en Compte, **L'Ermita and Finca Dofi
(Alvaro Palacios), Laurona, Mas Martinet** and **Scala Dei.**
Terra Alta Xavier Clua and **Bárbara Forés.**

EXTREMADURA, CASTILLA-LA MANCHA AND MADRID
Castilla-La Mancha Dominio de Valdepusa.
Valdepeñas Los Llanos.
Almansa Piqueras.

ISLANDS
Mallorca **Anima Negra**.

LEVANTE
Jumilla Casa de la Ermita.
Valencia Dominio Los Pinos.

NORTHERN COASTAL SPAIN
Rías Baixas **Lagar de Cervera**, Fillaboa, Lagar de Fornelos, Martín Codax, **Pazo de Barrantes**, **Pazo de Señorans**, Valdamor and **Valmiñor**.
Bizkaiko and **Getariako Txacolina** Bodegas Ametzoi and **Txomín Etaniz**.

RIOJA AND NAVARRA
Rioja Artadi, Barón de Ley, **CVNE**, **Contino**, **Marqués de Griñon**, Lopez de Heredia, Muga, **Marqués de Murrieta**, Navajas, **Remelluri**, La Rioja Alta, Roda, Viña Salceda, Urbina and **Marqués de Vargas**.
Navarra Agramont, Guelbenzu, Julián Chivite, Ochoa, Príncipe de Viana and Vega del Castillo.

USA
CALIFORNIA
Whoops, things still look awfully dear in California. This huge, diverse industry has no trouble in selling its wines locally and has taken its eye off the export market, so we have to put up with some hideously overpriced wines and miss out on most of the plum estates. Still if you are desperate to get into top Californian wines,

you will need a deep pocket and this list of serious producers. I have arranged the wineries in order of style of wine rather than regionally as most producers source grapes from far and wide.

Cabernet Sauvignon/Merlot/Cabernet Franc Araujo, **Arietta £**, Beringer, **Bryant Family £**, Cain, **Caymus £**, Clos LaChance, Corison, **Dalle Valle £**, **Diamond Creek £**, Dominus, Dunn, Etude, Flora Springs, Forman, Gallo Estate, **Harlan Estate £**, **Havens**, Paul Hobbs, Justin Vineyards, Lail Vineyards, Matanzas Creek, **Peter Michael £**, Robert Mondavi, Moraga, **Newton £**, Opus One, Pahlmeyer, **Paradigm £**, **Joseph Phelps £**, **Quintessa £**, **Ridge £**, **Shafer £**, Silver Oak, **Spottswoode £**, **Stag's Leap Wine Cellars £**, Philip Togni and **Viader £**.

Chardonnay Arrowood, **Au Bon Climat**, Beringer, Clos LaChance, Gallo Estate, **Hanzell £**, Paul Hobbs, **Kistler £**, **Kongsgaard £**, **Landmark £**, **Lymar £**, Peter Michael, Robert Mondavi, **David Ramey**, **Shafer £** and Sinskey.

Sauvignon Blanc Beringer, **Carmenet**, **Matanzas Creek** and Robert Mondavi.

Pinot Noir Au Bon Climat, **Calera £**, **Etude £**, **Gary Farrell**, **Hanzell**, **Kistler £**, **J. Rochioli £**, Sinskey, Talley Vineyards and Marimar Torres.

Rhône Rangers Alban, Au Bon Climat, Bonny Doon, **Jade Mountain**, Qupé, **Tablas Creek £**, **Sean Thackrey** and **Turley £**.

Zinfandel Cline, **Elyse**, De Loach, **Doug Nalle**, Ravenswood, Renwood, **Ridge £**, Rosenblum and **Turley £**.

Sparkling Domaine Chandon, Mumm Napa and **Schramsberg**.

Inexpensive estates: Avila, **Bogle**, **Fetzer Bonterra**, J. Lohr, Marietta Cellars, **Ramsay**, **Seventh Moon** and Wente.

PACIFIC NORTHWEST

Wines from Oregon and Washington State are sadly still hard to get hold of and consequently dear. Good luck with your search.

Oregon's best estates – **Adelsheim**, Archery Summit, Beaux Frères, Bethel Heights, **Cristom**, **Domaine Drouhin £**, Duck Pond, **Evesham Wood**, King Estate, Ponzi and Rex Hill.

Washington State's best estates – L'Ecole No 41, **Leonetti Cellar £**, **Quilceda Creek £**, Château Ste-Michelle, **Andrew Will £** and Woodward Canyon.

THE REST OF THE WORLD

This paragraph is my way of skirting around some of the less interesting countries and regions of the wine world. Once again a few areas in France didn't have any representation in my list. Jura, Savoie and Corsica were some of the omissions, but I am still convinced that these wines are better off drunk on hols when the sunset, ambience and local cuisine will help you get over their intrinsic quirkiness (and failings?). Swiss wines have also failed to pop up in any great numbers (i.e. zero). I prefer Austrian wines anyway, but if the Swiss will drink 98% of their production, how on earth do they expect us to get a look in? Eastern Europe still fails to light my fire. One or two bottles work, but in the greater scheme of things there is always a better wine from somewhere else. Please prove me wrong! I know you are going to suggest Tokaji from Hungary, so I'll get in first. This is still one of the great wine styles in the world, and as every year crawls by we are afforded a better selection of these historic and sumptuous wines – pity they are all bloody expensive. Three names to look out for if you are feeling flush are Disznókö, Oremus and the Royal Tokaji Wine

Company. Château Musar is still the Lebanon's one great wine. Greek wines are getting more more airplay and I'm nearly in favour. I have yet to crack open a bottle of Cypriot wine, although I did taste a shocker from Tenerife. North African wines, including those from Tunisia and Morocco, are increasingly seen on UK shelves – there are some useful Carignans around. Further afield, I have cunningly avoided wines from Mexico, Bolivia and Peru, but got caught in the headlights of a Chinese trio the other day and they were memorable – I will never forget the flavour! A winery in Bali has impressed me, as have the Monsoon Valley wines from Thailand, and by next year these may have a slot on a shelf somewhere in the UK – you'll read about it here if they do. I know Uruguay can produce good wine, but there is little of it in the UK. I am still not convinced by Indian wines, and it's rubbish to think that they are the only accompaniment to Indian cooking. And that pretty much covers it. For the time being the Gazetteer list is good enough for me, and I venture that if you kick off with Australia and head towards USA you'll only have made it to Chile by the time The Wine List 2005 comes out – that is if you are doing it properly!

DIRECTORY
OF UK WINE
MERCHANTS

This year there are a hatful of new entries in this chapter, but if your favourite wine shop is not listed, or you are a wine merchant and you're not in here, then do drop me a line for next year's book. The next few pages contain the vital contact details for the merchants responsible for selling nearly all of the top bottles of wine in the UK. Use this directory and get dialling. This list has every number you need to fill your cellar. If you spot a wine you like in the Top 250 don't delay, as some of the wines are in short supply. Phone up and reserve some stock today. The following list of merchants is sorted alphabetically and then regionally to help you access as wide a choice of merchants as possible. I have included the main contact number and e-mail address or website, where appropriate, for each company's HQ. Remember that every outlet mentioned below delivers wine around the country. So use this service if you are pushed for time, not in the area or have placed a particularly large order. Many of these companies have newsletters (either via e-mail or post), so ask to be put on their mailing list and you will be the first to hear about new releases. Most importantly of all, if you locate an independent wine merchant near to where you live, do your best to support them. These hardworking companies are the lifeblood of the wine trade. Supermarkets and chain stores have massive buying power and search out the best wines possible, but their orders are usually multiples of hundreds, if not thousands, of cases. Each year the supermarkets and the big wine chains increase their selections and buy better wine. They are very skilled at this and are often the place to go when buying big brand names. But the smaller outfits sniff out individual parcels, sometimes a case at a time, and you want to be the first to know about these rare gems. In the same way that your local butcher or fishmonger knows your likes and dislikes, your local wine merchant will get to know your taste. Now, what could be better than that?

KEY
✪ = Jukesy-rated wine merchant worthy of particular note
C = Wine sold by the case (often mixed) of twelve bottles
M = Mail order company, usually with no retail premises
F = Fine wine sales/wine broker/good range of expensive stuff!

RECOMMENDED LARGER CHAIN STORES AND SUPERMARKETS (PLUS ABBREVIATIONS)

Asda (Asd) 270 stores 0500 100055 www.asda.co.uk ✪

E.H. Booth & Co., of Lancashire, Cheshire, Cumbria and Yorkshire
(Boo) 27 stores 01772 251701 www.booths-supermarkets.co.uk ✪

Co-operative Group CWS (Coo) 1,763 stores 0800 068 6727
www.co-op.co.uk

Majestic Wine Warehouses (Maj) 104 stores 01923 298200
www.majestic.co.uk ✪C

Marks & Spencer (M&S) 332 stores 020 7935 4422
www.marksandspencer.co.uk ✪

Wm Morrison (Mor) 115 stores 01924 870000
www.morereasons.co.uk

Oddbins (Odd) 234 stores and Oddbins Fine Wine shops (OFW)
8 stores 020 8944 4400 www.oddbins.com ✪

Safeway (Saf) 485 stores 020 8848 8744 www.safeway.co.uk ✪

Sainsbury's (Sai) 489 stores 0800 636262
www.sainsburys.co.uk ✪

Somerfield Stores (Som) 600 stores 0117 935 6669
www.somerfield.co.uk

Tesco Stores (Tes) 737 stores 0800 505555 www.tesco.co.uk ✪

Thresher Group – including **Bottoms Up (Bot)**, **Thresher (Thr)**
and **Wine Rack (WRa)** 2,105 stores 01707 387200
www.threshergroup.com ✪

Unwins Ltd (Unw) 432 stores 01322 272711 www.unwins.co.uk

Waitrose (Wai) 142 stores 01344 825232 www.waitrose.com ✪

Wine Cellar (WCe) 62 stores 0800 838251 www.winecellar.co.uk

RECOMMENDED INDEPENDENT RETAIL SPECIALISTS, SMALL CHAINS, WINE BROKERS AND MAIL ORDER WINE COMPANIES SORTED ALPHABETICALLY

A & A Wines, Cranleigh, Surrey 01483 274666 AAWINES@aol.com C

A & B Vintners, Brenchley, Kent 01892 724977
info@abvintners.co.uk ✪ M C

Adnams Wine Merchants, Southwold, Suffolk 01502 727222
wines@adnams.co.uk ✪

Ameys Wines, Sudbury, Suffolk 01787 377144

Amps Fine Wines of Oundle, near Peterborough, Northamptonshire
01832 273502 info@ampsfinewines.co.uk

Arkells Vintners, Swindon, Wiltshire 01793 823026
arkells@arkells.com

John Armit Wines, London 020 7908 0600 info@armit.co.uk
✪ M C F

W.J. Armstrong, East Grinstead, West Sussex 01342 321478
www.wjarmstrong.com

Arnolds, Broadway, Worcestershire 01386 852427

Arriba Kettle & Co., Honeybourne, Worcestershire 01386 833024
C

Australian Wine Club, Hounslow, Middlesex 0800 8562004
orders@austwine.co.uk ✪ M C

Averys, Bristol 0117 921 4146 ✪

Bacchanalia, Cambridge 01223 576292

Bacchus Fine Wines, Warrington, Buckinghamshire 01234 711140
wine@bacchus.co.uk ✪ C

Bakers & Larners, Holt, Nolfolk 01263 712323 ctbaker@cwcom.net

Ballantynes, Cowbridge, Vale of Glamorgan 01446 774840
enq@ballantynes.co.uk ✪

Balls Brothers, London 020 7739 1642 info@ballsbrothers.co.uk M C

Georges Barbier, London 020 8852 5801 georgesbarbier@f2s.com
✪ M C

Barrels & Bottles, Sheffield 0114 255 6611
sales@barrels&bottles.co.uk

Bat & Bottle, Knightley, Staffordshire 01785 284495
mail@batwine.com ✪

Beaconsfield Wine Cellar, Beaconsfield, Buckinghamshire
01494 675545 thecellars@btinternet.com

Bella Wines, Newmarket, Suffolk 01638 604899
sales@bellawines.co.uk ✪ M

Bennetts Fine Wines, Chipping Campden, Gloucestershire 01386
840392 enquiries@bennettsfinewines.com ✪

Bentalls, Kingston-upon-Thames, Surrey 020 8546 1001

Bergerac Wine Cellar, St Helier, Jersey 01534 870756

Berkmann Wine Cellars, London 020 7609 4711
info@berkmann.co.uk ✪ M

Berry Bros. & Rudd, London 0870 900 4300
www.bbr.com ○ F

Bibendum Wine Ltd, London 020 7449 4120
sales@bibendum-wine.co.uk ○ M C F

Bideford Wines, Bideford, Devon 01237 470507

Bonhote Foster, Bumpstead, Suffolk 01440 730779
www.pinotpeople.co.uk M

Booths of Stockport, Heaton Moor, Stockport 0161 432 3309
johnbooth@lineone.net

Bordeaux Index, London 020 7253 2110 sales@bordeauxindex.com
○ M F

The Bottleneck, Broadstairs, Kent 01843 861095
sales@thebottleneck.co.uk

Brinkleys Wines, London 020 7351 1683 www.brinkleys.com

Burgundy Shuttle, London 07771 630826
mail@burgundyshuttle.co.uk M C

Butlers Wine Cellar, Brighton, East Sussex 01273 698724 ○

Anthony Byrne Fine Wines, Ramsey, Cambridgeshire 01487
814555 sales@abfw.co.uk M C

D. Byrne & Co., Clitheroe, Lancashire 01200 423152 ○

Cairns & Hickey, Bramhope, Leeds 0113 267 3746

Carley & Webb, Framlingham, Suffolk 01728 723503

Carringtons, Manchester 0161 832 5646

Castang Wine Shippers, Pelynt, Cornwall 01503 220359
sales@castang-wines.co.uk M C

Les Caves du Patron, Stoneygate, Leicester 0116 221 8221
wines@lescavesdupatron.com

Cave Cru Classé, London 020 7378 8579 enquiries@ccc.co.uk M C F

Andrew Chapman Fine Wines, Abingdon, Oxfordshire
0845 458 0707 info@surf4wine.co.uk ✪

Simon Charles Vintners, London 020 7228 3409 ✪

The Charterhouse Wine Co., London 020 7587 1302
info@charterhousewine.co.uk

Cheshire Smokehouse, Wilmslow, Cheshire 01625 540123

Chiltern Cellars, High Wycombe, Buckinghamshire 01494 526212

Chippendale Fine Wines, Bradford, West Yorkshire 01274 582424
mikepoll@freenetname.co.uk **M C**

Church House Vintners, Newbury, Berkshire 01635 579 327
chv@saqnet.co.uk **M C**

Clifton Cellars, Bristol 0117 973 0287
clifton@cellars.freeserve.co.uk

Brian Coad Fine Wines, Ivybridge, Devon 01752 334970
briancoad@berkmann.co.uk ✪ **M C**

Cochonnet Wines, Falmouth, Cornwall 01326 340332
sales@wineincornwall.co.uk

Cockburns, Leith, Edinburgh 0131 346 1113 sales@winelist.co.uk

Colombier Vins Fins, Swadlincote, Derbyshire 01283 552552 **M C**

Compendium, Belfast, Northern Ireland 028 9079 1197

Connollys, Birmingham 0121 236 9269 www.connollyswine.co.uk ✪

Constantine Stores, near Falmouth, Cornwall 01326 340226

Corks, Cotham, Bristol 0117 973 1620 sales@corksof.com

Corkscrew Wines, Carlisle, Cumbria 01228 543033
corkscrewwines@aol.com

Corney & Barrow, London 020 7265 2400 wine@corbar.co.uk ✪ **F**

Croque-en-Bouche, Malvern Wells, Worcestershire
01684 565612 mail@croque-en-bouche.co.uk ✪ **M C**

Dartmouth Vintners, Dartmouth, Devon 01803 832602

bill@dartmouthvintners.fsnet.co.uk
Decorum Vintners, London 020 8969 6581 www.decvin.com ✪ M C
deFINE Food and Wine, Sandiway, Cheshire 01606 882101
Rodney Densem Wines, Nantwich, Cheshire 01270 626999
sales@onestopwine.com
F.L. Dickins, Rickmansworth, Hertfordshire 01923 773636
Direct Wine Shipments, Belfast, Northern Ireland 028 9050 8000
enquiry@directwine.co.uk ✪
Direct Wines, Windsor 0870 444 8383 www.laithwaites.co.uk M C
Domaine Direct, London 020 7837 1142
mail@domainedirect.co.uk ✪ C
The Dorchester Wine Centre at Eldridge Pope, Dorchester, Dorset
01305 258266 ✪
Dunells Ltd, St Peter, Jersey 01534 736418
Du Vin, Henley-on-Thames, Oxfordshire 01491 637888
info@duvin.co.uk

Edencroft Fine Wines, Nantwich, Cheshire 01270 629975
sales@edencroft.co.uk
Ben Ellis, Brockham, Surrey 01737 842160
sales@benelliswines.com ✪ C
Ells Fine Wines, Portadown, Northern Ireland 028 3833 2306
rrwines@hotmail.com
El Vino, London 020 7353 5384 www.elvino.co.uk
English Wine Centre, Alfriston Roundabout, East Sussex 01323
870164 bottles@englishwine.co.uk
Eton Vintners, Windsor 01753 790188
sales@etonvintners.co.uk M
Evertons, Ombersley, Worcestershire 01905 620282

Evingtons Wine Merchants, Leicester 0116 254 2702
evingtonwine@fsbdial.co.uk
Farr Vintners, London 020 7821 2000 sales@farr-vintners.com ✪ M F
Fine & Rare Wines, London 020 8960 1995 wine@frw.co.uk ✪ M F
Fine Cheese Co., Bath 01225 483407 sales@finecheese.co.uk
Fine Wines of New Zealand, London 020 7482 0093 www.fwnz.co.uk
✪ M
Irma Fingal-Rock, Monmouth, Monmouthshire 01600 712372
Flagship Wines, Brentwood, Essex 01227 203420
julia@flagshipwines.co.uk M C
Le Fleming Wines, Harpenden, Hertfordshire 01582 760125 M C
La Forge Wines, Marksbury, Bath 01761 472349
kevin@laforgewines.com
Fortnum & Mason, London 020 7734 8040 ✪
Four Walls Wine Company, Chilgrove, West Sussex 01243 535360
fourwallswine@cs.com ✪ M F
Friarwood, London 020 7736 2628 sales@friarwood.com

Gallery Wines, Gomshall, Surrey 01483 203795
Garland Wine Cellar, Ashtead, Surrey 01372 275247
simon@garlandwines.freeserve.co.uk
Garrards, Cockermouth, Cumbria 01900 823592
admin@garrards-wine.co.uk
Gauntleys, Nottingham 0115 911 0555
rhone@gauntleywine.com ✪
General Wine Company, Liphook, Hampshire 01428 727744 ✪
Goedhuis & Co., London 020 7793 7900 sales@goedhuis.com ✪ M C F
Peter Graham Wines, Norwich, Norfolk 01603 625657
louisa@petergrahamwines.com

✪ = Jukesy-rated wine merchant worthy of particular note
C = Wine sold by the case (often mixed) of twelve bottles

Great Gaddesden Wines, Hemel Hempstead, Hertfordshire 01442
412312 sales@flyingcorkscrew.com M C
Great Northern Wine Company, Ripon, North Yorkshire 01765
606767 info@greatnorthernwine.com M
Great Western Wine Company, Bath 01225 322800
post@greatwesternwine.co.uk ✪
Peter Green, Edinburgh 0131 229 5925 petergreenwines@talk21.com
Patrick Grubb Selections, Oxford 01869 340229 ✪
Gunson Fine Wines, South Godstone, Surrey 01342 843974
gunsonfinewines@aol.com ✪ M C

H & H Bancroft, London 020 7232 5463
sales@handhbancroftwines.com ✪ M C
Hailsham Cellars, Hailsham, East Sussex 01323 441212
Halifax Wine Company, Halifax, West Yorkshire 01422 256333
www.halifaxwinecompany.com
Hall and Woodhouse Ltd, Blandford, Dorset 01258 452 141
Handford – Holland Park, London 020 7221 9614
james@handford-wine.demon.net ✪ F
Hanslope Wines, Milton Keynes, Buckinghamshire 01908 510262
charles@hanslopewines.co.uk
Roger Harris Wines, Weston Longville, Norfolk 01603 880171
sales@rogerharriswines.co.uk ✪ M C
Harrods, London 020 7730 1234 ✪ F
John Harvey & Sons, Bristol 0117 927 5006 M C
Harvey Nichols & Co., London 020 7201 8537
wineshop@harveynichols.co.uk ✪
Richard Harvey Wines, Wareham, Dorset 01929 481437
harvey@lds.co.uk M C

The Haslemere Cellar, Haslemere, Surrey 01428 645081
info@haslemerecellar.co.uk ✪

Haynes, Hanson & Clark, London 020 7259 0102
london@hhandc.co.uk and Stow-on-the-Wold, Gloucestershire
01451 870808 stow@hhandc.co.uk ✪

Hedley Wright, Bishop's Stortford, Hertfordshire 01279 465818
hedleywine@aol.com C

Pierre Henck, Wolverhampton, West Midlands
01902 897107 M C

Charles Hennings Vintners, Pulborough, West Sussex
01798 872485 sales@chv-wine.co.uk

Hicks & Don, Edington, Wiltshire 01380 831234
mailbox@hicksanddon.co.uk M

George Hill, Loughborough, Leicestershire 01509 212717
andrewh@gerorgehill.co.uk

Hopton Wines, Kidderminster, Worcestershire 01299 270734
chris@hoptoncourt.fsnet.co.uk M C

Hoults Wine Merchants, Huddersfield, West Yorkshire
01484 510700 bobwine@hotmail.com

House of Townend, Kingston upon Hull, East Yorkshire
01482 586582 info@houseoftownend.co.uk ✪

Ian G. Howe, Newark, Nottinghamshire 01636 704366
howe@chablis-burgundy.co.uk

Victor Hugo Wines, St Saviour, Jersey 01534 507977
sales@victor-hugo-wines.com

Inspired Wines, Cleobury Mortimer, Shropshire 01299 270064
info@inspired-wines.co.uk

Inverarity Vaults, Biggar 01899 308000

enquiries@inverarity-vaults.com
Irvine Robertson, Edinburgh 0131 553 3521 C
Jeroboams (incorporating **Laytons Wine Merchants**), London
020 7259 6716 sales@jeroboams.co.uk ✿
Michael Jobling, Newcastle-upon-Tyne 0191 261 5298 M C
The Jolly Vintner, Tiverton, Devon 01884 255644
L & F Jones, Radstock near Bath 01761 417117
buying.buying@lfjones.aclm.co.uk
S.H. Jones, Banbury, Oxfordshire 01295 251179
shjonesbanbury@aol.com ✿
Justerini & Brooks, London 020 7484 6400 ✿ F
Just in Case Wine Merchants, Bishop's Waltham, Hampshire
01489 892969

Joseph Keegan, Holyhead, Isle of Anglesey 01407 762333
enquiries@josephkeegan.co.uk
John Kelly Wines, Boston Spa, West Yorkshire 01937 842965
john@kellywines.co.uk M C
David Kibble Wines, Fontwell, West Sussex 01243 544111
Richard Kihl, Aldeburgh, Suffolk 01728 454455
sales@richardkihl.ltd.uk ✿ F C

Laithwaites, Reading, Berkshire 0870 444 8282
orders@laithwaites.co.uk M C
Lay & Wheeler, Colchester, Essex 0845 330 1855
sales@laywheeler.com ✿
Laymont & Shaw, Truro, Cornwall 01872 270545
info@laymont-shaw.co.uk ✿ M C
Lea & Sandeman, London 020 7244 0522

sales@leaandsandeman.co.uk ✪

Liberty Wines, London 020 7720 5350 info@libertywine.co.uk ✪ M C

O.W. Loeb, London 020 7234 0385 finewine@owloeb.com ✪ M C

J & H Logan, Edinburgh 0131 667 2855

Longford Wines, Lewes, East Sussex 01273 400012
longfordwines@aol.com M C

Love Saves the Day, Manchester 0161 832 0777
chris@lovesavestheday.co.uk ✪

Luckins Wine Store, Great Dunmow, Essex 01371 872839

Luvian's Bottle Shop, Cupar, Fife 01334 654820
v.fusaro@ukonline.co.uk

Magnum Wine Company, Swindon, Wiltshire 01793 642569 ✪

Richard Mallinson Wines, Overton, Hampshire 01256 770397

Map Wines, Bridgewater, Somerset 01278 459 622

Martinez Fine Wines, Ilkley, West Yorkshire 01943 603241
editor@martinez.co.uk ✪

Mayfair Cellars, London 020 7386 7999 sales@mayfaircellars.co.uk
M C

Mill Hill Wines, London 020 8959 6754
millhillwines@compuserve.com

Mille Gusti, London 020 8997 3932 millegusti@hotmail.com ✪ M C

Mills Whitcombe, Peterchurch, Herefordshire 01981 550028
info@millswhitcombe.co.uk ✪ C

Milton Sandford Wines, Knowl Hill, Berkshire
01628 829449 ✪ M C

Mitchells Wines, Sheffield 0114 274 5587

Montrachet Fine Wines, London 020 7928 1990
www.montrachetwine.com ✪ M C

Moreno Wine, London 020 7286 0678
   sales@morenowines.co.uk ✪
Moriarty Vintners, Cardiff 029 2022 9996
   sales@moriarty-vintners.com
Morris & Verdin, London 020 7921 5300 info@m-v.co.uk ✪ M C

New World Wines, London 020 8877 3450
   andy@NewWorldWines.co.uk
James Nicholson, Crossgar, Co. Down, Northern Ireland
   028 4483 0091 info@jnwine.com ✪
Nickolls & Perks, Stourbridge, West Midlands 01384 394518
   sales@nickollsandperks.co.uk
Nicolas UK of London, 20+ stores 020 7584 9318 www.nicolas.co.uk
Noble Rot Wine Warehouse, Bromsgrove, Worcestershire
   01527 575606 info@nrwinewarehouse.co.uk ✪
The Nobody Inn, Doddiscombsleigh, Devon 01647 252394
   info@nobodyinn.co.uk ✪

Oasis Wines, Southend-on-Sea, Essex 01702 293999
The Old Forge Wine Cellar, Storrington, West Sussex
   01903 744246 chris@worldofwine.co.uk
Oxford Wine Company, Witney, Oxfordshire 01865 301144
   info@oxfordwine.co.uk ✪

Thomas Panton, Tetbury, Gloucestershire 01666 503088
   info@wineimporter.co.uk M
Paxton & Whitfield, London 020 7930 0259
   sales@cheesemongers.co.uk
Thos Peatling, Bury St Edmunds, Suffolk 01284 714285

sales@thospeatling.co.uk
Peckham & Rye, Glasgow 0141 445 4555
stuart.barrie@peckhams.co.uk ✪
Penistone Court Wine Cellars, Penistone, Sheffield 01226 766037
pcwc@dircon.co.uk ✪ M C
Philglas & Swiggot, London 020 7924 4494
philglas-swiggot@aol.com ✪
Christopher Piper Wines, Ottery St Mary, Devon 01404 814139
sales@christopherpiperwines.co.uk ✪
Terry Platt Wine Merchants, Llandudno, Conwy 01492 874099
info@terryplattwines.co.uk ✪ M C
Planet Wine, Sale, Cheshire 0161 973 1122
sales@planetwine.co.uk M C
Playford Ros, Thirsk, North Yorkshire 01845 526777
sales@playfordros.com M C
Portal, Dingwall & Norris, Emsworth, Hampshire 01243 370280
Portland Wine Co., Sale, Manchester 0161 962 8752
portwineco@aol.com
Premier Cru Fine Wine, Guiseley, Leeds 01943 877004
enquiries@premiercrufinewine.co.uk

Quay West Wines, Stoke Canon, Exeter 01392 841833
sales@quaywestwines.co.uk C
Quellyn Roberts, Cheshire 01244 310455 sales@qrwines.co.uk

R.S. Wines, Bristol 0117 963 1780 M C
Arthur Rackham Emporia, Guildford, Surrey 0870 870 1110 C
Raeburn Fine Wines, Edinburgh 0131 3431159
sales@raeburnfinewines.com ✪

Ravensbourne Wine, London 020 8692 9655
sales@ravensbournewine.co.uk C

Reid Wines, Hallatrow, Bristol 01761 452645
reidwines@aol.com ✪ M F

La Réserve, London 020 7589 2020
redwine@la-reserve.co.uk ✪

Revelstoke Wines, London 020 8875 0077
sales@revelstoke.co.uk ✪ M C

Howard Ripley, London 020 8877 3065 info@howardripley.com
M C

Roberson, London 020 7371 2121 retail@roberson.co.uk ✪

Roberts & Speight, Beverley, East Yorkshire 01482 870717
sales@robertsandspeight.co.uk

Robert Rolls, London 020 7606 1166 mail@rollswine.com ✪ M C F

St Martin Vintners, Brighton, East Sussex 01273 777788
sales@stmartinvintners.co.uk

Sandhams Wine Merchants, Caistor, Lincolnshire 01472 852118
sales@sandhamswine.co.uk

Scatchard, Liverpool 0151 709 7073 info@scatchards.com

Seckford Wines, Woodbridge, Suffolk 01394 446622
sales@seckfordwines.co.uk ✪ M C F

Selfridges, London 020 7318 3730 and Manchester 0161 629 1234
wine.club@selfridges.co.uk ✪

Shaftesbury Fine Wines, Shaftesbury, Dorset 01747 850059

Shaws, Beaumaris, Isle of Anglesey 01248 810328
wines@shaws.sagehost.co.uk

Edward Sheldon, Shipston-on-Stour, Warwickshire 01608 661409
finewine@edward-sheldon.co.uk

H. Smith, Derby, Derbyshire 01335 342150

Laurence Smith, Edinburgh 0131 667 3327 vintnersmith@aol.com M C

Soho Wine Supply, London 020 7636 8490 info@sohowine.co.uk

The Sommelier Wine Co., St Peter Port, Guernsey 01481 721677 ✪

Springfield Wines, near Huddersfield, West Yorkshire 01484 864929

Frank Stainton Wines, Kendal, Cumbria 01539 731886
   admin@stainton-wines.co.uk

William Stedman, Caerleon, Newport 01633 430055
   info@wmstedman.co.uk

Charles Steevenson, Tavistock, Devon 01822 616272
   sales@steevensonwines.co.uk M C

Stevens Garnier, Oxford 01865 263303 info@stevensgarnier.co.uk

Stokes Fine Wines, London 020 8944 5979
   sales@stokesfinewines.com ✪ M C

Stone, Vine & Sun, Cosham, Hampshire 0845 061 4604
   sales@stonevine.co.uk ✪

Stratford Vintners, Cookham, Berkshire 01628 810606
   sales@stratfordwine.co.uk ✪ M C

SWIG, London 020 7903 8311 imbibe@swig.co.uk ✪ M C

T & W Wines, Brandon, Suffolk 01842 814414
   contact@tw-wines.com

Tanners, Shrewsbury, Shropshire 01743 234455
   sales@tanners-wines.co.uk ✪

Theatre of Wine, London 020 8858 6363

Topsham Wines, Topsham, Devon 01392 874501
   mail@topshamwines.co.uk

Totnes Wine Co., Totnes, Devon 01803 866357
   info@totneswine.co.uk

Trenchermans, Sherborne, Dorset 01935 432857
  steve@trenchermans.com
Turville Valley Wines, Great Missenden, Buckinghamshire
  01494 868818 info@turville-valley-wines.com ✪ M C F
Uncorked, London 020 7638 5998 drink@uncorked.co.uk ✪

Valvona & Crolla, Edinburgh 0131 556 6066
  sales@valvonacrolla.co.uk ✪
Helen Verdcourt, Maidenhead, Berkshire 01628 625577 M C
Vicki's Stores, Chobham, Surrey 01276 858374
La Vigneronne, London 020 7589 6113 lavig@aol.com ✪
Villeneuve Wines, Peebles, Haddington and Edinburgh
  01721 722500 wines@villeneuvewines.com ✪
Vin du Van, Appledore, Kent 01233 758727 ✪ M C
Vinceremos, Leeds 0113 2440002 info@vinceremos.co.uk M C
The Vine Trail, Hotwells, Bristol 0117 921 1770
  enquiries@vinetrail.co.uk ✪ M C
The Vineyard, Dorking, Surrey 01306 876828
The Vineyard Cellars, Hungerford, Berkshire 01488 681313
  jameshocking@vineyardcellars.com ✪ M C
Vino Vino, New Malden, Surrey 07703 436949
  vinovino@macunlimited.net M C
The Vintage House, London 020 7437 2592
  vintagehouse.co@virgin.net
Vintage Roots, Arborfield, Berkshire 0118 976 1999
  info@vintageroots.co.uk M
Vintage Wine Cellars, Luton, Bedfordshire 01582 455068

Wadebridge Wines, Wadebridge, Cornwall 01208 812692

wadebridgewines@eclipse.co.uk

Waterloo Wine, London 020 7403 7967 sales@waterloowine.co.uk

Waters Wine Merchants, Coventry, Warwick 01926 888889
info@waters-wine-merchants.co.uk

David J. Watt Fine Wines, Ashby-de-la-Zouch, Leicestershire
01530 415704 shop, 01530 413953 fwatt@lineone.net M

Weavers, Nottingham, Nottinghamshire 0115 958 0922
weavers@weavers.wines.com ✪

Wessex Wines, Bridport, Dorset 01308 427177
wessexwines@btinternet.com C

Whitebridge Wines, Stone, Staffordshire 01785 817229
sales@whitebridgewines.co.uk

Whitesides, Clitheroe, Lancashire 01200 422281

Whittalls Wines, Walsall, West Midlands 01922 636161 C

Wicked Wines, Pockthorpe, Kilham, East Yorkshire
01377 255725

Wilkinson Vintners, London 020 7272 1982
wilkinson@finewine.co.uk ✪ M C F

James Williams, Narberth, Pembrokeshire 01834 862200

Wimbledon Wine Cellar, London 020 8540 9979
enquiries@wimbledonwinecellar.com ✪

Winchcombe Wine Merchants, Winchcombe, Gloucestershire
01242 604313

The Wine Cellar, South Croydon 020 8657 6936
winecellarsnd@aol.com

The Wine Man, Streatley-on-Thames, West Berkshire 01635
203050 sales@wine-man.com M C

Wine Society, Stevenage, Hertfordshire 01438 741177
memberservices@thewinesociety.com ✪ M C F

The Wine Treasury, London 020 7793 9999
  quality@winetreasury.com ✪ M C
The Winery, London 020 7286 6475
  dmotion@globalnet.co.uk ✪ F
Wines of Interest, Ipswich, Suffolk 01473 215752
  sales@winesofinterest.co.uk
The Winesmith, Peterborough, Cambridgeshire 01780 783102
  cases@winesmith.co.uk
WineTime, Milnthorpe, Cumbria 01539 562030 M C
T. Wright, Bolton, Greater Manchester 01204 697805
The Wright Wine Company, Skipton, North Yorkshire
  01756 700886 ✪
Wrightson & Co. Wine Merchants, Darlington 01325 374134
  ed.wrightson.wines@onyxnet.co.uk M C
Wycombe Wines, High Wycombe, Buckinghamshire
  01494 437228
Peter Wylie Fine Wines, Plymtree, Devon 01884 277555
  peter@wylie-fine-wines.demon.co.uk ✪ F

Yapp Brothers, Mere, Wiltshire 01747 860423 sales@yapp.co.uk ✪ M C
Noel Young Wines, Trumpington, Cambridgeshire 01223 844744
  admin@nywines.co.uk ✪ F

M = Mail order company, usually with no retail premises
F = Fine wine sales/wine broker/good range of expensive stuff!

RECOMMENDED INDEPENDENT RETAIL SPECIALISTS, SMALL CHAINS, WINE BROKERS AND MAIL ORDER WINE COMPANIES SORTED REGIONALLY

(For contact details see alphabetical list)

LONDON
John Armit Wines, W11 ✪ M C F
Australian Wine Club, Hounslow ✪ M C
Balls Brothers, E2 M C
Georges Barbier, SE12 ✪ M C
Berkmann Wine Cellars, N7 ✪ M
Berry Bros. & Rudd, SW1 ✪ F
Bibendum Wine Ltd, NW1 ✪ M C F
Bordeaux Index, EC1 ✪ M F
Brinkleys Wines, SW10
Burgundy Shuttle, SW11 M C
Cave Cru Classé, SE1 M C F
Simon Charles Vintners, SW11 ✪
The Charterhouse Wine Co., SE11
Corney & Barrow, E1 ✪ F
Decorum Vintners, W10 ✪ M C
Domaine Direct, N1 ✪ C
El Vino, EC4
Farr Vintners, SW1 ✪ M F
Fine & Rare Wines, W10 ✪ M F
Fine Wines of New Zealand, NW1 ✪ M
Fortnum & Mason, W1 ✪
Friarwood, SW6

Goedhuis & Co., SW8 ✪ M C F
H & H Bancroft, SW8 ✪ M C
Handford – Holland Park, W11 ✪ F
Harrods, SW1 ✪ F
Harvey Nichols & Co., SW1 ✪
Haynes, Hanson & Clark, SW1 ✪
Jeroboams (incorporating **Laytons Wine Merchants**), W1 ✪
Justerini & Brooks, SW1 ✪ F
Lea & Sandeman, SW10 ✪
Liberty Wines, SW8 ✪ M C
O.W. Loeb, SE1 ✪ M C
Mayfair Cellars, SW6 M C
Mill Hill Wines, NW7
Mille Gusti, W13 ✪ M C
Montrachet Fine Wines, SE1 ✪ M C
Moreno Wine, W9 ✪
Morris & Verdin, SE1 ✪ M C
New World Wines, SW18
Nicolas UK of London 20+ stores
Paxton & Whitfield, SW1
Philglas & Swiggot, SW11 ✪
Ravensbourne Wine, SE10 C
La Réserve, SW3 ✪
Revelstoke Wines, SW15 ✪ M C
Howard Ripley, N21 M C
Roberson, W14 ✪
Robert Rolls, EC1 ✪ M C F
Selfridges, W1 ✪
Soho Wine Supply, W1

Stokes Fine Wines, SW18 ✪ M C
SWIG, SW6 ✪ M C
Theatre of Wine, SE10
Uncorked, EC2 ✪
La Vigneronne, SW7 ✪
The Vintage House, W1
Waterloo Wine, SE1
Wilkinson Vintners, N19 ✪ M C F
Wimbledon Wine Cellar, SW19 ✪
The Wine Treasury, SW8 ✪ M C
The Winery, W9 ✪ F

SOUTH EAST

A & A Wines, Cranleigh, Surrey C
A & B Vintners, Brenchley, Kent ✪ M C
W.J. Armstrong, East Grinstead, West Sussex
Bacchus Fine Wines, Warrington, Buckinghamshire ✪ C
Beaconsfield Wine Cellar, Beaconsfield, Buckinghamshire
Bentalls, Kingston-upon-Thames, Surrey
The Bottleneck, Broadstairs, Kent
Butlers Wine Cellar, Brighton, East Sussex ✪
Chiltern Cellars, High Wycombe, Buckinghamshire
Church House Vintners, Newbury, Berkshire M C
F.L. Dickins, Rickmansworth, Hertfordshire
Direct Wines, Windsor M C
Ben Ellis, Brockham, Surrey ✪ C
English Wine Centre, Alfriston, East Sussex
Eton Vintners, Windsor M
Le Fleming Wines, Harpenden, Hertfordshire M C

Four Walls Wine Company, Chilgrove, West Sussex ✪ M F
Gallery Wines, Gomshall, Surrey
Garland Wine Cellar, Ashtead, Surrey
General Wine Company, Liphook, Hampshire ✪
Great Gaddesden Wines, Hemel Hempstead, Hertfordshire M C
Gunson Fine Wines, South Godstone, Surrey ✪ M C
Hailsham Cellars, Hailsham, East Sussex
Hanslope Wines, Milton Keynes, Buckinghamshire
The Haslemere Cellar, Haslemere, Surrey ✪
Hedley Wright, Bishop's Stortford, Hertfordshire C
Charles Hennings Vintners, Pulborough, West Sussex
Just in Case Wine Merchants, Bishop's Waltham, Hampshire
David Kibble Wines, Fontwell, West Sussex
Laithwaites, Reading M C
Longford Wines, Lewes, East Sussex M C
Richard Mallinson Wines, Overton, Hampshire
Milton Sandford Wines, Knowl Hill, Berkshire ✪ M C
The Old Forge Wine Cellar, Storrington, West Sussex
Portal, Dingwall & Norris, Emsworth, Hampshire
Arthur Rackham Emporia, Guildford, Surrey C
St Martin Vintners, Brighton, East Sussex
Stone, Vine & Sun, Cosham, Hampshire ✪
Stratford Vintners, Cookham, Berkshire ✪ M C
Turville Valley Wines, Great Missenden, Buckinghamshire ✪ M C F
Helen Verdcourt, Maidenhead, Berkshire M C
Vicki's Stores, Chobham, Surrey
Vin du Van, Appledore, Kent ✪ M C
The Vineyard, Dorking, Surrey
The Vineyard Cellars, Hungerford, Berkshire ✪ M C

Vino Vino, New Malden, Surrey M C
Vintage Roots, Arborfield, Berkshire M
Vintage Wine Cellars, Luton, Bedfordshire
The Wine Cellar, Croydon
The Wine Man, Streatley-on-Thames, West Berkshire M C
Wine Society, Stevenage, Hertfordshire ✪ M C F
Wycombe Wines, High Wycombe, Buckinghamshire

SOUTH WEST
Arkells Vintners, Swindon, Wiltshire
Averys, Bristol ✪
Bideford Wines, Bideford, Devon
Castang Wine Shippers, Pelynt, Cornwall M C
Clifton Cellars, Bristol
Brian Coad Fine Wines, Ivybridge, Devon ✪ M C
Cochonnet Wines, Falmouth, Cornwall
Constantine Stores, near Falmouth, Cornwall
Corks, Cotham, Bristol
Dartmouth Vintners, Dartmouth, Devon
The Dorchester Wine Centre at Eldridge Pope, Dorchester, Dorset ✪
Fine Cheese Co., Bath
La Forge Wines, Marksbury, Bath
Great Western Wine Company, Bath ✪
Hall and Woodhouse Ltd, Blandford, Dorset
John Harvey & Sons, Bristol M C
Richard Harvey Wines, Wareham, Dorset M C
Hicks & Don, Edington, Wiltshire M
The Jolly Vintner, Tiverton, Devon
L & F Jones, Radstock near Bath

Laymont & Shaw, Truro, Cornwall ✪ M C
Magnum Wine Company, Swindon, Wiltshire ✪
Map Wines, Bridgewater, Somerset
The Nobody Inn, Doddiscombsleigh, Devon ✪
Christopher Piper Wines, Ottery St Mary, Devon ✪
Quay West Wines, Stoke Canon, Exeter C
R.S. Wines, Bristol M C
Reid Wines, Hallatrow, Bristol ✪ M F
Shaftesbury Fine Wines, Shaftesbury, Dorset
Charles Steevenson, Tavistock, Devon M C
Topsham Wines, Topsham, Devon
Totnes Wine Co., Totnes, Devon
Trenchermans, Sherborne, Dorset
The Vine Trail, Hotwells, Bristol ✪ M C
Wadebridge Wines, Wadebridge, Cornwall
Wessex Wines, Bridport, Dorset C
Peter Wylie Fine Wines, Plymtree, Devon ✪ F
Yapp Brothers, Mere, Wiltshire ✪ M C

MIDLANDS
Amps Fine Wines of Oundle, near Peterborough, Northamptonshire
Arnolds, Broadway, Worcestershire
Arriba Kettle & Co., Honeybourne, Worcestershire C
Bat & Bottle, Knightley, Staffordshire ✪
Bennetts Fine Wines, Chipping Campden, Gloucestershire ✪
Les Caves du Patron, Stoneygate, Leicester
Andrew Chapman Fine Wines, Abingdon, Oxfordshire ✪
Colombier Vins Fins, Swadlincote, Derbyshire M C
Connollys, Birmingham ✪

Croque-en-Bouche, Malvern Wells, Worcestershire ✪ M C
Du Vin, Henley-on-Thames, Oxfordshire
Evertons, Ombersley, Worcestershire
Evingtons Wine Merchants, Leicester
Gauntleys, Nottingham ✪
Patrick Grubb Selections, Oxford ✪
Haynes, Hanson & Clark, Stow-on-the-Wold, Gloucestershire ✪
Pierre Henck, Wolverhampton, West Midlands M C
George Hill, Loughborough, Leicestershire
Hopton Wines, Kidderminster, Worcestershire M C
Ian G. Howe, Newark, Nottinghamshire
Inspired Wines, Cleobury Mortimer, Shropshire
S.H. Jones, Banbury, Oxfordshire ✪
Mills Whitcombe, Peterchurch, Herefordshire ✪ C
Nickolls & Perks, Stourbridge, West Midlands
Noble Rot Wine Warehouse, Bromsgrove, Worcestershire ✪
Oxford Wine Company, Witney, Oxfordshire ✪
Thomas Panton, Tetbury, Gloucestershire M
Edward Sheldon, Shipston-on-Stour, Warwickshire
H. Smith, Derby, Derbyshire
Stevens Garnier, Oxford
Tanners, Shrewsbury, Shropshire ✪
Waters Wine Merchants, Coventry, Warwick
David J. Watt Fine Wines, Ashby-de-la-Zouch, Leicestershire M
Weavers, Nottingham, Nottinghamshire ✪
Whitebridge Wines, Stone, Staffordshire
Whittalls Wines, Walsall, West Midlands C
Winchcombe Wine Merchants, Winchcombe, Gloucestershire

EASTERN COUNTIES

Adnams Wine Merchants, Southwold, Suffolk ☻
Ameys Wines, Sudbury, Suffolk
Bacchanalia, Cambridge
Bakers & Larners, Holt, Norfolk
Bella Wines, Newmarket, Suffolk ☻ M
Bonhote Foster, Bumpstead, Suffolk M
Anthony Byrne Fine Wines, Ramsey, Cambridgeshire M C
Carley & Webb, Framlingham, Suffolk
Flagship Wines, Brentwood, Essex M C
Peter Graham Wines, Norwich, Norfolk
Roger Harris Wines, Weston Longville, Norfolk ☻ M C
Richard Kihl, Aldeburgh, Suffolk ☻ F C
Lay & Wheeler, Colchester, Essex ☻
Luckins Wine Store, Great Dunmow, Essex
Oasis Wines, Southend-on-Sea, Essex
Thos Peatling, Bury St Edmunds, Suffolk
Sandhams Wine Merchants, Caistor, Lincolnshire
Seckford Wines, Woodbridge, Suffolk ☻ M C F
T & W Wines, Brandon, Suffolk
Wines of Interest, Ipswich, Suffolk
The Winesmith, Peterborough, Cambridgeshire
Noel Young Wines, Trumpington, Cambridgeshire ☻ F

NORTH WEST

Booths of Stockport, Heaton Moor, Stockport
D. Byrne & Co., Clitheroe, Lancashire ☻
Carringtons, Manchester
Cheshire Smokehouse, Wilmslow, Cheshire

Corkscrew Wines, Carlisle, Cumbria
deFINE Food and Wine, Sandiway, Cheshire
Rodney Densem Wines, Nantwich, Cheshire
Edencroft Fine Wines, Nantwich, Cheshire
Garrards, Cockermouth, Cumbria
Love Saves the Day, Manchester ✪
Planet Wine, Sale, Cheshire M C
Portland Wine Co., Sale, Manchester
Quellyn Roberts, Chester, Cheshire
Scatchard, Liverpool
Selfridges, Manchester ✪
Frank Stainton Wines, Kendal, Cumbria
Whitesides, Clitheroe, Lancashire
WineTime, Milnthorpe, Cumbria M C
T. Wright, Bolton, Greater Manchester

NORTH EAST
Barrels & Bottles, Sheffield
Cairns & Hickey, Bramhope, Leeds
Chippendale Fine Wines, Bradford, West Yorkshire M C
Great Northern Wine Company, Ripon, North Yorkshire M
Halifax Wine Company, Halifax, West Yorkshire
Hoults Wine Merchants, Huddersfield, West Yorkshire
House of Townend, Kingston upon Hull, East Yorkshire ✪
Michael Jobling, Newcastle-upon-Tyne M C
John Kelly Wines, Boston Spa, West Yorkshire M C
Martinez Fine Wines, Ilkley, West Yorkshire ✪
Mitchells Wines, Sheffield
Penistone Court, Penistone, Sheffield ✪ M C

Playford Ros, Thirsk, North Yorkshire M C
Premier Cru Fine Wine, Guiseley, Leeds
Roberts & Speight, Beverley, East Yorkshire
Springfield Wines, near Huddersfield, West Yorkshire
Vinceremos, Leeds M C
Wicked Wines, Pockthorpe, Kilham, East Yorkshire
The Wright Wine Company, Skipton, North Yorkshire ✪
Wrightson & Co. Wine Merchants, Darlington M C

SCOTLAND
Cockburns, Leith, Edinburgh
Peter Green, Edinburgh
Inverarity Vaults, Biggar
Irvine Robertson, Edinburgh C
J & H Logan, Edinburgh
Luvian's Bottle Shop, Cupar, Fife
Peckham & Rye, Glasgow ✪
Raeburn Fine Wines, Edinburgh ✪
Laurence Smith, Edinburgh M C
Valvona & Crolla, Edinburgh ✪
Villeneuve Wines, Peebles, Haddington and Edinburgh ✪

WALES
Ballantynes, Cowbridge, Vale of Glamorgan ✪
Irma Fingal-Rock, Monmouth, Monmouthshire
Joseph Keegan, Holyhead, Isle of Anglesey
Moriarty Vintners, Cardiff
Terry Platt Wine Merchants, Llandudno, Conwy ✪ M C
Shaws, Beaumaris, Isle of Anglesey

William Stedman, Caerleon, Newport
James Williams, Narberth, Pembrokeshire

NORTHERN IRELAND
Compendium, Belfast
Direct Wine Shipments, Belfast ✪
Ells Fine Wines, Portadown
James Nicholson, Crossgar, Co. Down ✪

CHANNEL ISLANDS
Bergerac Wine Cellar, St Helier, Jersey
Dunells Ltd, St Peter, Jersey
Victor Hugo Wines, St Saviour, Jersey
The Sommelier Wine Co., St Peter Port, Guernsey ✪

If you are a wine merchant in the UK and would like to be
mentioned on this list, or if your details are listed incorrectly,
the author and publisher will be happy to amend later editions.
We have tried to make *The Wine List* as helpful as possible but if
you have any ideas as to how we could improve it then write to
The Wine List c/o Headline Book Publishing, 338 Euston Road,
London, NW1 3BH.

Matthew Jukes

AUSTRALIA

Margaret River, WA
2003 2002 2001 2000 1999 1997 1996 1995 1994 1993 1991 1990

Barossa Valley, SA
2002 2001 1999 1998 1997 1996 1995 1994 1991 1990 1986

Clare Valley, SA
2003 2002 2001 2000 1999 1998 1997 1996 1995 1994 1991 1990

Coonawarra, SA
2003 2002 2001 1999 1998 1996 1994 1993 1992 1991 1990

Yarra Valley, VIC
2002 2001 2000 1999 1998 1997 1995 1994 1993 1992 1991 1990

Hunter Valley, NSW
2003 2002 2001 1999 1998 1996 1995 1994 1993 1991

FRANCE

Alsace
2001 2000 1999 1998 1997 1996 1995 1990 1989 1988 1985 1983

Burgundy Chablis
2002 2000 1999 1997 1996 1995 1990 1989 1988

Côte d'Or
2002 2000 1999 1998 1997 1996 1995 1993 1990 1989 1988 1985 1983

Beaujolais
2002 2000 1999 1995 1991 1989 1988

Bordeaux	Left Bank	2001 2000 1999 1998 1996 1995 1990 1989 1988 1986 1985 1983 1982
	Right Bank	2001 2000 1999 1998 1996 1995 1990 1989 1988 1986 1985 1983 1982
	Sauternes	2001 1999 1998 1997 1996 1995 1990 1989 1988 1986 1985 1983
Rhône	Northern	2001 2000 1999 1998 1997 1995 1994 1991 1990 1989 1988 1985 1983
	Southern	2001 2000 1999 1998 1995 1990 1989 1988 1985 1983 1981
Loire	Sweeties	2001 2000 1999 1997 1996 1995 1990 1989 1988 1985 1983 1982
Champagne		2000 1999 1998 1997 1996 1995 1990 1989 1988 1985 1983 1982
Languedoc/ Roussillon		2001 2000 1999 1998 1996 1995 1994 1993 1990 1989 1988 1986 1985
Provence		2001 2000 1999 1998 1997 1996 1995 1993 1991 1990 1989 1988 1985 1982 .
GERMANY Mosel		2001 2000 1999 1998 1997 1996 1995 1994 1993 1992 1991 1990 1989 1988 1985 1983

Rheingau	2001 1999 1998 1997 1996 1995 1994 1993 1992 1990 1989 1988 1985 1983

ITALY
Piedmont	2001 2000 1999 1998 1997 1996 1995 1990 1989 1988 1985
Tuscany	2001 2000 1999 1997 1995 1993 1990 1988 1985 1983 1982
Veneto	2002 2001 2000 1997 1995 1993 1990 1988 1985

NEW ZEALAND
North Island Hawkes Bay, (reds)	2001 2000 1998 1997 1996 1995 1994 1991
South Island Marlborough, (whites)	2003 2002 2001 2000 1999 1997

PORTUGAL
Vintage Port	2000 1997 1994 1992 1992 1985 1983 1980 1977 1970 1966 1963

SOUTH AFRICA
	2002 2001 2000 1998 1997 1995 1994 1992 1991 1989 1987 1986

SOUTH AMERICA
Chile
2003 2002 2001 1999 1996 1995

Argentina
2002 2001 1999 1997 1996 1995

SPAIN
Rioja
2001 2000 1999 1998 1996 1995 1994
1991 1990 1987 1982 1981

Ribera del Duero
2001 2000 1999 1998 1996 1995 1994
1991 1990 1989 1988 1986 1983 1982 1981

Penedès/Priorat
2001 2000 1999 1998 1996 1995 1994
1993 1992 1985

USA
North Coast
2001 1999 1998 1997 1996 1995 1994
1993 1992 1991 1990 1987 1985 1984

Napa and Carneros
2001 2000 1999 1997 1996 1995 1994 1993
1992 1991 1990 1987 1986 1985 1984

Central Coast
2001 2000 1999 1998 1997 1996 1995
1994 1993 1992 1991 1990

Oregon/Washington
2001 2000 1999 1998 1996 1994 1992
1991 1990 1989

index 239